D1443058

Praise for

THE PE☀PLE PART

"The first time I heard Annie speak about leadership and team building was a near-mystical experience for me. I immediately knew that I needed her help to grow the functionality of my team. That was nearly a decade ago, and since then Annie has had a profound positive impact on my business. Now she's finally put her wisdom and practical approach into a book, and The People Part delivers. It starts with the first principles that most every other leadership book glosses over. This is a nutrient-dense book that will show you how to build a responsive and productive team."

— **Jeff Walker**, #1 *New York Times* best-selling author of *Launch*

"The productivity of your business, the effectiveness of your algorithms, your business's ability to grow—it comes back to how well you're able to get effective teamwork driving results. And Annie Hyman Pratt knows how to build teams that drive results. From having a visionary master plan that creates powerful team alignment, to helping your people reach their highest performance potential, this book can help you become the type of leader who attracts a growth-focused dream team. The people part of business is arguably the most important part . . . and with Annie's help, you can have an amazing team working together to achieve the results you want."

— **Joe Polish**, founder of Genius Network

"Annie's groundbreaking work in the area of team and leadership development helped our business undergo a remarkable transformation from one that Jim Collins would describe as 'A genius with a thousand helpers' to one led by a highly collaborative, incredibly cohesive team of senior leaders. Simply put: If you are an entrepreneur, small business owner, or leader in your company, read this book. It will transform your business—and possibly even change your life—forever."

— **Ryan Levesque**, five-time Inc. 5000 CEO of The ASK Method Company and #1 national best-selling author

THE PE🌼PLE PART

THE PEPLE PART

SEVEN AGREEMENTS ENTREPRENEURS
AND LEADERS MAKE TO BUILD
TEAMS, ACCELERATE GROWTH,
AND BANISH BURNOUT FOR GOOD

ANNIE HYMAN PRATT

HAY HOUSE, INC.

Carlsbad, California • New York City
London • Sydney • New Delhi

Copyright © 2022 by Annie Hyman Pratt

Published in the United States by: Hay House, Inc.: www.hayhouse.com®
Published in Australia by: Hay House Australia Pty. Ltd.: www.hayhouse.com.au
Published in the United Kingdom by: Hay House UK, Ltd.: www.hayhouse.co.uk
Published in India by: Hay House Publishers India: www.hayhouse.co.in

Cover design: theBookDesigners • *Interior design:* Karim J. Garcia
Interior illustrations: Jim McGonigal III • *Indexer:* Joan Shapiro

Cataloging-in-Publication Data is on file at the Library of Congress

Hardcover ISBN: 978-1-4019-5857-2
E-book ISBN: 978-1-4019-5858-9
Audiobook ISBN: 978-1-4019-5860-2

10 9 8 7 6 5 4 3 2 1
1st edition, April 2022

Printed in the United States of America

SUSTAINABLE FORESTRY INITIATIVE
Certified Chain of Custody
Promoting Sustainable Forestry
www.sfiprogram.org
SFI-01268
SFI label applies to the text stock

33614082863340

*For those brave enough to answer
the call of leadership—every challenge is an
opportunity to have a positive impact.*

CONTENTS

Introduction: Why the People Part Matters xi

Agreement 1: Learning Self-Leadership 1

Agreement 2: Defining Company Goals... 43

Agreement 3: Establishing Clear Roles.. 77

Agreement 4: Building High-Trust Relationships 103

Agreement 5: Making Conscious Agreements..................................... 135

Agreement 6: Recognizing and Responding to Change..................... 167

Agreement 7: Creating Your Company Culture 195

Conclusion: Your New Part 221

Your People Part Plan 227

Your Leadership Toolbox 235

Leadership Conversations Cheat Sheet.. 243

More People Part Resources 247

Index 249

Acknowledgments 257

About the Author 261

INTRODUCTION

Why the People Part Matters

"You're working on all the wrong things! If you'd prioritize better, I'm sure you could get it all done!"

My good friend Carol, an entrepreneur with a big heart and even bigger ambition, had reached her boiling point. Her successful health coaching company was in the midst of a rapid growth spurt. Her team was working hard to deliver consistently great service and to keep customers from being affected by the company's growing pains—but mistakes were being made and Carol's confidence in her team was starting to wane.

Feeling frustrated with the tumult in the business operations, Carol had decided to attend a business productivity conference that focused on metrics and dashboards. She had just returned and was fired up to make change happen, NOW. She'd always known she should track important numbers, but the team never seemed to have time to get the numbers together. The information at the conference was excellent, and Carol became convinced that these tools would not only enable her to directly manage the business's growth but also make her team significantly more productive and effective.

For more than a year, she had felt almost powerless to make changes in her business, because her team was always stuck in overwhelm and running behind. It seemed that every time she brought forward a new idea or improvement that she wanted implemented, she was met with an impenetrable wall of resistance. Sometimes it felt like she was just watching her team fail, because she didn't have the courage to confront them with stronger demands. She had to do something different or eventually her whole business would fail. And truth be told, she was flat-out angry that her business wasn't performing better. On the drive home from the conference, she decided that she would demand that the metrics be put in place and not allow the team to put her off again. If they couldn't accomplish her request, maybe it would provide the clarity she needed to definitively decide whether she had the wrong team. So she called an immediate team meeting and shared the conference information and materials.

From the start, the meeting was tense. But Carol, anticipating pushback from her team, was ready to fight for what she wanted. She shored up her inner resolve and insisted, "We've got to have metrics. I must be able to see how our business is performing at all times. I'm flying blind right now and this must stop! In fact, if we had a working dashboard, we'd be way ahead of where we are now." Andrew, Carol's operations leader, raised his hand to speak, but she pushed ahead, "We've got to do it now, and by 'now' I mean this week. And don't tell me that you're all too busy; you can easily prioritize better, because this is far too important to put off."

Andrew, having the most in-depth understanding of what the team was working on, found his mind flooding with conflicting priorities. He wanted to deliver an outstanding dashboard that would provide exactly what Carol requested. For more than a year, he too had been thinking they needed to measure and track certain numbers to decrease their costs without diminishing their clients' satisfaction. But Andrew knew that Carol's request couldn't be easily delivered; if it were easy, he would have done it months ago when he first thought of it. In order to get accurate and useful metrics for every department, many of the company's systems would need to be upgraded, making the project bigger and more complex than Carol likely understood. Bottom line, the team had more critical improvements to make before they could devote time and energy to creating a dashboard.

Before Andrew could sort out his thoughts and decide how best to respond, Carol left the room, allowing no space for discussion. Andrew and the team were already facing major challenges to meet the upcoming product launch deadline and now faced a new wrinkle. They didn't want to disappoint Carol, but something would have to give. The question was what.

Neither Carol nor Andrew knew how to effectively raise, discuss, and work through this difficult situation. As Andrew began planning how to circle back and address the issue with Carol, he remembered how a similar situation had backfired not long before—Andrew had raised challenges he saw on the horizon and Carol had exploded with anger. After the immediate flare-up, Carol had reluctantly adjusted her expectations to accommodate Andrew's concerns. But what haunted him now was that the conflict had significantly damaged their relationship, and it took months to return to normal. Andrew felt he couldn't handle the consequences of another conflict.

In the end, neither of them tried to have the much-needed conversation, because they both believed it would go badly. Absent a better solution, the team resigned themselves to trying their best to build the dashboard that Carol wanted without falling further behind in the product launch preparations—even though they all knew that they wouldn't succeed.

The net result? As everyone expected: big disappointment all around. The product launch was not only late, it underperformed by a lot. The dashboard was up, but it was missing data and full of errors. Both things got done—but poorly. Team morale was lower than ever. Carol was blaming Andrew and wanted to fire him; Andrew was blaming Carol and wanted to quit.

However, neither of them was in a position to act on those desires. Carol couldn't run her business without a leader as skilled and experienced as Andrew—she had grown past that point years earlier. To recruit, hire, and train a replacement would be slow and expensive, and the company likely couldn't survive that. Andrew had a young family and wasn't in a position to be without an income; finding a new executive position could take many months and might even require a move. Besides, he had invested major "career capital" in Carol's business, learning unique skills that weren't obviously valuable to another company, likely resulting in a pay cut. They were at a painful impasse.

PEOPLE ARE THE PROBLEM–AND THE SOLUTION

If we take a step back and look at the roles and business needs, Carol and Andrew were actually quite a good fit. They were both driven, hardworking, and strong critical thinkers. They both had long track records of demonstrated success. And they each had a unique, expert skill set that complemented the other's.

So what went wrong here? How could these leaders, who were both highly invested and shared a common desire for the business to succeed, have created such a dysfunctional relationship in which communicating, collaborating, and problem-solving weren't possible? Why would they behave in ways that deep down they *knew* would fail? It's as if all of their capabilities, experience, and ability to think clearly had evaporated when the stress got high!

It seems that way because that's exactly what happened: All good critical thinking went off-line and they reacted from their emotions instead. The reality is that this is a common occurrence when working with humans. A friend of mine summarizes the experience quite succinctly: "People, people, people!" (punctuated with an eye roll). People often behave in unproductive ways, even when they're accomplished professionals, and even when they know it will make things worse, not better.

As human beings, we're emotional, reactive, messy, and fallible. We are much less often in conscious control of our thoughts and behavior than we like to think. We tire easily and are slow to change, but fast to acquire bad habits. And maybe worst of all, when a situation is high-stakes, and challenging (as often happens in business), in moments when we most need to control our own thinking, behavior, and communication—we can't do it. In fact, we're biologically wired to automatically react without thinking.

I've spent 30 years observing how people interact and function in a wide range of businesses, and I've never met a company leader or team member who didn't have at least a few disaster stories in which people's behavior was the root problem. In this situation, Carol and Andrew were both behaving in very human ways: Carol was frustrated and impatient with her team, longing for a time long past when she could just do it all herself. Andrew was exhausted and burned out, hardly able to remember a time when he felt successful in his role. They were focused on valuable but conflicting goals—putting metrics in place to boost results versus stabilizing things before introducing more change.

When leaders and teams don't work together effectively, they assume the other people involved are doing something wrong, are on the wrong track, or are downright incapable. But the reason Carol and Andrew failed could not be summed up in some fuming reflection on team member incompetence, nor could the answer be found in any balance sheet or dashboard, no matter how many key performance indicators it contained. The answer was simply that neither of them had the skills to work effectively with each other and the rest of the team or to maintain their equilibrium under pressure enough to keep the business moving toward the goals they all shared.

In my career as a business and leadership consultant, I've seen this dynamic play out in countless iterations. I've coached solopreneurs, entrepreneurs, corporate executives, and industry leaders on how to look beyond systems and processes and learn to work effectively with the human beings who make their business run. I've worked with them to solve their biggest dilemma: "How can I activate my team's driven, hardworking, critical-thinking, and creative qualities in my business without getting tripped up by all the reactive, difficult, messy parts?" I've developed a set of tools to help them turn their people from their most perplexing challenge to their greatest resource and opportunity. I call this powerful tool kit the People Part, and whether you're a CEO, an entrepreneur getting a new business off the ground, or a leader within a larger company, I've written this book to put these same tools in your hands.

HOW I DISCOVERED THE PEOPLE PART

My story in business starts with the family business that hugely influenced every part of my life. As you read the next few pages, you'll see how my journey progressed through some of the classic phases of entrepreneurial business growth—probably some you'll recognize from your own experience—and also gave me a crash course in how to work (or how not to work) with the people around me.

My father, Herbert Hyman, a widely recognized and successful entrepreneur, was a visionary willing to take risks who had a gift for seeing opportunities from being in tune with the demands of the market. He was an ambitious, demanding parent with high standards, and the expectation was that if I wanted to work in the family business, I would get on board and follow his lead—which I did, at first.

As an undergraduate at UCLA, my father started his first business supplying sorority and fraternity houses with vending machines. It was so successful that he dropped out of UCLA just a few credits shy of graduation. He sold that business and then, witnessing the office building boom, in 1963 started an office coffee service in and around Los Angeles.

In 1966 he met my mother, Mona, and quickly married her, recognizing the gem he had found. On their honeymoon in Sweden (my mom's home country), my father tasted European coffee for the first time and had an epiphany. In 1968 that epiphany led my parents to open their first gourmet coffee store in Brentwood, California. My father and mother sold imported, freshly roasted, specialty coffee beans from behind the oak cabinets and countertops he made himself. This was years before you could buy imported, gourmet-quality coffee beans and well before the cappuccinos, lattes, and specialized coffee drinks that caught fire in the late 1980s and early 1990s. With its quality coffee and Hollywood-native celebrity customers, the store, The Coffee Bean, was distinct, before its time, and an instant success.

Over the next decade, the family business grew, and with the addition of exotic teas, it was named the Coffee Bean & Tea Leaf. As my parents rapidly added more stores, they faced many challenges in hiring and retaining talented store managers. As a teenager, I was steeped in the problem-solving discussions that were frequent features of dinner table conversation, including everything from coffee roasters to manager revolts. Without even realizing it, I was beginning my own business management education, and I hadn't even graduated high school!

While I was studying for college entrance exams, one issue started to stand out for my parents—the higher-performing managers were asking for more autonomy and authority than my father was willing to give. His traditional management model? You probably guessed it: top-down authority. Naturally, he had very strong opinions on how *his* stores should be operated, which created conflict with managers who wanted to do things differently, driving more than a few of them to quit. But in the 1960s and 1970s, his more authoritarian management model and leadership style was the norm and still able to sustain the business.

Impacts from a Changing Business Environment

Once the gourmet coffee beverage revolution hit at the end of the 1980s, bringing those lattes and cappuccinos with it, the business changed so dramatically that my parents couldn't keep up. They were feeling the impact of some big external factors, such as quickly increasing demand. The suburbs had mushroomed, with everyday commutes into the city becoming commonplace. Women who used to be at home making coffee were now entering the workforce with new careers. Busier than ever, women, just like men, were buying coffee on their way to work and creating even bigger demand.

But more than that, coffee began to occupy a different space in American life. My father was standing at the ready for when coffee morphed from a wake-me-up that "got the job done" to an affordable luxury and well-deserved treat, and a life experience that was meant to be explored and savored. The company's priority and challenge: *quality coffee beans first—brew it up best—keep the pace and go with the flow!*

To illustrate the change, in 1986 (before the coffee revolution exploded from Seattle to Los Angeles) on a good day, we sold $200 worth of coffee drinks at the "bar" counter, and $2,000 worth of beans and loose-leaf tea. By 1992, that ratio had completely flipped, and we had long lines of loyal customers waiting for our original Ice Blended Mochas (yes, we invented those). I had no idea that our store volumes would triple and quadruple in the next few years.

At this point I was studying at UCLA, and during summers I worked the beverage counters. With specialty drinks demanding much more skill to prepare than weighing out a pound of beans, our stores went from an average staff size of around 6 to 18 practically overnight, and I'll never forget my rocky beginnings as I started training people.

First, I was teaching fresh hires to make espresso drinks on Italian machines that behaved more like defiant stallions than coffee makers. Learning to steam milk was a lot like learning to ride a bucking bronco, and for a beginner (and everyone was a beginner back then) there were many tentative fits and starts. Painful accidents were practically unavoidable (that milk was hot!), and sprinkled in was the occasional angry customer who had waited 10 or 20 minutes only to have their day completely ruined by getting the wrong drink, or *no foam!*

Training new team members was a major investment in time and resources, and if an employee stayed only a short time, the entire staff felt the impact. This often turned into a cycle of overworking the trained people to the point of burnout, because there just weren't enough of them! My parents had little sympathy and frequently questioned why a store needed so many people in the first place. With no on-the-ground experience, and thus no practical understanding of the beverage-making work involved, they became suspicious that our store teams were becoming lazy and unproductive (which couldn't have been further from the truth!).

Around that same time, in 1990, I graduated from UCLA with an economics/business degree. I was always good with numbers, so right away I went to work at a "Big 8" accounting firm and got my CPA license.

But then the unexpected happened: My father needed a triple bypass, decided to semi-retire, and I became the general manager of the Coffee Bean & Tea Leaf at the age of 22. Almost two years later, I moved into the role of CEO. Keep in mind that this was before Zuckerberg and before the tech boom, when the idea of a CEO under 50 was outrageous—especially a woman!

I had always wanted to lead our company, so I dove right in, working 70-hour weeks, spending every day driving from store to store, and trying to do everything and be everywhere all at once. I went from feeling energetic and passionate to overwhelmed and dangerously close to burning out.

"This Isn't Working!"

Starting in 1995, the company had a lot more to handle than just those stubborn espresso machines. We were scrambling to remodel stores while at the same time opening a new store every month but failing to resolve our staffing and efficiency issues. Because our growth was mostly fueled by traditional bank borrowing, if we put money into stores that performed poorly, our entire growth plan could collapse, and then we'd have trouble paying our debts.

The slew of new (and stressful!) pressures made the company even *more* like a bucking bronco—so I dug in my boots the only way I knew how: adopting my dad's top-down management style. All these years later, I can laugh and admit that I am a "recovered micromanager." But back then, I wouldn't listen to my team. My management style forced store managers to wait on me and my decisions, when they should have been presenting *their* solutions to the issues that *they* were dealing with on the ground. Instead of asking, "What do our stores need?" their default was, "What does Annie want?"

I vividly remember the gut-wrenching day I realized I had to change. My HR manager and I had a major disagreement about management staffing, and while storming out the door, she didn't mince words about me and the "ivory tower" she felt I lived in (spicing in language that I don't dare repeat) and how my leadership style "wasn't working!" And she wasn't the only one who felt that way. Many other managers threatened to quit en masse, and for the first time it hit me that having an unhappy, overworked, under-inspired workforce could put us out of business.

In the undeniable reality of this painful moment, the light turned on, and I realized that a viable company isn't just a product or a service, nor is it a combination of systems or processes—*it's all about the people who work there.* After all, they are the ones who, day in, day out, deliver results. Their skills, their commitment, their teamwork, and their heart are necessary to drive a business forward. I couldn't have sustainable business success without my team.

Learning to Partner with My Team

I mulled over this thought: *How could I let people know they were an essential key to achieving our goals within our company?* How could I make the best use of our great employees—the people I now call A Players—and at the same time structure teams in such a way that they worked together like the well-tuned parts of an engine? I needed a business model that allowed me to step back to do the bigger strategic thinking while filling the gap with people who stepped up and took responsibility!

To make this happen, I had to radically change my management approach. I couldn't sacrifice our company values to get results, no matter how tempting, because then everyone who worked there would do the same. I realized I wanted a company whose reputation highlighted the *value of our products and our people*—people who were empowered to make decisions and encouraged to lead. I admit this transition was a challenge for me for a while. I had to learn to develop my team so I could reliably trust that they would think and act in the most effective, best interest of the company and its goals. And once they got developed, I had to trust that they had the skills and perspectives to do not only the operational tasks but also the ongoing managerial activities (such as problem-solving and decision-making) that I had kept control of for far too long.

These realizations were part of a humbling and growing season for me as a person and a business leader. After all of my running around, working long hours to continue our expansion and strengthen our reputation for having the best ice-blended mocha beverage on the market, I was still slammed with the fact that we could go under from poor operations. Up until this time, I had believed it was my role to figure everything out and then dole out the instructions to my team. My leadership shortcomings were the driving factor behind the challenges we were facing, and this harsh reality got my attention. At that point, I started to think, *I have to learn how to do this differently.* Our company would not survive if I didn't change my approach and transform into a leader who recognized the people who worked for me as my most valuable resource.

A NEW BUSINESS MODEL BEGINS TO TAKE SHAPE

To summarize this part of my journey, there were three major shifts I had to make. All were absolutely imperative to our business success then—*and to yours now!*

Business Is a TEAM Sport

The *first* shift was recognizing, and really owning, the fact that business is a TEAM sport. It's not a solo sport and you can't play it as if it revolves around one person, any more than you could play professional basketball without a team. This meant I could no longer behave as if it were a solo sport by telling others exactly what to do and by deciding everything important myself. When an entrepreneur starts a business, they do play many of the roles themselves, at first. But that becomes unsustainable as soon as the business starts to significantly grow. I realize this might seem obvious, but as someone who played almost no team sports growing up, I found it was completely outside of my experience to be part of a group achievement. All of my academic achievements and most of my extracurricular activities—things like gymnastics, tennis, and skiing—relied solely on me to perform.

When I had to shift responsibilities to others because I could no longer play so many roles in the business myself, it felt like I went from total control to zero control. I knew intellectually that I must make the shift to rely on others, but I wasn't ready for how difficult that shift actually was. As the business grew, the stakes went up, which exacerbated my urge to take over and control the exact things I should not be doing at all. It didn't take long to realize that by trying to do too much myself, I was on a path to self-destruction.

If I wanted the business to sustainably grow and succeed, it was imperative that I learn to work together with others, as a team. I had to learn how to harness the group's collective efforts, perspectives, and talents to achieve business goals—and trust that the result would be much better than trying to do so many things myself.

Trusting in a team is way easier said than done. Remember, my way of achieving up until that point was always to do important stuff myself. It wasn't clear to me how to trust others when they could so easily let me down and leave me suffering—wishing I had just performed the thing myself that time. I knew that I had to set people up for success so that they could perform well (maybe even better than I could). But honestly, I had no idea how to do that.

Effective Human Performance Has to Be Developed

Human performance, in my opinion, is the single most vital element of modern business success. In basic terms, we need the best, most effective human intelligence and behavior to show up and perform in our businesses. But humans don't have a simple switch to turn that part on, while turning off the ineffective, counterproductive human parts that are emotional, irrational, tired, scared, angry, etc. In fact, the very parts that we don't want to show up are always "at the ready" and engage automatically at the slightest provocation—no effort required on our part.

The opposite is true for the human parts we *do* want to engage. It takes a lot of effort, focus, critical thinking, and interacting effectively with the team to make good business decisions, solve problems quickly, form future plans, adjust strategy, and so on— not to mention performing regular job tasks like responding to an upset customer or designing a new product. So when the human parts we don't want get triggered, they basically shut down our access to the good parts, and we can't turn them back on until we turn off the reacting parts. It all has to do with how the human nervous (limbic) system is wired to kick in automatically for survival. We'll take a closer look at this a bit later in the book.

It's my experience that we ignore this challenge to human performance in the workplace, and instead of addressing it directly and developing skills to make us more effective, we try our best to exclude individuals whose reactivity is so problematic that they harm the business more than they contribute to it. We label them as unproductive, lazy, disrespectful, aggressive, and even toxic, as if these were innate personality traits of theirs. In reality, these people *couldn't* control their emotional reactivity, which is not a personality trait any more than lacking eye-hand coordination and repeatedly failing to catch a baseball is. All humans have trouble regulating their emotional reactivity, and it's something we need to learn and keep improving upon to reach our performance potential.

We call this ability to regulate our emotions so that we can think and behave intentionally "Self-Leadership." I liken it to athletic endurance in sports—some people have natural stamina and can run longer than others before pooping out. But anyone who wants to be a marathon runner will need to practice often and learn to keep running through all kinds of stress and challenges, such as steep hills, hot weather, blisters, and muscle pain. So if we want team members in our business to perform at a high level even during challenges and tough times (while also growing and improving), their Self-Leadership skills will need to be developed. Recognizing this was my *second* major shift.

Teamwork Is Built on Agreements

My *third* huge shift came from the observation that top-down authority, giving orders, making demands, and micromanaging made teams less productive, not more. At first, even when I recognized what didn't work, it wasn't clear to me what *did* work to lead an effective team. If I didn't tell people what to do, how would they do something productive that met my expectations? How could I give people freedom to make their own choices and yet make sure they would make good ones that contributed to a result? And how could I know more about what team members were going to do before they actually did it, since after something's done, it's much more difficult to correct?

Other leaders kept telling me that I just needed to "let go and trust my team," as if their performance would magically skyrocket as soon as I stopped asking them about their work progress and just let them do their thing. After giving that a disastrous try, I researched and observed how high-performing team members worked together. I discovered that they were constantly interacting and discussing what they were going to do before they did it. They always clarified the purpose or goal they wanted to achieve, and then basically negotiated an agreement for who would do what by when. And if things didn't go as planned, they got together and renegotiated.

It was so simple, and yet I had never thought of these types of internal interactions as real "agreements." In my mind, agreements were more like legal contracts or promises, something you only made when you were certain you wouldn't or couldn't break them—because the consequences would be dire. But when I started to think about things like running plays and forming game strategy in sports, I realized that the players make agreements all the time without any guarantees whatsoever. No one can promise to win a game or even make any particular basket in basketball—heck, they can't even promise to make a free throw! However, most of the time the team knows exactly what the other players intend to do in a specific situation, because they agreed ahead of time. For example, if a player misses a shot, another player will immediately try to grab the ball in the rebound to recover it and get another chance to score. It's such a clear standing agreement that no one even thinks about it. And when a team goes into the game with a certain defense strategy and it's not working, they will huddle to redo the strategy and leave with a new agreement for what they'll do on the court. Maybe it'll work, and maybe it won't, but they all know the actions they each intend to take.

Here's how I define "agreement" when we're talking about teamwork: An agreement is formed when *multiple team members define and align the future behaviors and actions they intend to take to achieve a result.* You can think of these agreements as including not just actions, but also expectations, commitments, roles, and plans, because the point is always the same—for the team members to reasonably predict and rely upon what the others will do so that they themselves can take the most effective actions to achieve a result.

I find it helpful to think of a basic agreement like a basketball pass. You have two players working together, agreeing that one of them will pass the ball and the other will catch it. Solo sports don't operate on agreements; you play on your own, with no need to understand what your teammates are doing. But team sports require agreements for the different players to do anything at all together—from the basics, like knowing one's position, to utilizing a sophisticated, multi-person play. The players involved in that basketball pass are actually demonstrating multiple competencies at once, such as remembering the game strategy, locating their partner on the court, looking out for the opposing players who want to steal the ball, identifying where to move next, and on and on. Without agreements, you have chaos, because no one knows what their part is in relation to the other parts. It's the same in business: Everything is an agreement, whether it's goals and roles, processes and plans, or an explicit renegotiation.

That's why I've structured this book around seven key agreements that effective leaders and teams abide by—and you'll read more about them in a minute or two. For now, I just want you to take this truth to heart: A highly successful, sustainable business is a TEAM sport that involves intentional HUMANS working together utilizing AGREEMENTS to achieve results. This is the essence of the People Part.

Spreading the Word of the People Part

We negotiated a successful sale of Coffee Bean & Tea Leaf at the end of 1998. I was only 30 when the company sold; in seven years we had grown from 7 to 70 stores, and I had gained enough experience swimming in the deep end of the pool to become a consultant for other companies' strategic business plans, operations, finance, and leadership performance. Over the next decade or so I performed as an interim executive (usually a CEO, CFO, or COO) and business consultant for a wide range of entrepreneurial companies. Everything from boutique consultancies to cutting-edge entertainment firms, from complex logistics to high-volume manufacturing, from post-graduate education to multi-unit dining and hospitality. I was usually engaged to help during a business inflection point, such as when revenue was racing up or racing down; or to help ready a company to sell, or integrate a new acquisition; or to help stabilize a major change in executive leadership. As I worked with diverse types of companies, I helped them adjust their business strategy, processes, and people to become much more effective through developing the team and teamwork. I filed away experiences from all the different companies in my head, expanding my operating knowledge as I evaluated the wins and losses and captured the learnings.

As I accumulated and put into place my experience, perspective, and knowledge, and was seen as one who recognized the value of people, managers no longer ducked behind counters to avoid talking to me (which actually happened in a Coffee Bean store once). I was on a roll to figure out a truly repeatable and systematic approach to prioritize—and train companies in—the People Part of business. I stopped doing interim executive work and started my business consulting firm, Annie Hyman Pratt Consulting, then went on to develop a highly successful training program and mastermind for business leaders of entrepreneurial companies, which became what's now Leading Edge Teams. For the last decade, I have specialized in ensuring that entrepreneurial businesses with huge potential, and the CEOs who founded them, achieve success—and don't burn out before they get there.

Effective leadership and teamwork is the burnout cure. Most entrepreneurs and leaders try everything else to improve their businesses before investing in their people and their own leadership development. Systems and processes (like Carol's dashboards) are often touted as "the only solution needed," and all too often consume the owner's attention and resources. Now don't get me wrong—systems and processes are 100 percent necessary for repeating situations and tasks. Systems and processes are all about eliminating the thinking part to increase efficiency and effectiveness. However, they don't do much, if anything, to enhance people's critical-thinking or complex-decision-making abilities, which are at the very heart of delivering better business results. Implementing systems and processes without addressing people and team development will set you up to fail. Building empowered leaders and a strong team who can do good critical thinking about your business while executing the expectations for their role is the only way to navigate the rapid rate of change in business today.

WHAT THE PEOPLE PART CAN DO FOR YOU

In my career, I've sometimes met CEOs and leaders who couldn't yet afford to work with a consultant like me but, respecting my experience, asked me for book recommendations to help them in their business. I had no books to recommend that I felt told the full truth of what it takes to succeed in entrepreneurial business today and for the long term. The market was full of quick-fix solutions that sounded lovely but, when implemented, left gaping holes that would ultimately sink the proverbial ship. That's why I've written this book: It's the book I wished I could recommend when those leaders asked.

Many books, and many consultants, can offer you systems, processes, and structure, and while these are often valuable, they will fail if the people using them do not work well with one another. You *cannot* leave the people out of your business solutions. They are essential to the success of your enterprise—and to your own success as a leader.

But I can honestly say there hasn't been a comprehensive tool kit for how to work effectively with your people until now. So this book is my attempt to offer a workable solution to as many CEOs, business leaders, and team members as possible. It's going to teach you the competencies that you (almost certainly) don't yet have (and didn't know you needed) so that you can:

- **Become a highly respected, successful leader**, achieving much greater results and more recognition with less frustration, overwhelm, and burnout while building a reputation that attracts talent and makes team members want to work with you.

- **Transform the interactive "people part" of your role** from difficult and draining to fulfilling and productive.

- **Experience your role as a vehicle to personally and professionally grow,** develop, and contribute meaningfully to your organization and to what matters most to you.

- **Develop effective leaders and teams** who sustainably grow and operate your business day to day, giving you the freedom, creativity, and success you desire.

The People Part Is for You If . . .

- You're just starting out: You will learn how to lay the foundation of your business so that you set it up for success.

- You have a business that is stalling: You will find team-driven solutions that will kick your business into gear and deliver real results.

- You're a leader feeling like you are just not good with people, but you really, really want to be: You will finally understand what has been blocking your success. You will up your teamwork skills and become the kind of leader who team members want to go above and beyond for.

- You're a member of a team within a business: You will hone your skills to work more effectively and happily with your team—and gain the perspective you'll need to move toward a leadership role.

I can say this confidently, because with Leading Edge Teams I've used the principles of the People Part to help real people in all those roles turn things around. Here's what some of our clients have to say:

"We were stuck in a cycle of stress and overwhelm that severely limited our ability to not only grow, but actually maintain the results we expected. Team morale was poor, and our best people were taking calls from headhunters that they had previously brushed off. Raising our game in the People Part not only got us out of the stress/over-whelm cycle, but our best people are now highly committed, successful achievers who are dedicated to growing themselves and the team, realizing it's the basis of a sustainable success."

"The team part used to be terribly difficult and frustrating, and I had resigned myself to believing that I'd never have a team that could operate the business as well as I could, let alone better. But here we are! I'm so grateful and impressed with my team! And now the team is my favorite part."

"I used to hate doing leadership duties—things like giving feedback and holding people accountable were not only stressful, but nothing even seemed to change no matter how hard I tried. Now I actually like my leadership duties because I know how to work with my team to actually make change happen."

"I used to stay in my silo and focus only on my part. I thought that doing my best individual work would always be enough. Until it wasn't. Applying the teachings in the People Part helped me to connect cross-functionally and come out of my solo silo. Only then did I fully realize the potential of my best creative ideas."

The Seven Agreements

As I explained a few pages back, teamwork relies on the mechanism of agreements for all that it accomplishes. Agreements are built into most everything we voluntarily do with other human beings, but too often agreements are mistaken, assumed, or completely ambiguous. To make agreements effective—that is, the kind of basketball passes that can outmaneuver the most challenging of opponents even when the team is under stress and pressure—they need to be explicit (generally spoken out loud), negotiated, and consciously agreed upon.

So, in the chapters ahead, you'll learn to make and keep conscious agreements in seven crucial areas. These seven agreements are how you shift your business from a solo sport to a team sport. Master them, and the People Part will soon become your favorite aspect of your business! Once you have a unified team of leaders who are as committed to achieving results as you are, you will never want to go back to the old model of top-down authority and control where you were the one carrying it all.

So what are the seven agreements of the People Part? To show you, I'll take you back to where we started this Introduction, with the story of Carol and Andrew.

When my team and I met these two, both their professional relationship and their company were in bad shape. But worst of all, they were both personally in bad shape, experiencing a mix of frustration, exhaustion, anger, resentment, doubt, and fear. They didn't trust themselves to make good decisions, and they certainly didn't trust each other. Neither of them could access any positivity for more than a few minutes when talking about the business, and what passed for "critical thinking" was finishing the sentence "That won't work because . . ."

Before we could address and transform the poor business performance, or help Carol and Andrew rebuild their relationship to interact productively and lead the company to success, we first had to get each of them to a more positive, compassionate, and confident place inside themselves so that they could clearly perceive and confront the real-world business situations they had.

We knew we couldn't achieve any meaningful results without first helping Carol and Andrew to regulate and moderate their negative thoughts and emotions in a reasonably sustained way. We call this capability Self-Leadership, and it's the basis of the first agreement you'll learn in this book: *We consistently show up in Self-Leadership rather than self-protection.*

Next, we helped Carol and Andrew form and agree upon a picture of the future state they wanted to reach, in which they're successful—in other words, their desired goals and outcomes for the business. We also helped them identify how they'd need to operate differently to achieve this state. And we updated their (and their team's) expectations about business growth, and how it works in today's world of rapid change. This is what the second agreement is all about: *We define and align on intended outcomes.*

Third, we worked on role clarity. Once Carol and Andrew's team knew who to go to for what, they saved time and resources by working together more effectively. When there is clarity on who is doing what, it is much easier to see how the organization operates, form functions, and fill any gaps that may arise. It's also easier to anticipate when someone's plate is becoming overly burdened and it may be time to shift resources or hire (thus allowing the company to keep pace with growth). This is the essence of the third agreement: *We clarify our parts and where they fit in the whole.*

Fourth, we worked on developing secure relationships within the team. Andrew and Carol needed to have safe space between them and trust that they each cared about how things turned out for the other, in order to discuss the real issues facing the business. And the entire team needed what's called psychological safety in order to be willing to step up and take greater responsibility in their roles. Here's where the fourth agreement comes in: *We consider our impact on others, have their backs, and repair relationships promptly.*

Fifth, we taught the entire team the importance of making explicit agreements to guide their day-to-day work so they could avoid guessing about how things were supposed to go, and they could count on one another to follow through. This is the fifth agreement: *We make collaborative, conscious agreements that we're confident we can keep.* (Yes, it's an agreement about making agreements!)

Sixth, we showed the team that those agreements were negotiable if things went differently than expected, but they would need to communicate and get a new agreement in place. Only then could they be sure that the team could be counted on to deliver. Gaining the ability to make, renegotiate, and keep agreements consistently is far more important than any KPI (key performance indicator) ever could be. Once the team could recognize that things weren't going well and were empowered to make changes accordingly, Carol's confidence in them soared. This is the sixth agreement: *We recognize change, anticipate impacts, and proactively adapt our agreements.*

Last, we took the time to strengthen the company's leadership and teamwork habits across the board. The culture of the organization became one that truly exemplified excellence. They collectively strove for progress and found ways to seize the opportunities that were related to or embedded within their challenges. The team was overjoyed by the changes in the organization. It was now a pleasure to come to work, thanks to the People Part. This is the seventh agreement: *We create a culture in which we make best practices habitual to achieve our highest performance potential.*

How to Use This Book

The People Part is like the "human business education" you never got—even if you went to business school! The seven agreements of the People Part address all the key components needed to successfully lead in business today. Learning and implementing these seven agreements will work with teams in all industries and at all growth levels. They are fundamental, foundational, and expand to meet the needs of the moment.

They may also seem like a lot to take in! But don't worry. In the chapters ahead, we'll unpack all seven agreements, one by one. I'll explain the key concepts and illustrate them with examples from my own and my clients' experiences. (I'll change some of their names and identifying details to, as we say, protect the innocent.) We'll look at some neuroscience along the way, and also share some basketball analogies (as you might have guessed), and you'll be with me just as if you're a client. The tools I'll share with you are the same tools my clients use every day. They work.

This book provides a deep dive of information far beyond what you'll find in the typical business "how-to" book. In this book, you're discovering what it really takes for humans to work together to achieve results. As such, you are learning how to think about business differently and take actions from a "people-centered" place. This is no small thing!

So I'd like you to think of this book, first, as a primer for how to successfully work with people in your business, and second, as a reference you'll go back to over and over to refresh and improve your skills. Because it's a new kind of education, it will take time to assimilate each agreement, and you will progress to higher levels within each—a bit like grades in school. And as your business evolves and you face new challenges, you'll find answers and support in these pages that you may not have recognized the first time around.

The agreements are in a particular order for a reason. If you think of Abraham Maslow's well-known hierarchy of needs—starting with essentials like food and sleep, and moving up to more rarefied qualities like self-actualization—you can view the People Part sort of like a Hierarchy of People's Performance Needs. They start with what's most fundamental—your own Self-Leadership, how *you* situationally "show up"—and move on to more complex interactions. Thus, as you work your way through the book, you'll find that each agreement builds on the ones before. And when you or your team hit challenges, you can use the agreements as a checklist, knowing that you need to meet each agreement in order before you can effectively move on to the next one.

To best support your learning and growth, at the end of every chapter I'll provide summaries of the key takeaways so this book can be easily reviewed and used as a rapid reference guide in your biggest moments of challenge and change. I'll also include questions to help you reflect on what you've learned in each chapter, and I'll share a success story showing how one of my clients solved a real business challenge using the agreement we've discussed in the chapter.

At the end of the book, I've laid out additional practical information and implementation steps you can take to put the People Part into action, starting right now—including:

- A handy toolbox with the tools you'll use most often

- A quick-reference guide to challenging conversations

- A seven-step plan with exercises for implementing the agreements with your team

- Links to download digital versions of helpful worksheets and cheat sheets, plus exclusive online-only resources

Your Journey into the People Part Begins Here!

Once you see that people are the most underleveraged, underutilized asset you have, you won't be able to unsee it. And once you master the seven agreements, you won't be able to unknow what you know. You will look forward to working with your team because your business results will clearly show that the whole is truly greater than the sum of its parts! By the end of this book, my hope is that you will have an entirely new model for what *being at work* can look and feel like—experiencing a sense of relief, fulfillment, and optimism that you haven't felt in years, if ever. :-)

THE PEOPLE PART

Seven Agreements Entrepreneurs and Leaders
Make to **Build Teams**, Accelerate **Growth**,
and **Banish Burnout** for **Good**

1 Self-Leadership:
We consistently show up in Self-Leadership rather than self-protection.
The basis of critical thinking, performance, and effective interaction

2 Defined Outcomes:
We define and align on intended outcomes.
The foundation of team achievement

3 Role Clarity:
We clarify our parts and where they fit in the whole.
The organized structure that enables teamwork

4 Secure Relationships:
We consider our impact on others, have their backs, and repair relationships promptly.
The condition for productive team interaction

5 Conscious Agreements:
We make collaborative, conscious agreements that we're confident we can keep.
The mechanism of effective teamwork

6 Recognize Change and Renegotiate:
We recognize change, anticipate impacts, and proactively adapt our agreements.
The formula for succeeding in an ever-changing reality

7 Culture That Drives Excellence:
We make best practices habitual to achieve our highest performance potential.
The collective behaviors for sustainable success

LEARNING SELF-LEADERSHIP

We consistently show up in Self-Leadership rather than self-protection.

The basis of critical thinking, performance, and effective interaction

When the gourmet coffee beverage revolution hit in the early 1990s, the Coffee Bean & Tea Leaf stores rapidly tripled in revenue. Keeping up with the growth was chaotic and difficult. If you've frequented coffee bars or small cafés, you've likely seen at least a few that you'd call dirty—with dish-filled tables, sticky floors, overflowing trash cans, and condiment stations covered in chocolate sprinkle powder and spilled cream. This became a significant problem for us when the stores got busy, so I worked with our director of store operations to create and implement clear "cleanliness standards" across the stores.

One day shortly after the rollout of the cleanliness standards, I visited one of our busiest stores, and it was definitely dirty! I got angry and immediately started cleaning the condiment station—with a rather contemptuous attitude. I wanted the store staff to feel guilty that they'd let the store get so disgusting that the Big Boss had to clean it up.

Then, as I approached the cash register, I noticed there was a sign on the espresso machine saying, "Out of Operation until 6 P.M." *What the hell is that?* I thought.

I was seriously triggered and went straight to the back room to have a talk with whoever was in charge of the shift. I found the assistant manager sitting at the desk reading a comic book and leisurely eating his lunch. He said, "I'm on lunch, but do you need something?" "Yes, I do," I said quite loudly. "Did you see how dirty your store is? I need an explanation. And why is the espresso machine out of operation until 6 P.M.? That's not only bad for business, it's not allowed. How could you think either of those things are okay? I'm shocked by how badly you're operating this store." The assistant manager didn't say anything; he just froze in place for two minutes, and then he left the store, saying he was "going to the bank to get change."

I went home that night and told my husband about my awful visit. He was equally appalled and suggested that I consider firing the manager for allowing the shutdown of the espresso machine and for not meeting the cleanliness standards. The next day I confronted our director of store operations and self-righteously told her about my horrible visit. I expected her to apologize profusely and tell me how she would make this right ASAP.

Instead, she became angry with *me*! It turned out that there were legitimate reasons that the store was in disarray and the espresso machine shut down. This particular store was terribly short-staffed and had been so for months, which created ongoing stress and extra-long work hours for the manager and assistant manager. The beverage work area in this store was particularly small and poorly organized, making it extra difficult to do the job (many of the stores needed remodels to the beverage area). This caused people to cry uncle and quit. The director of store ops was personally helping to hire and train to resolve this. Also, the store was so busy selling mostly our signature Ice Blended Mochas that customers often had to wait 15 to 20 minutes to get their drink. But when the store had to also make espresso drinks, which required a dedicated staff member and disrupted the Ice Blended production system, the wait time swelled to more than 30 minutes. A 30-minute wait time is definitely worse than closing the espresso station.

But the operations director's biggest beef with me was about *my* behavior in the store. My self-righteous attitude and criticism of the staff came through loud and clear. Considering everything in the situation, they did not deserve that. In fact, they deserved my gratitude for working so long and hard in such difficult circumstances. Instead, the assistant manager was so traumatized by my criticism that he quit that night.

My explosive response to the dirty store had created a full-on crisis. Instead of slowing down, getting curious, and giving my team the benefit of the doubt, I jumped to inaccurate conclusions and blamed and shamed my team for handling a difficult situation as well as they possibly could. This seems clear in hindsight, so why didn't I react differently? And why was I so confident in the moment about criticizing the team? What did I think I was going to accomplish? And why couldn't I anticipate that my actions would have negative consequences?

Questions like those are exactly what we're going to address in this chapter. As you can see, the crisis I created when encountering the dirty store had everything to do with how I was behaving in that moment. How we show up and conduct ourselves in any interaction with other people is fundamental to how we function in business. As you go through the chapter, I think you'll understand why I've chosen this as the first agreement to examine, because it's the foundation for everything else we'll explore in this book.

We're going to take a close look at the main two ways we "show up" in situations—in Self-Leadership or in self-protection; how we operate in each of these modes; and how we shift out of one and into the other. But first we need to know a few basic facts about human behavior.

THE WAY WE'RE WIRED

Our understanding of how human behavior and productivity works has undergone breakthrough changes in recent years thanks to new scientific discoveries. We now understand more fully what drives our behavior—meaning what causes us to take certain types of action and say specific things. To summarize and put the science in very simple terms, there are three main drivers of how humans behave, interact, and respond to other people (and the world around them): *intention*, *habit*, and *reaction*.

Intention

Humans have enormous intelligence and so many amazing capabilities that we could never list them all. The way we apply our smarts and talents is by making conscious, intentional choices for what actions we take and how we behave. We have "agency"—meaning we create our own future and learn to get what we want by choosing to act in a specific way, with a specific purpose or intention in mind. We make choices and then behave in accordance with them, in everything from choosing our clothing for the day to making dinner reservations to solving complex math problems to creating a new piece of art.

The thinking and mental processing that drives complex, intentional behavior happens in the prefrontal cortex, an area of the brain sitting right behind the forehead in the frontal lobe that's responsible for "executive actions." Critical thinking, assessing risks, weighing options, planning ahead, imagining the future—even deciding when to talk and what to say in an important meeting—all these things happen here. This is the area of the brain we want in charge when making business decisions and taking action based on them.

In business today, many team members are what we call "knowledge workers"—meaning the company desires their specialized skills and their ability to apply them to achieve intended results. Jobs today require people to use their own brainpower

4

more than ever, which means that we need people to engage their frontal lobe to access their intentional thinking and behavior.

But there's a catch: Intentional thinking and behavior take up a lot of energy—literally—meaning we each have a limit for how much we can do before we need to step away and recharge. For example, think about how you behave during a job interview or on a first date. If you're like me, to make a good impression, you painstakingly think through every word and action. Your levels of focus and awareness are greatly heightened while you're putting your best performance forward, and frankly, it's exhausting! Can you imagine having to behave with your steady partner as if you were always on a first date? Luckily, once we have the job or the partner, our behavior becomes much more relaxed and habitual—for better or worse!

Habit

Habitual behavior happens when we automatically do and say things that we've done many times before, without consciously thinking about it. We spend a substantial part of each day in habitual behavior, saving our precious and highly taxing critical thinking for the things that matter. For example, you don't have to expend thinking energy to go about your morning routine, from brushing your teeth to making your breakfast to getting dressed and driving to work; it's all autopilot! This frees you to use your thinking energy to prepare for something challenging in the day ahead, like having a difficult conversation, or proposing a change to an important schedule.

Habits are especially useful when we can take skilled behaviors and practice them until they become automatic. While reading this book, you're not thinking about the act of reading—you've read so many times in your life that it's a hardwired habit by now. This allows you to consider the content instead, thinking about the points I'm making and forming your own opinions about them! We'll talk later in the book about the importance of habits in teamwork.

Emotional Reaction

This is a second type of automatic behavior, but different from acting out of habit, in that these are reactions that are driven by our emotions. There are many types of human emotions that drive behavior, but the ones that we encounter the most in business involve reacting to threats. This happens when we encounter a perceived threat and automatically react to it from our emotional center in ways that are meant to protect us—so we call these behaviors "self-protection."

Humans have an extremely sophisticated system for identifying and taking immediate action against threats, and that's by design! Emotional reactions are centered in our amygdala, the almond-size "threat detection center" that cues the sympathetic nervous system, which controls our fear response. The amygdala sits directly on top of our brain stem, making it first in line for information from the central nervous system (the body's "information superhighway" that's connected to all our senses). Whenever the amygdala identifies a threat in the environment, say, the strong smell of smoke or unexpected heat on the skin, it sounds the alarm bells! This is when the sympathetic nervous system takes over and the "fight or flight" response kicks in. The hypothalamus then releases adrenaline and other hormones that speed up our heart rate and breathing while slowing down low-priority tasks like digestion, long-term planning, and complex thinking.

The protective reactions and behaviors of the sympathetic nervous system are extremely effective when the situation requires some immediate defense, like putting up your hands to block a rogue soccer ball. In fact, humans wouldn't have survived this long had we not adapted to take such swift action in dangerous situations. But this system isn't adapted well for complex, longer-term, or psychological threats. It's programmed to interpret things like our boss's raised voice and critical remarks in a meeting as a challenge to our survival, causing fight-or-flight reactions within our nervous system. Though we usually don't literally flee from the room, we may react by becoming highly defensive, or by pointing the finger at co-workers to deflect blame.

It's astounding how rapidly we assess others' behavior as being threatening. Have you ever been presenting to a group when you saw someone roll their eyes while you were making an important point? If so, it was probably difficult to keep your attention on finishing the presentation as your nervous system fired up to prepare your body to deal with this clear sign of disrespect. If it was your boss who rolled their eyes, your professional confidence probably disappeared in less than a second!

I think it's easiest to think of our emotionally reactive threat responses as belonging to four main categories, and it's worth knowing them so you can easily identify reactive behaviors. In addition to the well-known "fight" and "flight," there's also "freeze," which is withdrawing or shutting down, and "please," or reacting in an appeasing, placating way to de-escalate a situation. I'm a big "pleaser," and I can't tell you how many times during my career I've said "yes" when I was put on the spot, because it was too uncomfortable to say "maybe" or "no," which was my real answer. This means I would literally say, "Yes," even though I knew that I would need to renegotiate later because there was no way I could actually keep the commitment. During those times, my reactive nervous system took charge to save me from the immediate threat it perceived, but it had no ability to consider 1) that I could say "no" and still survive or 2) that I was creating an even worse situation that I'd need to confront later.

With the prefrontal cortex off-line when in self-protection mode, it can be easy to react to a psychological threat as if it were something much greater. But responding to an upset boss from an emotionally reactive place will undermine cooperation and compromise, only making the situation worse. Way worse! Relationship repair is much more taxing than slowing down before you do the damage.

To give you an example of what can go wrong when a leader is in reactive, self-protection mode, I don't have to look any further than my own story. When I was a young twentysomething CEO of the Coffee Bean & Tea Leaf, things were unfolding fast. Our main competitor was Starbucks, and we were both building stores all over Los Angeles. I thought that given their real estate expertise, if they were looking at a location then it must be THE place to be, so I would seek out a nearby spot for Coffee Bean to make its home. It was a strategy that brought me a good number of wins, but there was a dangerous blind spot.

To make a long story short, Starbucks had the capital to open 10 times the locations we could. They could afford a number of misses. So when I was reacting to Starbucks's actions, rapidly deciding about locations and applying the logic that if Starbucks wanted to be there then the Coffee Bean should be too, I was missing a higher-level strategic consideration. Were these locations really the best ones available or could I find better options if I did more research? I needed to slow myself down, perhaps spend more time with the local real estate agents and then talk it over with my executive team. Instead, my FOMO (fear of missing out) overrode the fuller strategic thinking I needed to make such significant long-term decisions—which left us with some painfully low-performing stores. I made poor choices because I wasn't aware that my FOMO was tanking my ability to think logically and anticipate that more good locations were coming too. Emotions are incredibly powerful and easily take control of our thinking and actions.

Shifting from Reaction to Intention

In business, an effective response to a situation—as opposed to an emotional reaction—requires the kind of critical thinking and processing that only the prefrontal cortex is capable of. You need the "thinking" part of your brain to sort out the complexities, process data, project forward consequences, and then *make competent business decisions.*

Unfortunately for us, the critical thinking part of our brain is easily overtaken by our much more powerful, emotionally reactive sympathetic nervous system. This is an enormous problem for any human being who's trying to perform well on the job. As a society, we seem to understand that professional athletes and performing artists need to conquer their fears, stay focused, and learn to manage stress and pressure so that it doesn't affect their performance. And while having a positive mindset is also important for performance, we know that the self-management part is an absolute imperative for athletes and artists. No amount of positive mindset will overcome an athlete's inability to tolerate and play through pain and discomfort, physical and psychological. However, in business, we believe that pain and discomfort should not exist and that these are indications of problems or stress we should not have.

You might now be thinking, *Of course businesses will have stress and problems, and we will handle those with a positive mindset!* But in my experience, that is practically never the case—ever. When stress and problems surface in business, people get scared, angry, upset, avoidant, blaming, and so on, as our reactive minds shout at us, *THIS problem is unacceptable! This exact stress should NOT be happening! Someone messed up, because if they hadn't, we wouldn't have the stress or the problem!*

The sympathetic nervous system is a powerful force, and when left untamed, it drastically limits individual performance and causes major problems in both thinking and relationships. Because "taming" it is imperative and also something that must be learned, I have developed a Self-Leadership process that supports leaders under stress and pressure to tame their reactions and get their critical thinking reengaged!

Self-Leadership is a skill that can be learned, like any other skill. And when Self-Leadership is your internal habit, you become a fully empowered leader able to actively choose a response in the present moment that will serve both the short term and the long term of your business goals. When you build a *team* of individuals who have all developed the skill of Self-Leadership, you will have an amazing edge.

Let's take a closer look at what happens within you and your business when you're in self-protection mode. That way, you'll be aware when it's happening, and you'll be able to take action to shift yourself out of it!

RECOGNIZE SELF-PROTECTION

It all begins with learning to recognize when you're in self-protection. Without awareness, you cannot make change.

Self-protection—the fight, flight, freeze, or please response—served us well when we were cave dwellers, under constant threat from the elements, wild animals, or invading warrior tribes. Today, the irony is that in modern scenarios these responses not only don't protect us, but they're counterproductive, creating all kinds of problems in business and personal relationships.

Behavioral scientists explain that these reactive behaviors are not adapted to modern-day human life, in which we encounter very few immediate threats, unlike our ancestors who encountered many. Instead, in today's society, we are continuously challenged with psychological stresses that involve anticipating the farther-away future. Humans living in wealthy industrialized nations rarely worry about starvation; instead, they worry about paying taxes, getting promoted at work, sending kids to college, et cetera. Our world has so many psychological threats that it's impossible to avoid ever going into self-protection. Frankly, it's a miracle we don't spend all our time in self-protection!

However, to perform well, we must spend as little time as possible in self-protection, and this is why it's incredibly important to recognize those behaviors in ourselves and others. So what do those thoughts and behaviors look like? There are way too many to list, but some of the most common include avoiding, hiding, blaming, judging, rationalizing, and being paralyzed in the face of overwhelm. You can see the downward spiral illustrated vividly in the graphic on page 10. I call it the "lower spiral" because, as you'll discover a bit later in the chapter, it's the lower half of a whole model, and when you're down there, you can easily get swept down the proverbial drain! Your best thinking is not available when you are operating from this destructive lower spiral. I constantly remind the CEOs and leaders who work with me that "Nothing good happens in self-protection!"

But of course, we all become emotionally reactive at one time or another. I usually recognize when I'm in self-protection because I feel an almost uncontrollable urge to say or do something immediately. My heart rate speeds up, my cheeks get hot, and I can't sit still. Most people can relate to that type of discomfort. Here's an example: Imagine you are in an important meeting and a teammate questions the progress of a big project you are leading. They express "concern" that it's not further along, phrasing it in a way that implies your performance is lacking. Let's add one more stressful element: The CEO is in the meeting too!

What happens in that moment? With a flush of embarrassment and your heart racing, a self-protective reaction usually plays out: You might defend yourself and go into explaining every aspect of what you are doing and show why the other perspective is wrong. This leads to a debate with the other team member, where you both engage in blaming, rationalizing, and defending, causing the meeting to totally veer off course. Now neither of you looks good, valuable time has been wasted, and your CEO is losing confidence and questioning the team's ability to resolve issues productively. You leave the meeting feeling unappreciated, misunderstood, and without having made any progress on the project. Plus, you now believe that others perceive you poorly.

Blaming, defending, and rationalizing were the main offenders in this example, but there's a whole slew of self-protective behaviors that crop up whether people are high-level leaders or individual contributors. Here are some of the most common.

Ignore and Avoid

The first (and most common) way that we get self-protective is to ignore and avoid. Often this happens when we get overwhelmed, and it can manifest as procrastination. To use myself as an example, in my early interim CEO jobs, I was frequently brought in to help a company turn around and was expected to restore profitability quickly. The quality of my work is high—when I'm not overwhelmed. But in these jobs the constant crises, ever-changing situations, and lack of any certainty overwhelmed me a lot. I began the work assuming one set of facts—usually that things were moderately challenging—only to then uncover super-serious issues that no one had told me about, because they didn't know either! These situations, where I kept uncovering more and more bad news, were some of the most stressful in my whole career. But if every time I got stressed and overwhelmed, I gave in to my introverted, protective instincts—denying or ignoring complicated situations or avoiding discussions that might trigger conflict—I not only would have failed at my job, I would have had a heart attack from bearing the stress alone, knowing the situation would explode at some point. You can't turn a truly difficult situation around without facing it head-on and letting the truth lead you—no matter how painful.

Moreover, when leaders are highly avoidant, other team members looking for direction and guidance can feel disrespected. Many years ago, I worked with an avoidant CEO who interacted so infrequently with his team that he made them feel that their input and needs were such a low priority that he couldn't make time for them. If a dynamic like this isn't carefully addressed, then when the team eventually starts to complain, the CEO is only going to get more avoidant. It wasn't until I taught him how to consciously and productively engage with his team that things shifted.

Deflect with Denial or Rationalize

Another two sticky spots in the self-protection spiral are denial and rationalization. Let's say you're working on a project with a deadline that you know you're going to miss. The internal dialogue might sound like this: *I know I'm behind. But maybe not really that far behind? I think I can do the next part pretty fast. I've probably got it from here. I'll do a very quick assessment and then not think about it again for a while.* Now you've deliberately chosen not to recognize the looming deadline as a possible problem; instead, you've explained it away so you aren't even thinking about it, much less taking any action.

Then, as the deadline approaches, you may go from denying that it's an issue to denying that it's your fault. This is where the spiral really kicks in: Denying turns to rationalization and leads to blaming as you think, *Okay, fine, I'm not going to meet this deadline. But it's not my fault. My boss gave me extra work that interrupted it, and I got sick one of the days, and my instructions weren't clear.* As the deadline looms and others start to notice you're behind, denial must give way to other self-protection behaviors, such as using blame and judgment to deflect your own responsibility, but ultimately that doesn't work either and you find yourself in a self-protection crisis.

Judge

Making evaluations of people and situations to discern if things are going positively or negatively, or to identify danger, is a human imperative for making effective decisions. When we do this well, it's often called "having good judgment." But when we make moral or value judgments by assessing people and situations as bad or wrong, we instantly close our minds and move deep into self-protection. That's not a problem if you're about to get mugged, but it's an enormous problem when you're trying to work effectively and cooperatively with other people. As humans, once we've decided that another person is against us or on the "wrong" side of an issue that impacts us, we feel instantly unsafe—as though we must watch our back with them, even if the issue is relatively small.

An example that happens in many businesses is when team members gossip or complain with each other about team members who aren't present, or about their bosses. In the moment, this usually doesn't seem like a big deal, especially if you agree with the complaints. But when you leave the discussion, it's almost impossible not to create negative judgments about the complainers that you then carry forward with you. The inner dialogue often sounds something like this: *Wow, that person was too critical of our co-worker and raised a sensitive issue behind their back! That wasn't just "for fun," that was mean and unfair to do that behind their back. I better be careful about what I say or do around that person or the same thing may happen to me! I think I'll distance myself and try to avoid doing projects with them from here on.* Now we have team members who are suspicious and actively avoiding each other, which is terrible for business productivity. Even if things were exaggerated and misinterpreted in the casual conversation, the judgment will remain and expand as the team members avoid each other.

Blame and Defend

"To make a mistake is human, but to blame it on someone else is even more human!" I love this anonymous quote because it reminds me just how automatic it is for humans to blame. If you've ever had a toddler, you probably know that they're naturally able to lie and blame others long before they even have the cognitive ability to make it believable. When I teach classes about self-protection, I often refer to a story about Koko, a gorilla living at the San Francisco Zoo in the 1980s, who was taught sign language and also raised a kitten. Koko knew 1,000 signs, plus how to blame and lie! She once ripped a sink out of the wall, and when her keepers confronted her about it, she blamed her kitten, signing, "Cat did it."

Brené Brown says that blame is how we discharge discomfort and pain, and I find that's a helpful way to think about it. It's difficult to experience anger and other types of emotional pain, and when we aren't able to manage those feelings, we do everything possible to direct that pain elsewhere.

Defensiveness may sometimes seem warranted, but don't be fooled, as it's just another form of blame. When someone defends themselves, saying something like "It's not my fault the deadline was missed—I had nothing to do with it!" they not only imply that it's someone else's fault (blame), but they also communicate that they don't care about their teammate's situation and are willing to leave them completely on their own to resolve it.

Blame and defensiveness can be particularly insidious and difficult to escape. Think of a personal conflict that happened in your life. I had one where I was arguing with my husband over who was supposed to take the lead in our tax preparation. When I said, "I'm absolutely right. You're absolutely wrong," I made things worse by backing myself into a corner. Because then when I remembered that I actually *did* tell him that I would do the prep and have it ready by Monday, I wouldn't admit it. Instead, as I got more indignant, I became terribly invested in him being wrong and me being right! In that emotional state, I couldn't handle the shame and embarrassment of being wrong, so I concealed the truth. Needless to say, the situation got worse, not better.

Bonus: Self-Blame

Another ultra-common self-protective behavior is *self-blame*, and it is just as unproductive as blaming others, if not more. *Self-blame is essentially conflict with yourself,* and it easily escalates to shame as the dialogue in your head becomes self-criticism, which never ends well. If you tell yourself, say, that you failed to delegate properly and thus a team member's mistake is really all your fault, or if you berate yourself for not holding your priorities when your workday gets derailed by last-minute requests, you'll end up spending a large part of your day with negative self-talk running in the background, inhibiting your ability to focus, think clearly, and get things done.

I worked with a company whose content manager was always behind on her deliverables. Before anyone could have a productive conversation with her about making organizational changes to support her and fix the chronic problem, she would work herself up into such a state of self-blame—castigating herself and putting herself down—that her team members didn't feel like they could talk with her at all. Even though the situation was negatively impacting them, they didn't want to add to her already anxious state by piling on more. So they stayed quiet until the company reached a point when missed deadlines and late content simply couldn't continue, and the content manager was let go. If she had been able to release the self-blame and work openly with the team to find solutions, the company could have retained a smart, loyal contributor, and she could have kept her job.

I've thought about and researched why we humans self-blame the way we do, considering that it's self-destructive. I believe it's because acknowledging that we live in a world where we have very little control over how each situation turns out—and how vulnerable we are to experiencing failure, disappointment, and emotional pain—is extremely frightening. We create a belief that if we do things "better" next time, we'll assure our success and won't have to feel this terrible pain again.

That belief is false, though, and self-blame is ultimately an emotionally driven, self-protective reaction like any other. It skews your thinking, clouds your perspective, and most often causes you to isolate, preventing people from helping you during the time when you need it most. Think about how effective your decision-making is when you're feeling guilt or shame. It's 100 percent unproductive. And it feels horrible!

Stealth Behaviors in the Self-Protection Spiral

When we work with clients, they usually grasp the concept of self-protective stress responses such as avoidance, denial, and blame pretty readily (with more than a few nods and eye rolls as they recognize themselves in the behaviors we're describing). Perhaps you're nodding in recognition right now! But what I've found is that after we teach people about the ways self-protection manifests, while they usually improve their most obvious behaviors, they have more trouble recognizing and addressing the more deeply rooted or nuanced ones. Below the surface can be a whole host of behaviors that can *seem* productive but that are secretly masking lower-spiral tendencies. That's why we call them "stealth" lower-spiral behaviors, and because they tend to be our automatic ways of acting—our defaults—they require extra awareness to discern and overcome.

The Trap of Over-Responsibility

A common example of a stealth lower-spiral habit is taking not just responsibility, but over-responsibility. On the surface this may sound positive, like, is there such a thing as taking "too much" responsibility? This is where the stealth part comes in.

Say a team just made a big, expensive error. The leader's inner dialogue may go something like this: *Ugh, this is a big, costly mistake that my team just made. But I should have known that they weren't ready to handle that project on their own. I should have anticipated that they'd make this mistake or checked on them way more so that I caught it earlier. So in reality it's my fault. After all, it is my department, so ultimately I'm responsible for everything that happens in it. I guess I just messed up big-time.*

On the surface this looks like a mature and effective demonstration of leadership, right? The leader is taking responsibility, being accountable for results, and therefore not blaming the team or deflecting the problem. So it's all good, right?

Wrong! This is just self-blame in a different and even more damaging guise. The logic is: *This thing that happened is ultimately my fault because I should have anticipated it would go badly and then personally done something different to have the situation go well.* But this logic is massively flawed.

First, humans are not infallible, and making mistakes is an unavoidable part of business. To presume that I myself, or you yourself, or anyone else, could have done things perfectly and controlled the outcome in a similar situation is a fallacy equivalent to a professional basketball player presuming they'll score on every shot they take. Second, business performance is situational, and every situation has many factors at play, some that we can control and many that we can't. When a professional athlete misses the game-winning shot, is it their fault they lost the game? Or is it the team's fault for not making sure they were far enough ahead that they didn't need a game-winning shot? Or is it the coach's fault for planning the wrong strategy? Or did the general manager mess up when choosing the player roster?

Bottom line: To say definitively that a business situation should have gone differently, and that it's ultimately your "fault" that it didn't, is flat-out impossible. Taking excessive responsibility on yourself is *not* a mature or effective demonstration of leadership; it's an emotionally reactive behavior that starts you on the spiral, just like all the others.

In our example, here's where the leader's negative inner dialogue then compounds: *Oh my gosh, my team isn't nearly as capable as I thought, and I'm going to have to take back lots of responsibilities that I don't have time for. I've invested a lot in my team, and now they can't even do the work that they signed on for. I guess I hired a subpar team. But I don't have the time to train them, and I can't fire them because then I'd have no one—this is an impossible situation I've gotten myself into.* With those thoughts and feelings running, the leader's next actions will most likely be to isolate, take more tasks on themselves, and hold even more resentment as they try to regain confidence in themselves by "figuring it out" alone.

To the team, the message sounds something like this: "Hey, everyone, thanks for meeting, but I don't think we really need to debrief this mistake. I get what happened and I know what I need to do next. So, my time is better spent just figuring out the new plan on my own. I'll get back to you all when I'm finished."

Hearing this, the team sits quietly, because these words squelch any contribution they'd hoped to make. This leaves them feeling like they've failed and, even worse, feeling dismissed and devalued, which ultimately makes them less committed. Now the team will not contribute their important perspectives and ideas, and so the leader will take on even more work that they can't really do, which will lead to *more* self-criticism and isolation. The end result is that instead of the team learning from the mistake and being empowered to step up, the leader's self-blame sets off a series of behaviors that sabotage the whole organization.

This leader and this team are stuck, unless they all become aware of the confusing muck that this leader's stealth lower-spiral behaviors have mired them in. It's fixable, but only when the leader sees how they have snowballed the situation into a bigger problem than the one they initially faced.

The Trap of Deflecting Responsibility

This second "stealth" behavior works in the opposite direction to the first—even though they're both stealth forms of blame. This is when the leader deflects responsibility, frames it as giving others autonomy, but then blames the team when things go wrong. I see CEOs do this all the time: sharing a task with the team and then quickly stepping away without explaining it or giving enough context. They frame it in their heads as, *This will be a good test of the team's abilities*! But of course the team fails, and the leader is left thinking this:

Ugh, this is a big, costly mistake that my team just made. I gave them such a great opportunity to really go for it, and they totally messed up. Ironic that they were saying that how I do things is the real problem! I get results! I guess they're not nearly as good as I thought they were, and not nearly as good as I need them to be.

Again, on the surface this sounds pretty plausible. After all, it sounds like the leader got out of the way so that the team could work unhindered and without being micromanaged. And the team didn't warn the leader that they couldn't be counted on to deliver the result, so it can seem like the team is to blame in this example.

You might be thinking, *Well, sometimes blame must be warranted. Sometimes it really is someone's fault. And how will they know they've messed up if I don't make that clear to them?* It's understandable that we might want to assign blame for something that goes wrong; it's a way of trying to regain control over the situation. But blame in *any* situation has negative consequences—it never works the way you intend.

Let's look at what happens if the leader goes back to the team with those thoughts and feelings of blame. The leader's next actions are probably to make clear that the team was at fault, followed by strong demands that they produce results, with some specifics for what the team should do differently to become more productive and effective. That usually sounds something like this:

"Hey, everyone. Well, I'm sorry to report that this project didn't go well at all. You guys and gals made several mistakes that cost us a lot of money. First there was the e-mail mistake with the wrong link and wrong date and time. Then there was an order-taking problem that compounded the situation, because we were totally unprepared to handle the swell of angry and confused customers. Because of this, it underperformed, so we're going to have to raise the targeted results for our next project and add in a few additional projects to reconnect with customers. So, first, to get more organized you're all going to use a new digital project management tool. Second, you're going to share with me each day what you're focusing on, so that I know what you're prioritizing.

Third, the next project has to go extremely well, or I won't be able to keep everyone on. For now, I will let you hire one more person, and that should be plenty to achieve the results."

Again, this sequence of thoughts and actions will almost certainly lead to the absolute worst results! This team will feel stressed, threatened, and insecure—and at the same time resentful of the entrepreneur for not taking any meaningful ownership of the poor results, nor seeking the team's perspective to get the best solutions. The team will also feel that their best next moves are to merely try to do exactly what they're told and certainly *not* to think on their own. Over time, this will lead to them taking less and less responsibility and achieving worse and worse outcomes.

The end result is that instead of both the leader and the team learning from the mistake and bearing mutual responsibility to achieve better results, a self-fulfilling spiral of poorer and poorer performance ensues, with the entrepreneur losing all faith in the team and then moving on to find another, "better" team. Except since the entrepreneur has learned nothing from the experience, nothing will be gained with a so-called better team. What's more, that new team might actually be a *worse* team if the entrepreneur's reputation for disempowering team members becomes more widely known and it gets harder to make good hires.

Stealth Self-Protection in Other Forms

There are a host of other ways that stealth self-protection shows up. See if any of these common behaviors ring a bell with you:

- Pleasing others by saying "yes" when you actually mean "maybe" or "no"

- Agreeing even if you have a different opinion or perspective

- Applying pressure or giving ultimatums, so that others have no real choice and must commit

- Pressing for speed and action, even though the situation would benefit much more from thinking and strategizing

- Taking back responsibilities even when others are reasonably capable, to "protect them" from uncomfortable feedback, which really means your own discomfort with giving feedback

- Giving others space when they really need connection, so that you can avoid confronting an uncomfortable situation

- Pausing decision-making so that you can "think more," when that thinking won't meaningfully change the decision you'd make if you decided right now (analysis paralysis)

- Staying overwhelmed or confused, trapped in a place of powerlessness where you avoid taking more responsibility to influence your task load or clarity

If any of these (or all of these!) resonate with you, don't be discouraged. Ultimately, being able to observe yourself and become familiar with your recurring self-protection behaviors—especially the stealthy ones you tend to default to—is one of your most powerful tools. Because once you gain awareness and recognize your self-protective behaviors, you are in a position to make a different choice. On the lower spiral you may very occasionally get some results despite your counterproductive thinking and behaviors— but it won't last. To achieve consistent, sustainable results, you need your best critical thinking available, and that means you need to be making decisions and acting from Self-Leadership! Which brings us to step two of the process of getting yourself into the Self-Leadership state.

PAUSE TO SELF-REGULATE

Leaders and teams who work with me learn to trust "the power of the pause." To shift from self-protection into Self-Leadership, you first must develop the ability to pause before your emotional reaction takes you off course. The power to pause creates space where you can begin to regulate your emotions and rein them in to a manageable level—one that allows you to see what has been stirred up inside of you, work with it, take a fresh look at the situation, and choose how you want to show up. Another benefit of the pause is that by allowing things to play out a bit, a situation may work itself out or move forward to a place where a new solution emerges.

In the last few pages, we talked about learning to recognize when you're in self-protection. This can't be overemphasized, because to use the power of the pause, you first must recognize when you need to pause! By getting to know your own triggers and reactions, you can much more easily disrupt the emotional cascade before it takes you down.

So how do you hit Pause when you're in the middle of a situation that feels out of control? Here's one trick to try: Ask a question—any question—out loud or in your mind. It doesn't have to relate to the situation at hand at all. It can be as simple as, "Where did he get those shoes?" or "Why did she set up the billing like that?" It works because the process of asking a thoughtful question (not a rhetorical one) pulls blood back into your prefrontal cortex, which, as we saw earlier in the chapter, is the seat of rational decision-making.

Here are some other ways to pause and self-regulate:

- Count to 10, slowly

- Take a few slow, deep breaths

- Walk around the block

- Do some jumping jacks

- Take a dance break

- Take your dog out for some play

- Engage in exercise

- If words need to be spoken, say something like, "Let me think about this; I'll get back to you in a moment" (or "a little later today")

Try some of these and see which suits you and your workplace best. There are a host of other techniques to build emotional regulation and emotional endurance to stay present and neutral, even when the discussion gets heated. We have a list in the Resources section, and one of them is sure to set you on the path to increased emotional endurance.

Stay Focused on Intended Outcomes

Before we move on, there's one more thing you need to know about the pause. Once you've slowed down and shifted out of your emotional reaction to a situation, you next need to anchor your focus on the intended *outcome* for the situation. Intended outcomes, which we will cover in depth in the next chapter, are the shared goals of the team. Every project, every meeting, even every conversation has an intended outcome. When you anchor your focus on the business outcomes in the pause, it serves to align and ground you and your team, no matter what else is happening. When you approach a challenge consciously choosing to stay focused on the outcomes you are going for, it clarifies the situation and prepares you to think and act in the highest capacity.

RESOLVE WITH THE CCORE EMPOWERMENT PROCESS

Now that you've learned about getting out of self-protection, let's move forward to resolve the triggers or issues that got you there in the first place. We'll do this with the five-step process I've developed through my work with my team and my clients—the CCORE Empowerment Process.

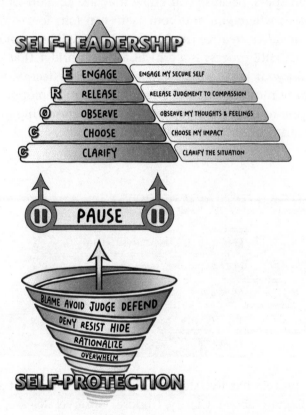

The path out of self-protection to Self-Leadership.

Taking yourself through the steps of my CCORE Empowerment Process is the way to be sure you are applying your best thinking and finding the best resolution for the issues that arise in your business. Quick emotional responses, aka self-protection, lead to

Band-Aid solutions that keep you stuck in a pattern of fighting one fire after the next, yielding poor results and ultimately burnout. Let's free you from the cycle of overwhelm, burnout, and frustration by giving you a surefire habit to build, one that strengthens your emotional endurance and allows you to bring your best thinking forward. I want you to be able to take on challenges in the most effective ways, so that you even begin to look forward to the tough spots, because you know they are actually opportunities—places where you and your team can join forces, do high-level, innovative creative thinking, and succeed faster and better.

The CCORE process is a critical mindset bridge that prepares you to do your best, most creative, intuitive, effective thinking and communicating. It gives you a mental and emotional clearing routine to use before engaging in problem-solving, decision-making, and connecting and working with others.

The process has five steps, and you can see them at a glance in the diagram above: Clarify, Choose, Observe, Release, Engage. It may seem like a lot to learn at first, but stick with me; every step serves a necessary purpose. Remember, we are building a new healthy habit to serve you better in modern stressful settings than the original hardwired habit of self-protection. Intentionally moving through these steps is the way to build a new default setting. Once you know the purpose behind each step, you will want to practice until it becomes habit because it works so well. Soon you will find you can move yourself through this process in mere minutes, and more importantly, you'll find it is worth the time it takes, because of the results it yields. In fact, many of the leaders I have worked with over the years report back with great joy how this process has improved all of their relationships across the board, both personal and professional.

When you're beginning to utilize CCORE and build the habit, we recommend that you start by writing down each step as you do it. As you gain proficiency with repetition, you will soon be able to conduct the process mentally without the need to write it down.

Step 1: Clarify the Situation

Make a list of the primary facts of the current situation. Be sure that you list only the clear facts—not your opinions or assumptions about the situation, or the stories and associations you may find yourself attaching to it through your self-protective judgments or fears. Then look at the list and remind yourself that these are the facts you cannot change and that you must accept them exactly as they are.

Step 2: Choose My Impact

Based on the intended outcomes you've anchored yourself in, the facts of the situation you've just clarified, and the current state of the business and team, ask yourself the following:

- How do I want to show up and have a positive impact?

- What do I most want to contribute to the situation?

- How can I be a positive influence toward achieving the desired outcomes?

- What opinion of myself do I want to have when I reflect back on my part in this situation?

Step 3: Observe My Thoughts and Feelings

The point of this step is for you to acknowledge what you are thinking and feeling. When you take the time to observe your thoughts and feelings, you naturally gain perspective and are able to move through them.

By labeling and describing your emotions, you shift yourself into the "thinking" part of your brain and gain the ability to control your words and actions. Labeling is a simple, solid technique to help emotionally self-regulate so you can consciously choose how you think and act with others, thereby modeling Self-Leadership.

Step 4: Release Judgment to Compassion

This step is a big one. "Release judgment to compassion" is my shorthand for a critical process: Release all the judgments, even the ones you don't want to—*especially* the ones you don't want to—until the feeling of compassion naturally comes forward inside of you. True compassion cannot be forced, which is why the wording of this step is purposefully chosen to remind you to keep going with the inner work of releasing judgments, all the way until you feel genuine compassion for yourself, others, and the situation.

Releasing judgment means letting go of all of your stories, opinions, evaluations of right/wrong or good/bad, predictions of the future, and everything else you've attached to the facts of the situation.

It's easiest to recognize judgments by noticing where you've got strong positions on what is right and wrong, or good and bad. Having a strong sense of being "right," and proving that "right-ness" in your mind (or out loud) with evidence, is a telltale sign that you're making a judgment. So is projecting how things will go badly in the future. Complaining, criticizing, blaming, and defending are strong signs of negative judgments too.

I've articulated three techniques to help you drop your stories, gain expanded perspective, and release judgments. They involve questioning your certainty, your evaluation, and your effectiveness.

The Wizard Test

First, question your CERTAINTY. What do you *really* know? Ask yourself:

- Am I an all-knowing wizard with a crystal ball to predict the future?

- Do I really understand what's going on here given my single, limited perspective?

- Is it possible that I'm missing facts and perspectives that would impact my thoughts and opinions on this situation?

- Am I making assumptions or attributing meaning that may not actually be true in the situation?

- Do I know and understand all the elements and interconnected factors that led up to this situation?

- Given how many business factors are out of my control, can I effectively predict the future?

- Is there a way this situation may positively impact the future of the business, the team, my relationship(s), and myself that I just can't see now?

The Villain/Victim Test

Second, question your EVALUATION of the situation. Is this *definitely* a negative situation? Ask yourself:

- Am I *sure* this is all bad or wrong with no positive opportunities or consequences, now or in the future?

- Am I sure this is all about me and that I'm all *villain or victim*?

- Am I *attributing negative intent or selfishness* to others' behavior that really isn't there?

- Am I *misinterpreting others' behavior* as disrespectful of me when they might be in a high level of fear, emotional pain, or self-protection?

- Am I *seeing myself as a victim* because I can't figure out what to do differently to change or influence my situation?

- Is there a *greater opportunity* for me, my team, and the business hidden in the current challenge, making it highly positive that this came forward?

- Is this situation coming forward because I'm ready to *learn and grow* and I can't do that while staying comfortable?

- (If experiencing conflict or disagreement) Is there a way we're actually *in agreement* beneath the surface issue that I'm not seeing?

The "How's This Working for Me?" Test

Third, question your EFFECTIVENESS. Will your thoughts and behaviors achieve positive results? Ask yourself, given the facts:

- Am I choosing the thinking, attitudes, and behaviors that are most likely to generate a positive result?

- How am I treating myself and others in this situation; is it helping any of us?

- Will I be proud of how I conducted myself in hindsight?

- What can I tell myself that would be more supportive to me now?

- If the main purpose of this situation was for the learning and growth of the team, the business, and me, how would I/we approach it differently?

- If there were a giant opportunity included in this situation, what might it be? Since I'm definitely not a wizard, villain, or victim, can I give myself and others a break for being human?

- What assumptions, biases, and judgments can I just drop for my greater good?

Holding on to judgments will keep you stuck in self-protective behaviors. Remember, no good thinking, relating, or creating happens while you are buried in self-protection.

Here's the really good news about this step: The process of releasing the judgments you hold about yourself, others, and the current situation will free you and automatically engage your natural compassion for yourself and everyone involved. It's a generous, kind, and super effective habit to offer to yourself and others.

The experience of compassion often includes:

- A sense of unity and oneness, that we're all in it together (whatever the situation)

- Competition dropping away as win-win becomes extremely important

- A sense of caring and wanting good things for others and yourself

- A desire to be of service and truly interested and curious about others

- A sense of abundance and confidence that you are able to contribute to others

- A heightened sense of trust and psychological safety, which allows you to risk sharing your perspective and creative ideas while supporting others to do the same

Don't underestimate the importance of reaching this place of compassion before taking action, especially when you are experiencing a high degree of negative emotions.

If you're not feeling compassion after Step 4, allow the time and space to keep regulating your emotions and releasing judgments. Like I mentioned earlier, sometimes it is better to give things a little space. Emotions are energy and will dissipate as you allow yourself to feel them and let go. And when your energy is shifted you can take another look at the situation, see if there are any other stealth judgments to release, and then choose how you would like to proceed.

Here's one important thing to keep in mind: Top performers like you are often the most critical and judgmental toward themselves. If a situation is extraordinarily challenging, take another look after you release judgment. Is there anything else you are telling yourself about this situation that you need to let go? If you are still holding on to something (that one thing you are "right" about), do the work and release that too.

Step 5: Engage My Secure Self

You will know that you have completed the CCORE Empowerment Process when you feel the inner ease and freedom that accompanies authentic compassion and security within yourself. This connection to what I call your Secure Self is a high-level characteristic of Self-Leadership. Rather than being concerned so much about yourself, you can now focus outward and contribute your best in teamwork. It moves you out of being self-focused (which causes you to separate from others and seek power and control) to being mutually outcome-focused, open, neutral, and curious. Once you are engaged in your Secure Self, you are then able to develop secure relationships with others to develop the psychologically safe environment that is needed to work together as a united team. (You'll read more about psychological safety and relationships in Agreement 4.)

PUTTING IT ALL TOGETHER

We've covered a lot of ground in this chapter! I hope you're seeing the importance of choosing how you show up in business, and the tools you can use to do so. To help you see how the pieces fit together, let's look at an experience one of my clients had in moving from self-protection to Self-Leadership.

Tony was the CEO of a rapidly growing online business. His team was remote, which made it hard for him to be sure what his team was working on. He had a misguided belief that if he wasn't constantly in contact and pressuring his team, they would be relaxing, not realizing the true urgency of their upcoming deadlines. What's more, his team was expanding, and he was fearful about meeting the payroll—another reason he felt compelled to make sure the team was always on its toes. He would jump into Slack throughout the day and question team members on the progress of their projects. With each message, the team responded immediately (it was the CEO, after all), but this meant that their workflow was disrupted, and they felt they were wasting time repeating information he was already aware of. He would pop into meetings and take over the helm, dominating the meeting time and interrupting the team's ability to get the information they most needed from one another to meet the tight timelines.

Ironically, although Tony was highly concerned about the team's efficiency, he had become the main hurdle to the team taking swift action because he was reacting to the stress of the rising payroll with self-protective behaviors, including judgment and blame (not to mention micromanaging). When I explained to him the ripple effects he was causing, he was more than a bit embarrassed. But I was quickly able to assure him that this was a common spot for a CEO to be in. It was totally understandable that his financial concerns were triggering him to respond from self-protection. He just needed the tools to shift out of that mode.

As Tony worked the CCORE Empowerment Process in our coaching session, he was able to see ways he could hit Pause in those moments when his fear was urging him to take over a meeting or send a bunch of Slack messages reminding the team how urgent everything was. He clarified the facts of the situation (essentially, that a certain amount of revenue was needed to meet payroll) while clearing away all his stories around it (for example, that his team couldn't be relied on and he was the only one who understood the seriousness of the situation). He chose the impact he wanted to have (to support his team through a successful, on-time Internet launch). He observed and labeled the thoughts and feelings that came up (fear was a big one here) and worked to release judgments (such as the idea that his team wouldn't be "on it" if he weren't riding them).

Finally, engaged in his Secure Self, Tony could acknowledge that it all worked out for the best. From a place of Self-Leadership, he and his COO made conscious decisions to put additional systems in place that would give him a snapshot of team activity. They also made sure their one-on-one weekly meeting had priority on the schedule no matter how busy Tony got, because that was the most effective way for him to get the full picture and get his questions and concerns addressed—not by pinging team members individually throughout the day. Best of all, Tony now had the tools to regulate his emotions and shift into Self-Leadership anytime he needed to.

The ability to shift out of reactive self-protection mode and into Self-Leadership is a critical skill not just for CEOs but for every member of the team. As a team develops, each player needs to demonstrate higher levels of security and confidence, teamwork, leadership, communication, critical thinking, endurance, and self-control. A team of self-leaders can work together and collaborate in the face of unexpected challenges and together find the opportunity in the situation they are facing.

A Word about Discomfort

I'll be blunt: You will likely experience major discomfort when you're learning Self-Leadership and the CCORE Empowerment Process. This is okay. Discomfort is good! It means you are moving through change for growth and learning as you persevere. Staying comfortable is tied to staying with what you know, and doing things differently requires a willingness to stretch yourself while you find your new way. (You'll learn even more about the positive effects of discomfort in Agreement 4.)

As you move forward to strengthen the skills you are learning in this book, you will be able to endure higher levels of discomfort in the face of challenge and change. You will build the emotional endurance needed to perform well in situations that before were too difficult. And your ability to stay in Self-Leadership will keep increasing, allowing you to make the best choices to achieve results, no matter the situation.

As humans, we often do not have a choice about what happens, but we always have a choice in how we respond. Working the CCORE Empowerment Process, just like anything, is a habit you must build through everyday practice. And it gets more and more important as your business grows. We will talk in the next chapter about how, as a company grows and expands, everyone is required to perform at ever-higher levels, including being able to shift and change. Think about it: Even if a business owner desires to keep the business static, saying, "Hey, we've hit our stride; let's just keep doing this," the external world keeps changing, including customer expectations, and the business will have to respond and adjust or become obsolete. The good news for you is that in this chapter, you've gained the tools you need to build a team of individuals who can function in Self-Leadership, even during stress and challenge, so that they can collaborate and innovate to set you up for ongoing success. I want that for you, and I know you can achieve it!

Annie Says:

**"You always have a choice
in how you show up!
Choose Self-Leadership!"**

O O O

SUCCESS STORY
Self-Leadership Can Turn Everything Around

Oscar Quinn, CEO—Real Estate Development Company

THE SITUATION

I hated approaching my team with possible project changes or problems I saw, because they reacted so negatively, even though the problems needed fixing and the changes would make a big, positive difference. I had to work hard to convince them to take action, and sometimes I resorted to demanding that they do it, or I just did it myself. It was exhausting. I was starting to think I should just start over with a new team.

WHAT I DID DIFFERENTLY WITH SELF-LEADERSHIP

First, I had to recognize that even though I thought my team's behavior was the problem, my own (self-protective) behaviors were sabotaging my interactions with them.

I had to look inward and admit to myself that I was often in a bad mood, which made me quickly react and blame the team whenever something went wrong. Whenever my team approached me with a problem, I got anxious, huffy, and impatient, sometimes cutting them off as they were trying to explain an issue. I'd say things like "I don't want to hear it" or "Just get it done." We were stuck in a vicious cycle: I would get angry or disappointed, and they would get overwhelmed and defensive. Sometimes I would even vent my feelings by making a sarcastic comment like "I got into business for this?"—which only made things worse.

Second, when my feelings of anger or disappointment hit, I had to learn to take a deep breath and count slowly to five before saying anything. This was my way to PAUSE and stop myself before saying something blaming or sarcastic.

I trained myself to say a few different phrases instead: "I need a moment to regroup. It has been a busy day" or "Before we dive in, let's all take a quick pause, then meet back here in two minutes." Having these phrases handy helped me to interrupt myself when feeling emotionally triggered and regain my footing. When I couldn't shift my energy, I rescheduled meetings until after I calmed down.

More often than not, I found a deliberate pause was all I needed to rejoin my team from a much calmer place. I also told them that I was working on becoming less reactive, and when I messed up, I apologized.

THE DIFFERENCE IT MADE

It turned out that I didn't need to fire everyone! My team was better than I thought, and I had two leaders in particular really step up.

Right away I noticed that one of those two leaders stopped avoiding me and started to raise issues before I found them myself. The second leader identified mistakes before they escalated and approached me with proposed solutions. The team also said they could see me trying to do things differently, which they really appreciated. Over time, they became more effective and proactive, which increased my confidence in them and created a virtuous cycle.

I almost can't believe that all I needed to do was learn Self-Leadership. When I stopped blaming and reacting, my entire team stepped up and fully took charge of their work, so much that I stopped needing to police them and I was able to work on the things that were important in my role!

AGREEMENT 1 TAKEAWAYS

We consistently show up in Self-Leadership rather than self-protection.

_____

- There are essentially two ways we can show up in any situation—self-protection and Self-Leadership—and the great thing is we get to choose!

- Self-Leadership is the ability to regulate our emotions so that we can think and behave intentionally, even under pressure and stress, to tame our reactions and get our critical thinking reengaged.

- Our actions aren't always based on our critical thinking and deliberate choices—as humans, we only sometimes act from our conscious intention. Other times we act out of routine or unconscious habits, or we react from perceived threats and emotional triggers.

- RECOGNIZE when you're in self-protection, even when it's stealthy, because remaining there will sabotage your relationships and performance.

- REGULATE your emotions by embracing the Power of the Pause. This can include activities such as taking several slow deep breaths, counting to 20, going for a walk, or dancing to some music!

- RESOLVE the issue that triggered you with the CCORE process to engage your Secure Self and empower your best thinking from Self-Leadership.
  Follow the steps of CCORE: *clarify* the situation, *choose* my impact, *observe* my thoughts and feelings, *release* judgment, and *engage* my Secure Self.

FOR YOUR REFLECTION

Take some time to think about what you've learned in this chapter. Write about what you're thinking in a notebook, on a device, or right on this page!

1) What one or two past situations (business or personal) come to mind that you recognize could have gone better based on what you know now?

_____

_____

_____

2) What insights did you gain about yourself from this chapter?

_____

_____

_____

3) What is one next action or interaction you intend to do differently moving forward?

_____

_____

_____

AGREEMENT 2

DEFINING COMPANY GOALS

We define and align on intended outcomes.

The foundation of team achievement

"We define and align on intended outcomes." This agreement may seem so obvious that you're probably wondering why we are devoting a whole chapter to it. But when I ask leaders and their teams about their main obstacles to performance and what prevents them from achieving results, the number one answer—*by far*—is "Not having clear goals." They say things like: "I don't really know what we're doing," or "I don't understand the bigger picture here," or "We keep changing our plans, and I'm confused about what we're really going for now."

My CEO clients are routinely shocked when I share this with them, saying things like "What do you mean, they don't understand the goals? I talk about them every week! Plus I just explained them in depth at our all-hands meeting a month ago! And what about all the strategic planning we did? My entire leadership team attended those sessions and said they loved the vision and goals!" I remember my leaders saying the same thing to me at Coffee Bean, and thinking to myself, *What the heck more could I tell them? I've given sales goals, and new store counts, and customer satisfaction targets—what else could they possibly need?*

I was perplexed about this for years until I realized that when team members said, "I don't really understand the goals," what they usually meant was, "I don't know how to achieve the goals, nor do I know the plan to make them happen," or "I don't really understand my part and how it will contribute to the goals," or "I don't believe I can achieve those goals, but I don't know how to say so." No one wants to commit to outcomes when they can't see a reasonably clear path to achieve them. As soon as we focused the leaders and team on creating the strategy and plans to achieve the results, the confusion and uncertainty disappeared, which then made alignment and agreement easy.

But how do we form those original goals in a way that everyone can understand them and have confidence in achieving them? How do we form goals that the team commits to achieving, and then does? And what about when the goals change?

In this chapter we will teach you exactly how to create effective goals and an overall plan to achieve them. Our process produces what we call your "Visionary Master Plan," and after Self-Leadership, it's the most important element that enables teams to achieve desired results. In the Visionary Master Plan, you'll learn how to articulate clear goals along with the "big why" behind them so that everyone knows what success looks like. You'll also learn how to identify the strategic and internal projects that create the path to get you there.

But before we dive into that, we need to temporarily back up and discuss how business happens in the "real world" today. The old ways of working, where unusually smart, driven people gave orders from the top and everyone else did what they were told, are completely obsolete. As I shared in the Introduction, the modern business environment changes faster and faster—technology innovates at blazing speeds, customers demand better quality for fewer dollars, and competitors pop up everywhere. So how do we grow a business amid such rapid change?

THE JOURNEY FROM A TO V: HOW BUSINESS GROWTH WORKS IN THE REAL WORLD

You have likely heard people talk about going from point A to point B. To describe the process of business growth today, I use a model that, instead, charts the journey from point A to point V. Point A in this model represents your current state, and point V represents your Vision State—the state you want to get to, where your vision for your business is made manifest.

You're probably now wondering, *But what does "vision" really mean in this context?* Well, this V State is a set of high-level goals that you can describe in relatively concrete terms, as if you're standing three or four years in the future and have actually achieved those goals.

And this V State doesn't just describe the business results you are aiming for—it also includes the level of operating excellence needed to achieve them. I've found that most small-business owners don't give the quality of their operations much thought. They think that if they just focus on achieving results, then good performance will happen naturally. But as with any activity in which you want to reach a mastery level, your company will hit a plateau if you don't take deliberate measures to improve. So when you are planning your future V State and defining the outcomes you want to reach, you also need to think about *how* you and your team will operate to achieve those outcomes. When you have successfully reached the V State, what level of professionalism, teamwork, communication, structure, and processes will you have in place that have propelled you to reach that point?

Thinking from Your V State

Thinking from your V State is a simple concept, yet it's a major empowering mindset shift. Picture yourself in the future, already having achieved your goals, and then imagine what your work and the work of your team members will look like. What kinds of things will you be doing differently from the way you operate now? For example, if your team currently plans everything at the last minute, how will that work when the revenue doubles? If you make all the important decisions yourself and haven't yet developed your team to take on more responsibility, how will you focus more on strategy and innovation? And if your customer service team currently has to enter the same information into three different software systems, how will that work when your volume triples?

When you think about these things from your current A State, you may realize that things are getting difficult and that you need some extra resources, or more planning time, but you aren't thinking of what will be different about the business at scale; you're just thinking about what would solve the problem *right now*. In fact, each of these issues needs to be addressed not only to solve the problem for now but also to work effectively for a bigger future that's coming soon! This V State mindset should inform all of your strategic planning, major decision-making, and problem-solving, because it both widens your perspective and moves it into the future. Thinking from your A State, or doing what's easy and convenient in the short term, does the opposite. In business, long-term, sustainable success is tied to your ability to face the problems of the current moment and address them with thought-out solutions that not only resolve the issue in the moment but are also in service to your future V State. Short-term-only solutions are likely to cause even more problems down the road, keeping you and your team locked in a perpetual state of running fire to fire, so it's worth thinking ahead in the "now."

Here's how this played out at Coffee Bean. As we sped up the pace for opening new Coffee Bean & Tea Leaf stores, training new store managers became a gargantuan challenge. Early on, our process was to recruit a manager for each new store about four months before the projected opening, and then assign them to an existing store in Los Angeles for training. This worked great—when we were opening at a pace of four to five new stores a year.

But then that shot up to 12 stores a year, and suddenly we didn't have enough local "training stores" to accommodate all the manager trainees. Our first solution came from A State thinking: We'd simply have trainees travel farther, to newer stores outside of LA, and have them train for several months. This solution did prevent the pain of making major investments right then, but expanding a "store-based" training program quickly became a nightmare. Some managers were great trainers, while others were awful; quite a few managers were barely trained themselves and weren't ready to develop other managers; and implementing a consistent curriculum across separate, unique stores proved way more difficult than we thought. More than a few trainees quit halfway through because they got frustrated and lost confidence in our organization. And on top of all that, our best, most seasoned managers got upset about having to constantly train new managers when they also had their own growing stores to run. This caused big stress and unanticipated turnover among the managers we most wanted to keep! It wasn't long before we were struggling to staff both new and existing stores with competent managers, and the problem compounded month over month.

As the situation continued to worsen, we realized we needed to think about the problem in a different way, taking the bigger-picture future into account. We started by estimating how many managers we'd be training over the next 12, 24, and 36 months. Using our growth plans and the regular turnover we anticipated, we ended up with a shocking number: Over only three years, we projected 75 manager trainees *per year* by the end. I knew we were growing fast, but I hadn't really thought about the specific implications and how something that had been relatively simple (training one store manager every few months) now required a ton of resources and a whole new process and approach! We were thinking from what I've now come to call the V State.

Now, with our V State in mind, we ended up building a training center. Instead of having trainees spend four months at a random store, we brought them to our designated training location just north of LA, where they spent about a month learning the ropes (and the milk steamer!). We restructured our entire store manager training program, redoing much of the curriculum so that we developed better managers in fewer weeks. More importantly, during that time, we went from training being something we did every now and then to becoming experts in producing a high number of highly qualified store managers. The benefit of having consistently trained managers trickled down to the rest of the store employees too, since better-trained managers were better at training employees! Solving our challenges with V State thinking was a huge positive shift. And soon enough, developing managers became sort of a mini-business within our company.

Of course, I look back now and see that we could have saved so much time and expense if, when we were first confronted with the training struggle, we had asked ourselves, "Are we approaching this from our A State? Or from our V State?"

Successfully Navigating from A to V

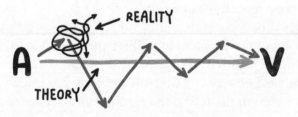

In reality, the straight line is not available!

When visualizing the journey from A to V, entrepreneurs and leaders want so badly for it to be a clear, straight line. They don't want to imagine any big problems or conflicts, downturns or negative outside influences; they think (or hope) that everything should go as planned. But I have to tell you, if a straight line were available, I'd be writing my book on that! Or, on second thought, business would be so simple that I wouldn't have to write a book at all!

Unfortunately, there's no way to avoid challenges, mistakes, unexpected changes, and failures along the way. You'll get better as you go, but it's a long voyage that demands education, commitment, practice, and a willingness to endure difficult feelings and situations.

The journey from A to V usually goes something like this: You make a plan for the direction you want to go, you take a few steps, and then you assess what actually happened. (You can see this illustrated in the graphic below: Look for the chaotic squiggle labeled "Business Happens," because that's what it feels like!) Sometimes things go exactly as you expected, but most of the time it's something pretty different that requires you and your team to address issues, make changes, and plan pivots—all while learning in the process. To decide which changes to make, realign to your V State and make the adjustments based on what will put you back on track to achieve those future desired outcomes. Then, you take a few more steps and see what happens. Be open to new information as it comes forward. Adjust. Repeat! And take heart from this quote I love, from an author who's unknown but, to me, brilliant: "The bend in the road is not the end of the road, unless you refuse to make the turn."

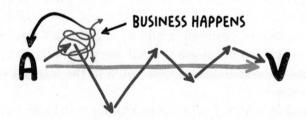

You will probably want to go back to A. But A is no longer available.

One more word to the wise: When you step off of A and things go differently than you anticipated, do not waste time, energy, and resources trying to return to A because it felt better than these new challenges. That option is no longer available! Seriously, once you step off of A, it no longer exists. This is because the world keeps moving forward. You can't go back to how things were before. Even if you tried, your customers' needs and expectations have likely changed, or one of your competitors could be gaining market share, or perhaps a popular product of yours is about to go obsolete. You can change your direction, but you still have to move forward, because returning to the past isn't possible.

Leveling Up

There's something else that happens as you move forward on your journey from A to V. The range of what I call "acceptable behaviors" narrows. The whole team's performance needs to improve, to become more masterful and professional, from the CEO to the leaders to the individual contributors. Because business and sports really do have a lot in common, I often use my stepson's basketball journey to illustrate this point.

In elementary school, Justin, my stepson, was the best player on his community basketball team. He had fantastic eye-hand coordination and was great at scoring points. Being so young, all that was expected of him was to show up for games, get the ball, dribble toward the correct basket, and shoot. The finer points of the game, such as positioning and strategy, didn't matter. Justin made loose plays and hogged the ball every now and then, but his wonderful natural ability carried him and the team to winning many games.

By middle school, Justin was in a local youth basketball league and more was expected of him. He had to learn positions and pass the ball—a LOT. He had to attend practice twice a week, learn fundamental strategies, and make multistep plays that involved other players. His coach made them do some running and skill drills to increase their ability and stamina.

In high school, he joined the freshman team, attending practice three to four days a week and regularly working out to build his strength. Then he moved to the varsity team, where he was practicing every day, including the weekends before the season started. Justin had also grown quite tall and was required to play a defensive position instead of being a player who took lots of shots at the basket. Varsity basketball is an enormous commitment for a high schooler, and before his senior year, Justin reevaluated whether he was up for it. He decided that he'd rather take all that time and energy and apply it to his studies to better ensure his place at a college of his choice, especially since he wasn't a candidate to play college basketball.

If he *had* gone on to college ball, he would've faced even higher expectations that required an even bigger commitment, as he would have competed against and played with only the most talented players who had continued on from high school. Some of those players, those who aspired to go pro, would be making basketball their main focus and relegating their studies to just getting by.

For players who do go pro, the performance expectations are so extreme that their daily lives revolve entirely around their sport. Trainers, physical therapists, dieticians, sleep specialists, and others give specific guidance that must be followed. As the level of commitment and performance keep increasing, the range of acceptable behaviors (even outside of the game) continues to narrow. Professional basketball players don't question the requirements because they know full well what it takes to succeed in pro leagues.

The point here is not only that expectations rise as you grow and get better at what you do, but also that you typically have fewer choices about how you do it. You must do things the proven way that works best. For example (allow me to switch sports for a moment), beginner skiers are taught how to stop by wedging their skis into the shape of a pizza slice. As an intermediate skier, I can do the more advanced parallel turns and stops, but I still use my pizza move to slow myself and regain control on a steep hill (more often than I like to admit). However, I've never, ever seen a professional skier use a pizza wedge to regain control while navigating a slalom course. That method won't work at their level. If you want to be a professional skier, no more pizza wedge—you must use the best practices and techniques that deliver the best results.

Leadership and teamwork habits follow a similar development path. Most people understand this is true for skills, such as engineering or software development, but many don't realize it's also true for personal and interactive behaviors. We'll cover this more in subsequent chapters, but for now, just know leadership is a competency that develops through a process of continued mastery much like sports or the performing arts. And when it comes to the skills that must become sharper as you advance in your career, what most needs to up-level is not your technique for executing specific tasks; it's the People Part.

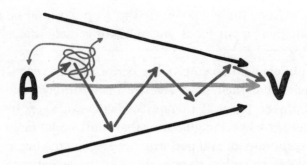

As you move closer to V, the range of acceptable behaviors narrows.

And here's something else to know: As you grow, you won't ever hit a spot when further improvement and development is optional. As much as you may want to stay at your, say, high-school level of play, the way you perform *must* keep going up—if you're going to keep playing. Why can't you stay steady at a certain level if you don't have a desire to grow? Because the external environment keeps shifting and changing in ways that you must respond to. Client expectations increase, technology brings new opportunities and makes old ways obsolete, and economic factors require constant reexamination of profitability and even business viability.

Think about the products and services your company offered only two or three years ago and all the ways you marketed, distributed, and served customers. Has anything changed? Where would you be now if you had decided to stop improving and didn't change anything in your business? What if you had just rolled along as is, sitting on the sidelines, not alert and in the game, but simply chose the status quo regardless of the circumstances?

Standing still will not stop the rest of the world from moving forward. And because the expectations of the outside world continue to rise, the pressure for continuous improvement only increases, which includes how the business operates. Team members must keep improving or they eventually find themselves out of jobs, either because they didn't improve their own skills and performance or because the business didn't keep up and ultimately failed.

When a Team Member Won't Level Up

Robert's company was growing, and his team of seven people could feel it. Expectations and team member performance were increasing organically, right along with the growth. So he wasn't sure how to handle it when one employee, Sarah, hit a bump in the road. She had been a steady team member, but suddenly she wasn't communicating issues early enough, and client service was slipping.

When Robert decided to confront Sarah, she became defensive, insisting she was communicating the same way she always had. As they discussed it further, it became clear that Sarah was correct—her performance actually hadn't changed! Instead, the company's pace of work production had increased to a point where she needed to raise issues much earlier than she used to, and to coordinate with others instead of trying to solve things herself. In the past, one or two clients might have been negatively impacted by an issue she was taking a long time to resolve on her own; now it was dozens, and this was not tolerable for the business.

Sarah was at a choice point. Robert explained to her that if she didn't choose to step up and level up her performance in her role, there would need to be a change (her exit). Because of Sarah's long history with the company, Robert made it clear that if she wanted to stay and was willing to step up, he would support her by checking in regularly and giving her feedback. For Sarah, though, it was too big of a shift. She did not feel able to give more focus and energy to improving in her role, given the demands of her personal life. She had been a perfect match for the company when they were early in their journey (able to play at the high school level, let's say). Since the company had evolved and she was unable or unwilling to match the new pace, she chose to take a role at another company that was a better fit.

These choice points are extremely common as a company advances toward its V State. You can see this illustrated in the graphic below: It's pretty clear when an employee's steady-state trajectory collides with the narrowing range of acceptable behaviors!

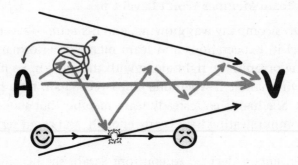

Falling out of the range of acceptable behaviors brings you to a choice point.

HOW TO GET THERE: THE VISIONARY MASTER PLAN

Now you have a sense of what the journey from A to V looks like, and how important it is to think from your V State when you're running and growing your business. But how exactly do you chart the course from A to V? You'll need to define and align clear, executable goals for leaders and teams, and involve others in the conversation so that it's a shared responsibility rather than a top-down decree. My clients do this by first defining their V State and then creating their Visionary Master Plan, which is the path to reaching their V. I've developed a simple process to chart this course.

Before we jump into how to effectively define your V State, I want to share a couple of common yet tragic mistakes that I find almost all entrepreneurs make at this stage. Visioning and goal setting are skills that take lots of practice to do really well no matter what—but if you start off with the wrong idea of what the V State should look like, no amount of practice will get you there.

A Vision That's Too Perfect

One of my clients is a brilliant entrepreneur who has helped thousands of people create their own successful online businesses while also improving their quality of life. She is truly remarkable.

When I was first engaged to develop her team, she excitedly invited me to the upcoming company retreat. On the first day of this all-team gathering of about 10 people, my client jumped to the front of the room and unveiled a five-year plan. This was something her team had been asking her to articulate, so the room was full of anticipation.

My client's vision for the next five years was spectacular. It included growing the business from less than $5 million to over $50 million in revenue, expanding into products (as yet unidentified) that had a "live-your-best-life" focus instead of a business focus, expanding internationally, opening a mountain retreat center, and being a progressive employer by paying all the team members full salaries for a 20-hour workweek. I loved the vision, but it's what I consider to be an ideal scene—a vivid, aspirational picture of big, bold ambitions for the business. I mean, who wouldn't want to work in a company that aspired to meaningfully impact the lives of not only customers but also team members, instead of focusing only on enriching the founder?

The vision had some super inspiring parts. However, as a guiding map for the team to begin executing upon, my client's vision was actually quite problematic. Instead of presenting the vision as a broad aspirational picture, meant to get people excited about what the future could bring, she presented an incomplete set of far-off, yet highly specific, goals along with vague assumptions for what would be needed to get there. It included details like revenue numbers and timelines (from $5 million to $50 million in five years) and big physical results like building a retreat center, but left out other important details, such as the products the company would sell to generate the revenue needed to realize these lofty aims. There was just enough information to leave her team simultaneously inspired, skeptical, and confused.

How did the team react? First with silence, then with some questions about what exactly was being asked of them. Frustrated, my client exclaimed, "You all said you wanted a clearer picture of the goals! I spent three days on this! Here it is!" Sensing her frustration and wanting to smooth things over, the team quickly switched to praising her and sharing all the things they loved about the vision.

The end result of this exercise? The entrepreneur felt disappointed and personally rejected by the team, while the team felt like they had let their wonderful boss down and were super anxious about how expectations were going to be set from here. Each side lost trust in the other. Think about it: How does an entrepreneur trust a team that doesn't believe in achieving the leader's vision? How does a team trust a leader who sets huge goals that they can't see any way to achieve? From something that was supposed to provide the win-win of inspiration, clarity, and alignment, instead they both experienced a lose-lose of mistrust and disconnection.

Experiences like this are so common. In the entrepreneurial business world, it's extremely popular to create a highly detailed, over-the-top "vision" for your business. Leaders get shamed for "thinking small" and not believing in themselves. I've seen visions that were dozens of pages long in which the entrepreneur described a scenario five years in the future where they worked four hours a week, did yoga and cardio every day, had a personal chef to cook healthy meals, owned a beach and mountain home, reached millions of people with their product, received a "best place to work award" from a top magazine, and sold the business for $100 million. Who wouldn't sign up for that?

Now, I do genuinely want every entrepreneur to achieve more success than they ever thought possible. And it's a good thing that entrepreneurs are inclined toward such sunny forecasts, since it's this rare and priceless "glass-half-full" attitude that enables someone to start a business in the first place! But the downfall here is that they're making a list of what they would achieve *in an ideal world*, IF they had all the resources they needed, and the external environment didn't pose any problems or unexpected change. Holding on to a vision that's overly optimistic and translates into unachievable goals is an entrepreneur's mistake number one, which leads directly to mistake number two: dumping that overly optimistic vision on their team and expecting them to commit to the overall goals—without any understanding of what it all really means or what it might take. This combination of setting the bar too high and expecting the team's commitment without a clear understanding of how to succeed creates a "worst of all worlds" scenario in which the team gives up on the vision early because they don't see how they can succeed, while the entrepreneur is left infinitely disappointed by a team that didn't live up to his or her high expectations.

The Three Fundamental Keys

At first it was puzzling to me that most leaders and key team members couldn't identify and describe their company goals when my team started to work with them, even though the CEO had shared enough information that they should have been able to articulate at least the biggest goals. I wondered: Were they confused by the business language? Or were they distracted, lazy listeners? Or actively ignoring the goals to escape accountability? I decided to investigate what the heck was going on.

What I found was NOT incompetence or ill intent, but instead that CEOs and high-level leaders were making the same mistakes I just described—without even realizing it. They *thought* they had clearly laid out practical goals for their team, when in reality they hadn't. The issue, I found, wasn't that the team didn't get what the CEO was going for in a big-picture sense. They did. It's that the gap between "what they want" and "how we get there" was huge, because the goals weren't articulated in a way that clarified the different elements that would add up to a successful outcome. For example, when a CEO says, "Our goal is to double our revenue this year," unless they also specify how the company plans to do that, it wouldn't mean much to the team. No one commits to a goal like that without also understanding at least the basics of the plan to get there. And because that type of goal is so abstract without a plan, it's not considered a practical goal by the team; it's just an aspiration.

It took attending many meetings and strategic planning sessions, but ultimately, I found three fundamental keys to setting goals that a team can both understand and commit to:

1. **Goals must be clear, concrete, and measurable.**
   Company *goals*, *mission*, and *vision* have lately become interchangeable terms and lost their distinct definitions. This leaves it to individual team members to decipher the meaning on their own without a common definition. For example, if a CEO of a vegan products company says, "In twenty years, we aim to lower U.S. meat consumption by fifty percent," is that a specific goal? Or is it part of the overall vision and mission that the company aspires to achieve but isn't making specific plans to reach in the near future?

   I define goals as clear, concrete, measurable (or recognizable) targets that team members are actively working toward achieving. Goals are the short- and mid-term definitions of winning, and without them, it's almost impossible to succeed in the near or long term.

2. **Goals must take into account "external drivers."** These are environmental or market factors that impact a company in a way that the company must respond to. A classic external driver for every company is technology. Most companies today have multiple types of technology they utilize, both inside and outside the company, that change often. Every company I work with is impacted by changes in things like accounting and CRM software, sales transaction technology, and using online platforms. Any company that provides a decent volume of customer service has been forced to interact with clients in multiple ways—meaning answering a phone from 9 to 5 no longer cuts it.

    Other external drivers that require addressing include changing customer expectations, shifts in the labor market or supply of materials, economies that expand and contract, and many others. The economic collapse of 2008 was one of the largest unexpected external drivers I had encountered in business, until the 2020 pandemic hit. So keep in mind that these are often unpredictable and yet must be addressed. Setting a goal without addressing these drivers is equivalent to making a wish instead.

3. **Goals must include team input.** Setting and clarifying goals is often left exclusively to the founder/owner/CEO in entrepreneurial businesses. But without input and context from the team, the team can't commit to achieving the goals. However, a team will rarely push back when an entrepreneur creates the major, high-level goals, as it's his or her business, even if team members don't believe they

can achieve them. Being excluded from the process of
setting goals makes the team completely dependent
on the entrepreneur having effectively thought
through all the major parts of how to achieve them.
If the entrepreneur slips up and commits to a goal
that has no chance of being achieved, or chooses two
conflicting goals that can't be resolved, the team has
no way to reach a successful result.

Business Evolution: Why You Need a Visionary Master Plan

The Visionary Master Plan, or VMP, is a process I created to
help leaders set effective business goals. Before I explain the process, I'd like to share a story that illustrates why you need it.

Some years ago, I worked with a small New York–based advertising agency that had been in business for 40 years. As the Internet
grew, media businesses had to scramble to keep up with the seismic
changes. Large network television (ABC, NBC, CBS) was overtaken
by hundreds of cable channels (such as Discovery, History, AMC),
streaming services (like Netflix), and so much online media that
it's impossible to list. Clients no longer wanted to create traditional
big-budget television campaigns. Instead, they wanted to place specialized ads in all the different channels where their customers now
engaged—TV, cable, streaming, social platforms, and online.

This huge market change turned the business upside down.
The agency had to shift from producing a handful of highly pol-
ished, one- to two-minute TV ads to producing a couple dozen different spots ranging from 5 to 30 seconds for placement on cable
channels, streaming services, social media platforms, and all over
the Internet—for basically the same client budget. A compound-
ing negative consequence was that internal costs didn't shift pro-
portionately with the business—that is, it didn't cost 10 times
less to produce a 6-second spot than a 60-second spot, because
many of the creative and production costs were fixed. Think
about it: Coming up with a central creative idea is going to take a

certain amount of time, whether the eventual ad is 10 seconds or two minutes.

Additionally, the ad firm had to rapidly learn about all the new digital marketing channels that they had very little prior experience with (think Instagram, YouTube, Facebook, WhatsApp, Google, etc.). They tried to learn and respond as quickly and effectively as they could, but they struggled to make the shift while also delivering on the traditional work that still made up about half of the agency's revenue, though that percentage was declining every year. It was like half the company was the same, but the other half needed to be built from scratch for the new digital advertising environment. And they needed to reach a point where they were succeeding in the digital advertising space before the traditional space could no longer anchor the business.

When management shared their diversification plan with the company leaders, it was more like a few ideas rather than an actual plan. I'd sum it up like this: "We're going to add new departments to do digital and streaming work." They said nothing about a new overall business strategy, or how those new departments would interact with the ones they already had. Even though management had an overall *vision*—to become successful in the new media space by leveraging both their creative talent and their specialized production processes for making entertaining ads—they had no organized, concrete plan. However, the pressure was enormous to do something ASAP! So they hired a few expert individuals to lead some new departments, but without a plan, they ended up taking chaotic, expensive, uncoordinated actions that generated poor results. By the time they hired me to help them, they were in serious trouble.

Creative company CEOs typically have tons of language to describe both the 40,000-foot-level and the 4-foot-level goals but have trouble describing everything in between. I immediately facilitated a Visionary Master Plan process to help them identify the specific strategy and near- and mid-term goals that would drive the business pivot. Creating the VMP itself took several two-hour sessions that included all the operational and client-service leaders in the company, which was intense! But once they defined their primary strategic goal—to provide large brand clients a "one-stop shop of superior media advertising and promotional solutions"— then all the other goals and deliverables became easier to define.

Once the strategic piece was in place, the senior leadership team then broke down the goals into projects and plans. To give you an example, in support of their primary strategic goal, they set up a priority project to build and strengthen the relationships they had with the executives in the streaming space. They discussed who had the best foot in the door in the major streaming companies and developed a coordinated plan to do this.

They then set goals for internal improvements. Across the company, they learned to communicate cross-functionally (something you'll learn more about later in the book) and interact a lot more effectively. Each new department needed to know what the other areas were doing so they could coordinate to achieve the best client outcomes. Bottom line: Implementing the Visionary Master Plan process jump-started their growth and business performance, and they were able to turn the company around in less than two years, which then led to a high-value sale.

Now let's bring this back to *you* and *your* business. You've already learned about thinking from your V State, and you've got a big-picture view of how the VMP works. But where do you start to actually make the plan?

Charting the Path to Your Desired Future

In the very beginning of a business, the vision and goals exist only in the head of the entrepreneur. And that's okay when it's just you! However, as you grow, you need to articulate the goals so that others can help you achieve them. The more people you have on your team, the more clear, specific, and comprehensive you need to be when describing your goals. But this is surprisingly difficult, *unless* you follow the process I'm sharing with you now.

I recommend the Visionary Master Plan process initially be done with the CEO and the executive or senior leadership team. In a small business, that may be everyone! In a slightly larger organization, a solid draft of the plan can be shared with different teams to confer, gather important input, and ensure the plan is doable and nothing major has been missed (or adjust it if needed).

Ready? Let's get started!

To create your Visionary Master Plan, I am going to have you think of your business goals for the next 12 to 18 months in four main buckets: financial goals; strategic goals; new client-facing priority projects, products, or services (to achieve those goals); and internal improvement projects. One simple way to approach this is in "back of the napkin" style—writing quick top-level notes on everything you know in the four main groupings without getting bogged down or feeling unclear.

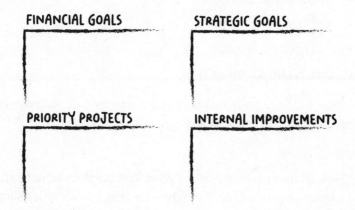

Whether you're typing in a document, writing on a whiteboard, or literally jotting on a napkin, you're going to fill out the top two buckets first: Financial Goals and Strategic Goals. Let's start with the finances.

1. Financial Goals

The easiest way to zero in on your financial goals is to start by listing all of your revenue sources and assigning numbers to them. Then list your other financial goals—these might include margins, profits, return on investment (ROI), expense reductions, or capital outlays. Early-stage companies often create and focus only on revenue goals, which is perfectly acceptable when meeting those goals puts the company in an overall financially healthy position.

Here are some examples of annual financial goals:

- Retail Product Revenue: $2,500,000
- Editorial Services Revenue: $15,500,000
- Digital Courses Revenue: $4,400,000
  - Gold Course: $900,000
  - Silver Course: $1,500,000
  - Bronze Course: $2,000,000
- Returns and Refunds: 5%
- Gross Margin: 60%
- EBITDA Margin: 18%
- EBITDA: $1,700,000
- Net Profit: $1,400,000

Once you have your financial goals written out, move over to the next bucket, Strategic Goals.

2. Strategic Goals

These goals should articulate what you hope to achieve that's new, highly improved, or different—meaning it includes significant change from what you do or achieve now. Strategic goals are meant to be meaningful "needle movers."

To make sure you consider everything you may want to do that's new or different in the year to year and a half ahead, think about these main categories:

- Products, new or major improvement
- Services, new or major improvement
- Brand or image
- Market positioning

- Customer experience
- Company purpose or impact
- Company reputation

Here are some examples of annual strategic goals:

- Create new flagship digital course
- Revise and relaunch our original healthy body supplement
- Gain a minimum of 6 well-known "high-prestige" clients
- Diversify client base and resolve client concentration risk
- Broaden our "anti-aging" cosmetics brand audience (from 40+ women only to also include 40+ men who use cosmetics)
- Provide clients a "one stop shop" for all their human resource needs (not just payroll and benefits) by adding a Talent Management Division
- Launch the "Community Give-Back Career Coaching Program" (for adults transitioning careers)
- Shift brand perception and position to "personal growth based with a spiritual component" (instead of spiritual only)

Now that you have the top two buckets filled out, you're ready to look at the bottom half of the document (or whiteboard or napkin). These two buckets represent the "how"—the ways you'll achieve the outcomes in the top two buckets.

3. Priority Projects

Given the financial and strategic goals you have clarified, what specific key projects and deliverables will be needed to reach those goals?

The projects you list here lay out your approach by identifying the major (priority) projects and deliverables you plan to complete so that you reach your goals. Each project should connect or contribute to a financial or strategic goal. You don't want to go too granular with this list. You want to capture the major projects and subprojects. These will later be communicated to your team, who will help break them down further.

Sometimes only a single project is needed to achieve a goal. For example, you may have a strategic goal to boost client loyalty by hosting a new live event—which is likely a single "live event" project. Other times it will take multiple projects to achieve a goal. For example, you may have a financial goal to increase your restaurant's lunchtime revenue by 35 percent by introducing a new lunch menu and also conducting a new community outreach campaign.

What new products or services will you be selling this year to reach those higher numbers? Will you need a shift in how you deliver a service? Or perhaps you want to increase your marketing efforts and investment to reach a bigger audience? Whatever the case, you have some important information to capture in this bucket.

4. Internal Improvements

These are the things you need to improve internally *so that* you can achieve your financial and strategic goals. If you have sizable new projects and deliverables in the third bucket, they most likely create internal company needs, such as growing your customer service team to serve the greater volume of customers coming in. A good problem to have, right? But one that does require you to make a plan and prepare.

Internal improvement goals typically involve human resources (people), leadership and team behaviors, organizational structure, systems, process, and/or infrastructure. This could include hiring/training new people, improving facilities, changing software, bringing a function like sales or marketing in-house, acquiring or upgrading expertise, restructuring and improving team meetings, or increasing cross-functional effectiveness. For example, many companies implement project management software systems, but the time to do this is when the benefit of tracking many projects and tasks in a software system outweighs the costs of putting it in place, including training, upkeep, and fees. Until that time, using spreadsheets to track projects works just fine. The point here is that having high-tech project management software isn't a goal in and of itself—it's valuable when it empowers the company to more effectively achieve its goals.

I'm sure you can think of all kinds of internal improvements you would like to make, but keep in mind that they need to be for the specific purpose of achieving the financial and strategic goals you've laid out in steps 1 and 2. I can't emphasize that enough. Internal improvements must have a clear relationship to the larger company goals; otherwise, they waste scarce time and resources that are needed elsewhere. So instead of asking yourself what could be done better in any possible area of your business, ask yourself specifically: "What do we need to improve upon internally this year to achieve our financial and strategic goals?"

SMART Goals

Here's a helpful acronym you can use for quick reference to create clear, actionable goals for your team. This is not my acronym; it has been around for a long time now, but it remains very sage advice.

Review your goals and make sure they are SMART:

Specific – Measurable – Achievable – Relevant – Time-Bound

For example:

- Not-so-SMART goal: *Upgrade the membership program to generate rave reviews from fan members who aggressively refer others.*

- SMART goal: *Upgrade the membership program to improve retention by 30 percent and increase referrals by 2X by December 2022.*

- Not-so-SMART goal: *Implement an effective live-event project management system that everyone uses consistently and that improves customer service.*

- SMART goal: *Improve virtual live-event performance by reducing unexpected issues by half, resolving customer complaints in five minutes or less, and improving customer service rating by 2 points by the next virtual event.*

The Living Document

In a constantly changing world, a Visionary Master Plan is your most powerful tool to create aligned, achievable goals that gain the team's commitment. For a Visionary Master Plan to function fully, it needs shared responsibility, the engagement and participation of the whole team—as far as that's practical—and not just the big boss or bosses. The entire purpose of the VMP is to keep everyone clear and aligned on the outcomes they are intending to achieve, and keeping the key players in your organization clear and aligned requires that they have access to and understand the Visionary Master Plan. The easiest way to do this is to bring the VMP forward during team meetings and measure progress against it. With my clients, I insist that this take place consistently (usually weekly) during meetings with the executives and leaders who have the most responsibility for achieving the goals.

Some companies choose to share the entire plan with the whole team—yes, including all the numbers for revenue and even the profits! It's important to note that not every company or team needs nor is ready for that. I suggest that transparency, especially financial transparency, be carefully considered, because you can't take it back once it's out there! The first criterion for sharing information should be responsibility: If someone is responsible for a financial outcome, or they have a large impact upon it, then they need the info to be transparent. The next criterion is business acumen: If the team doesn't understand how the business model works and the financial risks involved, then I don't recommend transparency, because the numbers can be widely misinterpreted. A common example is when employees think, *Oh my gosh, they're making sooooo much money, I don't understand why we can't hire more people!* but they don't have the full picture that includes all the costs (direct costs, overhead costs, taxes, refund reserves, uncollectible accounts, etc.). Even if your company or team isn't ready for full financial transparency, the specific goals that are impacted by a team member's work *should* be shared, as everyone needs to know what they're going for! Keep in mind that senior leaders must know the VMP if they are responsible to achieve it.

Remember, the Visionary Master Plan is a living document because all the time, even as you are executing, change happens. It could be external changes to the market, technology, the economy, new legislation, or shifting customer demands. Or it could be internal changes, such as shifting goals, new strategy, leadership or team changes, mistakes to learn from, or other experiential insights. As a result, any VMP you make will have to change and adapt to stay relevant.

Changes to the VMP usually happen in two ways: 1) The leaders or team miss or anticipate missing a milestone or meeting an expectation, or 2) they discover new information that impacts the goals or the plan. For example, as the team drives forward, you may find that some projects need more resources, and some can get away with less. As these discoveries pop up, you'll have to update the plan. If you don't, the plan becomes obsolete as it is no longer achievable.

I've found that entrepreneurs are often reluctant to do this, because they perceive it as decreasing motivation and letting their teams off the hook. They think, *If I allow us to lower our goals, the team will think it's acceptable to miss goals, and they won't try as hard in the future.* This couldn't be further from the truth. Missing a goal is psychologically painful for anyone who cares, and my experience is that team members care a ton about their performance and the company's achievements—way more than CEOs realize!

It is true that teams can recover from missing goals, and they do learn from their mistakes. Missing a goal can also be motivating, spurring the team to double down to reach the next set of goals. Then when they achieve the next set of goals, they gain confidence in themselves to continue their commitment to great performance. However, when a team faces an ongoing stream of unachievable goals, it's not only demotivating, it's demoralizing. No one wants to play a game they have zero chance of winning. In fact, your star players won't stand for it and will leave if they can't win a considerable amount of the time. What I want CEOs, leaders, and teams to always be thinking is, *How do we win the game given where we are and everything we currently know? Did something change? If so, let's deal with it right now!*

Reviewing and updating the VMP is essential, and sometimes you do need to lower goals—but other times you may need to raise them! Often, you'll need to reallocate resources, or perhaps add a new internal improvement goal, or change the strategy and plan behind achieving a financial goal. Because changes and unexpected situations happen often, I coach executive leaders to be familiar with their VMPs, so familiar that if they were asked, "What is your company up to this year?" they would be able to outline it quickly on the back of a napkin. This knowledge will help them as they perform in their role, because when anything new, or different, or unexpected happens they can check in with themselves first: *Does this impact the plan?* I also coach them to schedule quarterly sessions to do a full review that considers new opportunities and major or complex challenges. And my clients usually conduct an annual VMP meeting, where they plan another 12 to 18 months forward, though they may also do this during an earlier quarterly session when a bigger pivot or change is needed.

In our discussion of defining outcomes for your business, I'm sure you've discerned one key point: Clarity is crucial for successfully identifying your V State, framing your Visionary Master Plan, and executing to reach your goals. And now that you have your game plan, it is time to get clarity at another level—around the roles in your organization. You would be surprised how many resources get wasted in organizations when the team members aren't exactly certain who executes what part of the plan. That's why the agreement we will look at in the next chapter is all about role clarity. Makes sense, right? No pro team would show up to a game without knowing their positions. If they did, it would look more like a free-for-all than professional play!

Annie Says:

"Business is a team sport! Everyone must up their skills and teamwork in order to achieve the future vision and goals!"

OOO

SUCCESS STORY

Having Clear Outcomes Is 80 Percent of Staying on Track

Jasmine Rios, Founder—Fitness Company

THE SITUATION

This is how I used to approach my team when I had a new idea: "Hey, fitness pros, circle up. I jotted down a new idea I had while I was working out today. As you know, I do my best thinking on the treadmill. Anyway, I think it will work great for our clients, and I want us to implement it immediately."

The team wanted to please me and to be perceived as flexible and open-minded, so they said yes to my requests and tried to do them all. However, like any entrepreneurial business, they had resource constraints and weren't able to execute on every single idea, no matter how good it was. Over time, these extra "small" projects added up, and we got stretched too thin and eventually became overwhelmed. This prevented us from achieving our most important goals, and the team realized that if they kept saying yes to all my new ideas, they wouldn't be able to move the needle on the big, meaningful goals.

We all realized that we couldn't continue saying yes to everything, but it wasn't clear which ideas were worthy of doing and which weren't. In fact, things got pretty chaotic until we created clear goals and a real road map for achieving them, which we then used as criteria for deciding what to do with new ideas.

WHAT I DID DIFFERENTLY WITH DEFINED OUTCOMES

After coaching with Annie, my team and I created, for the first time, a Visionary Master Plan. This provided the road map to creating clear goals along with the projects and plans needed to achieve them. We were finally all aligned and confidently committed in a way we had never been before. Once we were on the same page, whenever I presented new ideas, they were added to our leadership meeting agenda for review. During our meetings, those new ideas were discussed and evaluated not only for their positive opportunity but also for their potential negative impacts on our bigger goals.

The team learned to push back on new ideas in a way that worked for me. They would say things like, "Jasmine, we are totally committed to our Visionary Master Plan. We like this new idea, but we don't think we have the time or resources to do it now. It could easily prevent us from achieving our biggest strategic goal of building our brand recognition. If we did add this new approach into our plan for the year, we think we might need to delay the brand building initiative for nine months out. So given that, what do you think?"

Being able to hear my team present their strategic thinking with this level of clarity made it easy for me to understand the potential impact of trying to implement a new idea without considering how it fits with the overall goals. Now we had the mechanism to stay on the same page by coming back to the Visionary Master Plan.

THE DIFFERENCE IT MADE

The first time the team added a new idea to the leadership meeting agenda and we talked about its impact on our Visionary Master Plan, I was able to see the impact of my pop-up ideas in a different light. I saw that even good ideas needed to be properly timed if we wanted to achieve our priority goals.

My team and I also decided to add a "New Ideas" tab to our Visionary Master Plan. It was in a shared doc, and we agreed to add new ideas to this tab that we wouldn't do immediately but would consider for another time. Then we'd review them during our quarterly strategic planning process and decide if it moved the company goals forward in ways that would justify either adding it to or changing the Visionary Master Plan.

Everyone involved felt we had arrived at having a "grown-up business," and I was relieved to have good thinking partners at my side who were looking out for the big vision. Bottom line: By creating clear goals, we could meet every new idea with curiosity instead of fear. It would either be better or not good enough to make the cut—a total win to be on the same page! Plus, team productivity skyrocketed!

AGREEMENT 2 TAKEAWAYS

We define and align on intended outcomes.

- Expect that the path will always go differently than planned. Learning to work with the inherent up-and-down nature of the A to V journey allows you to succeed in the ever-changing real world.

- Once you step off of Point A, it no longer exists. There is only one direction you can go, and that is forward.

- As you grow, your level of operational excellence will need to increase; thus there is a narrowing of acceptable behaviors as you get closer to Point V.

- Communicating goals effectively includes providing the purpose and benefits of the goal, the "why" behind what you're doing. Everyone involved needs to be working toward the same outcomes, with the same purpose in mind.

- Your VMP is a "living document"; reviewing and updating it is essential, making sure it reflects your active goals and your plan to get there. This aligns the team to perform at the highest level of efficiency and effectiveness.

- **NOTE:** You can find a fully worked out example of a VMP—and get more support for creating your own— at thepeoplepartbook.com/resources.

FOR YOUR REFLECTION

Take some time to think about what you've learned in this chapter. Write about what you're thinking in a notebook, on a device, or right on this page!

1) What one or two past situations (business or personal) come to mind that you recognize could have gone better based on what you know now?

_____

_____

_____

2) What insights did you gain about yourself from this chapter?

_____

_____

_____

3) What is one next action or interaction you intend to do differently moving forward?

_____

_____

_____

AGREEMENT 3

ESTABLISHING CLEAR ROLES

We clarify our parts and where they fit in the whole.

The organized structure that enables teamwork

In the previous chapter, I said that the most common complaint I hear from leaders and teams is that they don't know enough about the desired results to actually achieve them. The second most common complaint? "I don't know what my role is!"

Role clarity, in its simplest form, indicates the level of comprehensive understanding people have about their duties and responsibilities. It means that team members know their part in the business and how it fits with the other parts to achieve the desired results. It's usually communicated through a structure of some kind, like an organizational chart in a company or a chain of command in the military. We do it a bit differently from the military (most businesses aren't run like the Marines!), but still, getting role clarity in an organization is essential—and yet quite challenging. It's hard to figure out how a company's people should be structured to operate best and what each role should be when a company expands, adds new business lines, adds or changes functions, and keeps shifting roles. It's especially difficult when goals and roles have to shift often to keep up with major business changes. This is why role clarity works best as a responsibility shared between leaders and team members—as no one person has enough knowledge and insight into every role and how they're impacted every time things change. We'll talk more about this shared responsibility later in this chapter.

STRUCTURE IS FOUNDATIONAL TO SUCCESS

To help you understand why so many companies don't have the structure they need—and what can happen when they don't—I am going to share an example from a longtime client's business. I'll start by introducing you to Judy, the founder, because I'm guessing you'll have a lot in common with her. Judy is awesome; she is extremely positive, a welcoming people person, a super independent and bright woman, *and* the creator of an incredibly effective weight-loss method grounded in cutting-edge psychology and neuroscience. She has an amazing list of academic accomplishments, and yet none of them prepared her for leading a wildly successful entrepreneurial company. So, as effective as her program was and as popular as it proved, she ran into some very common entrepreneurial rough spots in the beginning.

Judy and her husband, Paul, started out with a few employees—mostly friends with varied careers but who had had firsthand success with Judy's approach to weight loss. After coming together as a small team, they produced their first virtual (fully online) event, where they sold their flagship weight-loss program, and the results were outstanding! Then their second event blew up (in a good way), resulting in five times the sales of the first one—and at the third event, they brought in even more. Sounds great, right?!

Well, here's the catch: Having successful events meant having way more customers, which their customer service systems and program delivery weren't prepared to handle. This resulted in many customer complaints and plenty of chaos trying to serve everyone. Judy and Paul hired seven people super quickly to try to resolve the issues as soon as possible. And Judy's directions to them could best be summarized as "So glad you are here; jump in and do something good." With very little training and no role descriptions, they were plopped into still-forming functions and roles and basically asked, "What role and title would you like?" Judy's intention was positive: to demonstrate confidence in her team members and allow them to define and take strong ownership of their roles, despite the roles being brand-new. But this backfired because everyone was trying to design a role that was tailored to their own desires, instead of designing roles that the business needed and that coordinated with the others. This led to chaos, confusion, and competition among team members as they each defined their role by themselves and asserted how it had been promised to them by Judy.

Remember, the digital (online) business was just getting started, so outside of the online events, Judy and her team had to do everything from scratch—things like developing video courses, hiring community coaches, putting customer service software in place, and much, much more. They were moving very fast and reacting to the most urgent crises, so they didn't think they had enough time to plan ahead and organize their projects, processes, and structure. This situation, where growth outpaces the ability to develop adequate infrastructure, is very common among entrepreneurial businesses in the early stages; with my clients, I refer to it as "building the plane as you fly it, while also having passengers on board!"

Judy fully understood that she needed more team and infrastructure, so she sped ahead with hiring—without first organizing the business, setting clear goals, laying out the strategy, and identifying roles. This stage reminds me of how young kids play soccer: You've got a bunch of kids on the field who don't know their positions or how to run plays between multiple people, so they all huddle directly around the ball, hoping to gain control of it so they can personally score a goal. There's usually one or maybe two kids on a team who have natural talent, and as no one has been trained yet, these kids end up controlling the ball and scoring the vast majority of the goals. Which means that all the other players are trying to do something productive but end up mostly watching the star players do their thing.

Judy was *the* star, and she did all the important stuff even after she hired a team, because the team wasn't organized or developed. Since Judy was the only one who knew what needed doing and what the results should be, she was the only one who could handle anything meaningful—but this setup is unsustainable; it leads to burnout and eventually to failure.

This is how Judy's business functioned for more than a year. If they hadn't gotten help, their business would have eventually fallen apart because they were not finding enough time to build the infrastructure and develop (not just hire) the team needed to sustain their rocketing success. We began by identifying the V State she was going for in her business and using that to help her create her Visionary Master Plan. With that defined, we could then take a closer look at how her business functioned, so that we could clarify roles and get a team structure in place.

DEFINING YOUR BUSINESS STRUCTURE

What kind of structure does a business like Judy's (and perhaps yours) need? To help you visualize it, I've developed a framework I call the Business Operating Triangle, to more easily define and clarify how a business is organized to operate. The big goals and outcomes—the kind we talked about in the previous chapter—are at the top, and the tasks people do to achieve the outcomes are at the bottom. As the company grows, the types of tasks become more specialized and eventually group together into roles, and then into functional areas. For example, early on a project manager or executive assistant may be able to handle any customer issues. As the number of tasks and the time needed for customers grows, a full customer service role is created. Eventually, as more employees come on board in customer service roles, a team of customer service representatives is formed and then evolves into a customer service function or department. Functions like this, or IT or marketing, are the vertical slices on the image on page 81.

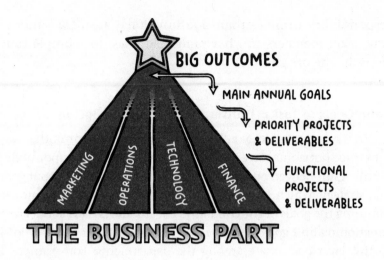

BIG OUTCOMES

MAIN ANNUAL GOALS

PRIORITY PROJECTS & DELIVERABLES

FUNCTIONAL PROJECTS & DELIVERABLES

MARKETING OPERATIONS TECHNOLOGY FINANCE

THE BUSINESS PART

Creating Functions

The reason we use the term *functional tasks* is because as the number and variety of tasks increase as the business grows, we start to group tasks by function (so managing social media ads falls under marketing, and payroll is a functional task of the human resources department). Many companies use the term *department*, but we prefer *function* because it implies something specialized is happening in the area. Also, when you consider the structure that will best support your business, you really want to understand how your organization *functions*. In fact, when starting to define your business structure, I advise you to start by creating a chart that lays out the different functions in your business across the top, then lists the different roles within each function. Lastly, add in the names of the people performing those functions. Unlike a more traditional org chart that focuses on who reports to whom, this is a functional org chart. What's different? In the traditional approach, team members are put on the org chart in one spot with their title. In the functional approach, the way the business operates determines the varied functions on the org chart; therefore, someone's name can show up in more than one spot on the org chart if they hold a main responsibility in more than one functional area. Said another way, team members can have multiple roles, in multiple functions, in one org chart.

From Goals to Tasks: Translating from Top to Bottom

In the image below, you'll see the triangle divided another way, into three horizontal layers, which represent levels of responsibility within a full-fledged business structure. The top layer is about goals and strategy, which includes the CEO and the big-picture thinkers outlining the goals of the company. The middle layer is about cross-functioning and goal execution, so the department heads who sit in this layer coordinate among the departments: For example, if a big goal for the year is promoting a new product line, then the head of marketing needs to talk with finance to work out a budget. And finally, in the bottom layer we have the functional tasks. Team members in this layer actually execute the strategies and take action from plans formed in the middle layer. They're the front line or "boots on the ground" of any company.

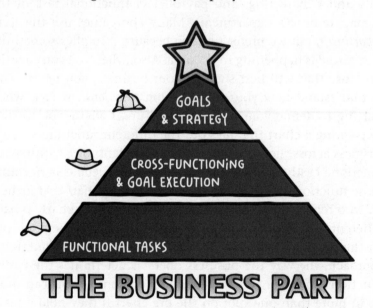

It's helpful to know what hat you are wearing.

STAGES OF BUSINESS GROWTH AND DEVELOPMENT

To summarize what we've just covered: As a business grows, it expands its operations and adds team members. The structure becomes more defined, and the functions (departments) become more specialized. It's important to identify where your company is on the "structure development" journey, and it's easiest to think of it in stages: At each stage the role responsibilities shift, and none more so than the entrepreneur's role. In the graphics on the pages ahead, we'll use the Business Operating Triangle to illustrate what's going on at each stage.

Stage 1: I Can Do It (No Structure Needed)

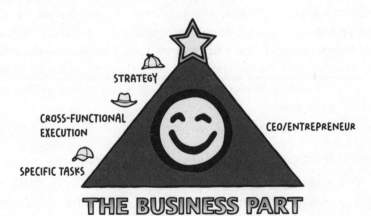

The very first stage of a business is about proving viability. It's about testing ideas for products and services in the real world. Typically, proof of good business concepts is measured by revenue, and business sustainability is determined by achieving consistent profits, or at least having the clear path to get there.

At this first stage, the entrepreneur is not only the creative visionary but also the main person who executes the vision. There is no organized structure because none is needed. The ideas and plans live in the entrepreneur's mind, and he or she is going to personally execute most, if not all of them. Because most start-ups are funded with little capital and a lot of the entrepreneur's talent, drive, and determination, the hiring step (up next!) happens when that entrepreneur can no longer do it all because the business is getting solid traction. The first hires are almost always for administrative and task support, like an executive assistant and/ or project manager, so that the entrepreneur can focus their time on developing the business to achieve their picture of success and reach financial viability and sustainability.

As the business starts to meaningfully grow, more specialized helping hands are needed, but they're usually part-time and often contractors. Examples are IT people, marketing or PR firms, copywriters, and bookkeepers. Even with a few extra team members, all the responsibility for achieving major results—including doing the important critical thinking, decision-making, and problem-solving—remains substantially in the hands of the entrepreneur. In short, the entrepreneur is performing duties all over this triangle in the early stages! This first stage needs little organization or structure because the entrepreneur is still in the driver's seat doing most everything that's important to the success of the business.

Stage 2: Define and Assign (functions and roles)

The next stage of development is about solidifying the business model and expanding on what's working. This is the stage when functional areas are beginning to form and delegation starts—as similar tasks get grouped together and shift from the entrepreneur to the assistant, to the project manager or operations officer, or to a part-time contractor/specialist. It's also when the entrepreneur hires or promotes a highly productive generalist, such as a strong assistant or project manager, to an organizational, management-type role. This right-hand person (sometimes it can be two people) then helps to organize the work, define roles and tasks, and performs some key responsibilities that then come off the plate of the entrepreneur.

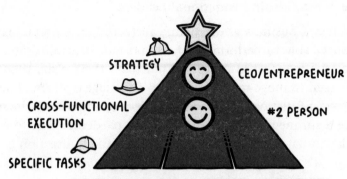

STRATEGY

CEO/ENTREPRENEUR

CROSS-FUNCTIONAL
EXECUTION

#2 PERSON

SPECIFIC TASKS

THE BUSINESS PART

Moving through this stage relies on the combination of an entrepreneur hiring or developing an appropriately skilled person who knows the business and can be trusted to perform well with very little supervision, and then giving that right-hand person the balance of responsibility, autonomy, and guidance they need to succeed. This person will be the entrepreneur's partner in driving the business forward. They will help keep the entrepreneur on track to reach their goals, doing tasks as needed and managing contractors who come in to play parts in accomplishing key projects.

This stage is the most variable in terms of how long it lasts. I know of a few businesses with stable revenues that have operated in this stage for three to five years, while others move through it in a matter of months. The complaint I most often hear from entrepreneurs and their right-hand people who are at this stage for too long is that they're burning out. They have too much to do and too little time and resources to accomplish it all—time to hire more team members and develop leaders!

Stage 3: Establishing Functional Leaders

When a business grows significantly and an entrepreneur is no longer able to perform all the important functions, and the operations manager also has too much on their plate, then the business must move to the next stage. This stage is all about developing clear functions and leaders for those functions. It's the stage where team members start working in a particular lane to carry out day-to-day tasks, while the leaders (in the midsection of the triangle) also do cross-functional planning, coordinating, collaborating, and decision-making.

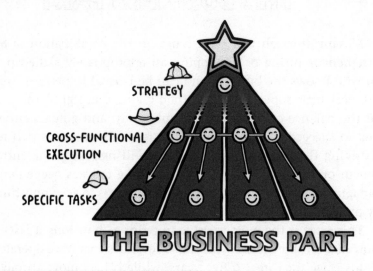

The first responsibility of a functional leader, or department head, is to supervise their function/department and ensure it delivers the results and performance that the business expects. CEOs often fill the functional leadership roles by promoting people within those functions, so when hiring team members, it's helpful to look for people who can specialize in a function and also have potential to take on a leadership role within it. For example, a CEO might ask themselves, *Can I hire an IT person who is able not only to do the tasks, but also to grow and take responsibility for the whole function being achieved?*

The second responsibility of functional leaders, and it's a big one, is to perform cross-functional coordination and communication. The cross-functional leadership team is the heart of your business—the pistons to your engine. The cross-functional team is meant to engage in regular communication with the other team leaders in the other functions (departments), to talk about the goals and projects and how they are progressing. This team makes sure, for example, that the marketing department knows of any changes in finance, and that finance knows of any changes in research and development. Each cross-functional leader's responsibility is to communicate and manage down within their function and across with the other leaders to integrate the parts and achieve the goals. When leaders fulfill the responsibility of leading their functions while also doing cross-functioning with the other department leaders with the purpose of achieving goals, we call this cross-functional goal execution. When you get this operational, it powers the engine of your business.

Stage 4: Establishing Executive Leaders

Once the functional leadership team is operating solidly, it may be time to bring in a COO or an upper-level management person who will supervise and develop the functional leaders while also engaging in the overall company goal setting, strategy, and planning.

It can be tempting to bring in a professional COO (a seasoned executive from outside the company) much sooner—right around the time you're moving toward Stage 3 and forming functions and leaders. At this stage you're still heavily needed to keep the most important business functions going. It seems like an experienced COO could take over the development of the org structure and roles (meaning they could put in place the functions and leaders) and also run the operations so that the CEO could focus on the aspects of their role that have the highest value.

However, in my experience this almost always FAILS! In fact, I've never personally seen it work! I've heard stories from others who've heard stories of other people for whom it *may* have worked—but seriously, I have never seen it work myself. Here's the thing: A COO is primarily an executive role meant to supervise functional leaders and to work through those leaders to achieve results. A COO may also lead a function or two but does not have task-level expertise in every function. So, if an outsider COO comes into a company that has no functional leaders yet, that COO has to manage all the functions at the most basic task level—performing decision-making, problem-solving, complex thinking, and giving guidance about things *that they know little or nothing about!*

Professional COOs are, however, experts at managing, developing, and working with other leaders to perform complex critical thinking and execution *above* the task level. So when you have functional leaders in place, that's when bringing in an executive leader such as a COO can really add value to your business.

ONGOING COLLABORATIVE
STRATEGIC THINKING

CEO/ENTREPRENEUR

EXECUTIVE LEADERSHIP TEAM

CROSS-FUNCTIONAL
LEADERSHIP TEAM

FUNCTIONAL ROLES

THE BUSINESS PART

Communicating within the Business Triangle

In the early days of a business, when the Business Operating Triangle is very small with just a few people, the distance isn't so big between the top and the base. The CEO can easily translate the big vision into the concrete outcomes, and then into the plans and tasks that need to get done. But as a company grows, it becomes more and more difficult to organize and supervise the ever-increasing number of projects and tasks happening every day. This means the organizational structure, role clarity, and teamwork need to improve at the same pace. Information needs to travel up to the CEO, across the departments at the cross-functional level, and down to those deep in the task level. This is what I refer to as translating up, down, and across the triangle. To make a significant change or to implement something new, word needs to travel to inform all the levels and functional areas, so everyone can get aligned and agreed. In short, as the company gets bigger, it becomes more important for people to know exactly what their role is.

The cross-functional leadership team is responsible for communicating with the other verticals, or functions, keeping the team abreast of developments so that any decisions that might impact the other areas are surfaced promptly.

In that sense, these middle leaders are the first group that is involved in almost everything—whereas before it was just the founder plus the right-hand person. They're leading up, they're leading across, and they're leading down. When they're effective as a team, the CEO is freed up to do the strategic and long-term thinking the business needs. This freedom leads to innovation and greater movement toward the V State.

Slow Down to Speed Up

Now, back to my earlier example of my heart-centered, trail-blazing CEO Judy. Once the structure I've outlined in the last few pages was put in place in her company, along with the needed leadership and team roles, she was able to transition responsibilities and focus her efforts on goal setting, strategy, and doing the important marketing and community development that was instrumental to the company's success. When Judy was stuck in firefighter mode, getting involved in everything from customer service to writing e-mails to website design, she unintentionally prevented her team from learning and doing those things. She also caused confusion in the team, leaving them uncertain of their role because she was doing so much. By getting functional clarity and role clarity, she was able to develop her team in an orderly way, which then freed her!

Often when we are introducing these new structural pieces to an organization, I will put it this way: "You have to slow down to speed up." Because entrepreneurial companies are so often running very fast, it can feel really risky to slow down, but please hear me: It is riskier not to!

It's also important to take the time to slow down and reevaluate your business's structure as the business evolves and grows. Your org chart is not stagnant; it's a visual representation of how your business is organized to operate in real time. You should revisit it often in the life of your organization, updating it to reflect a current snapshot of how your business functions.

Role clarity is a gift you give everyone on your team. And the clarity it provides around who does what and who holds the main responsibility for any given area is so helpful when it comes to the team knowing who to go to for what in the daily teamwork. Role clarity, as represented in a functional org chart, is integral to increasing efficiency, and I have not met a single business owner who is not concerned with increasing their team's efficiency; the challenge is that they often do not realize how unclear their team is on their roles and responsibilities. And in the chaos of putting out fires they often don't realize the lack of clarity that is all around, keeping the business stuck in a perpetual loop of urgency.

WHAT'S MY PART?

Now that we've seen the way roles and responsibilities shift and progress as a business grows, let's talk about those from the individual perspective of the people in them, and what it takes for both your people and your business to thrive. After all, an individual's first agreement with a company is their role—meaning they agree to perform their role in exchange for compensation.

So for starters, we need to know what really makes up a role. It's easiest to think of a role as a set of expected responsibilities, tasks, and behaviors intended to produce the business results we want. These are based on both the function and the level of organizational responsibility.

We can group these expected responsibilities into three main categories. Thinking about them this way is useful both for leaders creating roles and for the team members who are *in* the roles!

1. Role responsibilities

    a) Functional responsibilities and results—these are things like:

- Answering customer service inquiries
- Preparing marketing materials
- Producing monthly financial reports
- Planning the new season's products

    b) Leadership responsibilities and results—these are things like:

- Supervising and developing team members
- Cross-functional coordination, problem-solving, communication, and decision-making (such as between marketing, operations, and finance)
- Allocating and planning resources, in alignment with a company budget
- Putting in place new structure, systems, or process

2. What the team or company expects me to do as part of my role

    a) Participate in team meetings

    b) Use designated systems and process (such as a project management system)

c) Do ongoing reporting and communications (weekly updates, flash reports, dashboards)

d) Complete administrative tasks (like time sheets, HR stuff, etc).

3. How I'm expected to conduct myself

a) Self-Leadership

b) How I interact with others and build relationships

c) How I handle change and unexpected situations

If you don't have a role description for your own role, you can create one simply by making a list using these categories we've just looked at. Even if you received a job description when you were hired, it's important to review and update it by adding new responsibilities and removing ones that no longer apply. It's also important to think about how you're meeting expectations and how you're behaving, so that you don't drift off track without you or anyone else realizing it. And no one can do this for you but you.

Role Clarity Is Everyone's Responsibility

My clients have all at one time or another heard me say, "No one is coming to save you!" The reason I say this is because no one knows what is on your plate better than you do, so no one knows when you need saving! Time and again I have heard leaders share, from a frustrated spot, that their workload is completely unreasonable. They have a false belief that their supervisor or CEO understands everything they are busy doing. Their frustration usually sounds something like this: "I can't believe they keep giving me more to do! They know we have back-to-back big projects coming up, and that we are in the midst of upgrading our systems, and that my department is short-staffed, but sure, no problem—let's add another big project right now!" They fall into self-protection and stay firmly planted there, resenting that no one has noticed or addressed how unmanageable their workload has become. This is what I want all team members—and you—to understand: Communicating about how things are shaping up in your role is up to you. No one else in the organization knows what it really takes to get your part done. Even if your supervisor, or the CEO, has done your exact role themselves in the past, their understanding isn't current—they carried your role and responsibilities at a different stage of the company's development; often when the company was delivering to fewer clients, the tech involved was less complex, and decisions could be made faster because there weren't as many significant projects happening inside the company at the same time.

This is why I say that role clarity is a *shared* responsibility that involves the people creating the structure and the people actually doing the roles. It's imperative that you, as an individual team member or leader, raise your hand when your role either needs greater clarity or needs to be reviewed for how to make it more productive or effective. It might be that your parts of the company goals are too fuzzy, so you spend too much time trying to figure out what you should do. It might be that the tasks your role encompasses have now become so many and so frequent that it is time to consider shifting some of your responsibilities. But in all situations, the team member needs to take the lead in surfacing when their role isn't working well.

In Agreement 2, we discussed how the team performance continues to level up on the journey to the V State. One of the ways this shows up is that roles become more specialized with unique functional expertise—such as having a full-time programmer who only works on software. Another way is when roles shift "up the triangle" during growth and expansion, so that you now need to spend more time in high-level critical thinking and strategy and less time in functional tasks or executing projects. You could try to do the tasks and projects you have always done, but when you're stretched too thin, spending precious time in the weeds, the business suffers from the vacancy at the top.

THE PROFESSIONAL DEVELOPMENT JOURNEY

We've talked about how team members grow in their roles, and how leaders move "up the triangle" and take on greater responsibilities. But exactly how does that happen? It goes without saying that they need to start out as A Players, right? But hiring an A Player is not itself an end point, it's the beginning of a development journey.

A Players are typically strong individual performers who have a proven track record of success in past similar roles. The A Player joins your company with specific skills, aptitude, and often strong experience in a functional area. To apply their expertise and reach their performance potential in your business, the A Player must first adapt and integrate their skills to your specific business. From the start, they should demonstrate their ability to learn quickly and to competently perform the tasks of their role within a relatively short period of time. If a new team member is having trouble with the most basic tasks of their role for considerably longer than the training period, then it's time to reevaluate if they're a fit for the role.

As their journey continues, to leverage their expertise and contribute at a higher level, they next develop into an ACE Team Member who works effectively within the team. ACE Team Members not only perform their functional tasks well; they have also developed the Self-Leadership to consistently perform well, even while under stress, during change, and when facing challenges. They demonstrate the interpersonal skills and behaviors to effectively interact with others to achieve results—in other words, teamwork! (I'll explain exactly what "ACE" stands for when we talk about conscious agreements in Agreement 5. For now, if you like, you can take the common-sense meaning—these team members are aces!)

Next, an ACE Team Member can further develop into an A+ Leader who takes on greater levels of responsibility and makes strategic contributions. A+ Leaders not only possess a high level of business skills, Self-Leadership, and teamwork behaviors; they also possess the leadership skills that are all about guiding, supporting, and developing others to achieve results.

This is a journey that cannot be skipped or shortcut, meaning someone can't develop into an A+ Leader if they don't possess the interaction and teamwork acumen of the ACE Team Member first. Trying to skip levels—say, promoting your recent hire from an experienced, "star" customer service representative to a director of customer service with cross-functional and management responsibilities—is a recipe for failure. If you're familiar with the classic "Peter Principle" in management (the idea that employees who succeed in their roles tend to be promoted to higher roles until they reach a level where they're no longer competent, because skills from one role don't necessarily translate to the next), you'll see that this is a prime example. It happens most often because companies don't recognize that the "People Part" of teamwork and leadership expertise takes real development—that these competencies are completely different from functional skills. As an example, an A Player marketing person should know how to design a successful marketing campaign—that's what gets them in the door—but after that, it's up to you and your company to develop them into highly effective ACE Team Members and then into A+ Leaders who can lead the company to achieve the goals from your Visionary Master Plan! Take a look at the graphic on page 96 to see a visual representation of what the journey looks like.

If you are an A Player reading this book, I hope you are hearing loud and clear that there is a necessary arc to every A Player's journey. You enter a company by taking a role that utilizes your particular skills or zone of genius. Then, to be truly successful, you leverage and contribute your skills to achieve the company's desired goals. You work in a unified team with close co-workers and cross-functionally with other team members, who are also strongly skilled in their zone of genius, so that the whole truly becomes greater than the sum of the parts. Once you're an ACE Team Member, you have confidence in how you're going to show up—no matter what. Now you can operate with curiosity, asking, "What's my part right now, the most valuable role that I can play right now to get the needed result?" You can expect greater opportunities and greater contributions to come forward as you continue on your journey to A+ Leader.

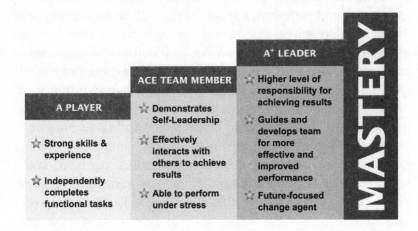

From Entrepreneur to CEO

If you are an entrepreneur in the fast-paced environment of business today, you have a development journey of your own. First, you need to develop *yourself* from an A Player into an ACE Team Member, and then into an A+ Leader. Entrepreneurs are actually quite prone to getting stuck at the A Player level, mainly because when they started their company, they were innovative experts, doing most everything in the business themselves. And growing a business has so many demands that most entrepreneurs don't advance their business leadership skills—or even realize they need to.

Once you have formed a functional team with leaders, then you move to mentorship of those leaders. The point here is that you do actual tasks less and less, and instead you provide the greater context, input, and support on decision-making and problem-solving, while the team executes. To function this way, you also have to get comfortable with having less control, which can be a journey in itself. But when your team knows the outcomes they are going for and why; when they are set up with systems, structure, and processes that facilitate their teamwork; when they know how to communicate up, down, and across, then giving up control is the wisest approach. Then you can let go of execution and focus on the big picture: strategic planning, creation, and innovation.

Remember, role clarity is a gift—to you and to everyone on your team. When everyone understands their parts and where they fit in the whole, they understand how the business itself works, how it actually operates. It's like chess: You need to understand the full game, even though your role is only to perform the knight's moves. And that's what makes this agreement essential: It provides the structure that allows a team to work effectively together and achieve the desired results.

Keep reading, because in the next chapter, we'll look more closely at what working *together* really means.

Annie Says:

"Role clarity is critical! No pro team would show up to a game without knowing their positions. If they did, it would look more like a free-for-all than professional play!"

○ ○ ○

SUCCESS STORY
Role Clarity Inspires
Confidence for Everyone
Maria Taylor, COO—Entertainment Company

THE SITUATION

The first thing I said to my mentor was, "I'm stepping into a new role as COO at a fairly new company, and I can't make heads or tails of who does what and when. Everyone seems to want to pass the buck and to 'stay in their lane,' but I don't even know what the lanes are, let alone who's in them!"

I'd been hired as the COO, brought in from outside of the company to replace an executive who wasn't working out. This company was practically brand-new, and the rest of the team had been together for about a year. Coming in, I knew exactly what my role was, but it didn't seem like any of the team knew their own roles, and it was super frustrating. I couldn't seem to get a straight answer from anyone about who did what without the team becoming defensive or shutting down completely. They seemed to get basic things done, but when it came to addressing an issue, coordinating between areas, or asking for a change, that's when I ran into problems. I had to change things fast in order to be successful as COO and reach the CEO's intended vision.

There was so much confusion all around from team members not knowing enough about their own roles and also knowing practically nothing about each other's! The team didn't know who to go to for what, nor who had the final say for decisions. And the teamwork was totally stifled from the constant tension. I knew that if we didn't get clear on roles right away that we'd keep hitting roadblocks and never reach any of the company's goals.

WHAT I DID DIFFERENTLY WITH ROLE CLARITY

I knew that to establish role clarity with the team, I first had to understand the goals, projects, and plans that the business currently had in place. I met with the CEO and CFO to discuss the strategic plan and the projects needed to fulfill it. This allowed me to start defining roles based on how we needed to operate to achieve the goals. I then met with each team member to discover what they'd worked on and what their expertise was to begin defining roles based on our new projects and goals. This helped create safety and build the trust of the team as we moved forward.

THE DIFFERENCE IT MADE

When the team's roles were clarified, they felt relieved. They began to really own their roles and stopped deflecting responsibility because they knew exactly what was expected of them. The defensive reactions and blame games stopped—each team member took responsibility for their parts and knew who to go to for other parts. One team member declared, "I'm not even sure how I ever got things done before. I mean, I know it happened, but it always felt like I might be working on the wrong things because I really didn't know what I was going for or what my part was until now." With this newfound role clarity, we could now function more optimally, and it even boosted everyone's confidence.

AGREEMENT 3 TAKEAWAYS

*We clarify our parts and where
they fit in the whole.*

- Role clarity means that everyone knows their part in the business and how it fits with the other parts to achieve the desired results.

- As a business grows, it expands its operations and adds team members. The structure becomes more defined, and the functions become more specialized.

- Clarifying roles is a shared responsibility: As roles and duties shift, it's up to each team member to proactively communicate what's changed, so the team can review the impacts and adjust their roles if needed.

- Clear organizational team structure and functional leadership is key to freeing up a CEO, so they can focus their role on the visionary, strategic, and innovative parts of the business.

- Hiring an A Player is only the beginning. A Players develop into ACE Team Members and then into A+ Leaders so that they become integrated with your team, align to your vision, and are developed to effectively apply their skills in the ways that will best serve your organization.

FOR YOUR REFLECTION

Take some time to think about what you've learned in this chapter. Write about what you're thinking in a notebook, on a device, or right on this page!

1) What one or two past situations (business or personal) come to mind that you recognize could have gone better based on what you know now?

_____

_____

_____

2) What insights did you gain about yourself from this chapter?

_____

_____

_____

3) What is one next action or interaction you intend to do differently moving forward?

_____

_____

_____

BUILDING HIGH-TRUST RELATIONSHIPS

We consider our impact on others, have their backs, and repair relationships promptly.

The condition for productive team interaction

Have you ever been presenting to a group or discussing something important and noticed another person react by rolling their eyes? Or heard them make a dismissive sigh? Or saw their eyes narrow and lips purse with resentment? Or recognized a wide-eyed look of shock on their face? Or maybe you even saw the ever-so-slight twitch of someone struggling to hold back tears?

It's mind-boggling to me how incredibly sensitive and accurate humans are when it comes to reading other humans' emotions, especially ones that could indicate a threat. Seriously, we automatically process dozens, if not hundreds, of cues all at once to determine how a fellow human is relating to us in the current moment. We're so effective that I think of it as another sense, and one that you *cannot* turn off. In the same way that you will smell smoke and instantly process many bits of information to determine whether it's coming from a backyard barbeque or the neighbors' roof, if someone rolls their eyes while you're talking, you will instantly conclude whether it was a sign of disrespect or your co-worker got something in their eye. If you're a human adult, you've experienced millions of situations where you've had to decide if someone else's behavior indicates a threat that you need to pay attention to.

In fact, in the workplace it's especially important to understand and learn not only how to interpret others' behavior but also how to manage the relationships among humans. Working with a team requires being in relationship with other people—there's no getting around it. But sharing ideas, considering options in a collaborative way, and finding the best solution for complex business situations are not easy things to do. This chapter will give you the tools to build the secure relationships and safe environment you need for your business to succeed.

Obviously, the point of teamwork is to work well together and accomplish amazing results—the kind that couldn't ever be accomplished alone. But we all know of terribly unproductive teams in which gossip is prevalent, backstabbing is a fact of life, and power struggles reign. And for every team like that, there is another team that's in constant anxiety about what their boss will say or do next, and so they learn to "avoid and appease" instead of "surface and resolve." And finally, there are teams of individuals so resigned to avoiding conflict and interaction with others that they don't even *try* to work together, instead opting to do everything on their own until they can no longer avoid their teammates and they *must* send that pesky e-mail asking for information and input from outside of their silo. Their primary thought about their work? *I'll just do my job, keep my head down, and leave promptly at 5 P.M.*

There's a reason this lone-wolf attitude has dug its roots so deep: Most employees in the United States describe their workplace as "dysfunctional." Self-protection, the human default hardwiring, is running the show, with individuals stuck in a paradigm of competition, self-promotion, and survival mode. This includes behaviors like throwing others under the bus to avoid looking bad, taking the meeting floor and not giving it up for others to talk, or refusing to speak up even though you have info critical to a project's success. (You may remember from Agreement 1 that holding strong positions about right and wrong, or good and bad, is a hallmark of self-protection.) When team members are in self-protection, it's impossible to build secure relationships. It will look like everyone is out for themselves, and it will be difficult, if not impossible, to come together and cooperate with others in the face of challenges, large and small. So how do you create relationships between individuals and within a team where people will drop their self-protection and willingly cooperate with one another to achieve business results?

The first step is to create what I call *secure relationships*.

A LOOK AT SECURE RELATIONSHIPS

What exactly is a secure relationship? It's a relationship where individual team members trust one another to keep each other's interests in mind before they act, to avoid taking actions that negatively impact them. Team members should be able to assume that another member won't throw them under the bus to avoid looking bad themselves, nor will they steal an opportunity because a teammate happens to be out at that moment. When relationships are secure, team members direct their full thinking power to the business benefit, instead of thinking, *Who's making me look bad? Who am I competing with to get the next plum project?* or *With whom do I need to watch my back?*

This all may sound rather obvious. The fact is, secure relationships are a simple concept to explain but a difficult thing to create and maintain. And working with relationship problems is often a major blind spot for us humans, since in terms of our evolution, relationships are frankly secondary to survival. In my years working as a consultant, I've seen entrepreneur after entrepreneur suffer in work environments they didn't know lacked secure relationships, and no one exemplified that better than a client I'll call Joe.

Joe had a commercial bakery specializing in high-end pastries. His baked goods were impeccably made—gorgeous and delicious—and also in high demand. I met him when he was nearing retirement and wanted to sell his business, but he had one big issue: He had a great baking facility and a robust corporate clientele, but he had no seasoned bakers who could reproduce the baked goods *without him*. He told me that he'd tried for years to train and mentor another head baker, but one person after another quit the job after just a couple of years. He tried more than a dozen hires before resigning himself to doing all the highly skilled parts of the baking himself.

When I asked him why all these people hadn't worked out, he told me a detailed story for each one, articulating their faults and detailing how they couldn't produce the flaky, delicately layered, perfectly buttery croissants and French pastries that his customers had come to expect. He was adamant that he would NOT let his customers down, and if that meant he had to do the baking himself because he couldn't find a competent baker—then so be it.

However, his non-baking team members, who had been around for a while in various other roles (prep cooks, cleaning staff, delivery drivers, bookkeeper) told me a different story. Joe had brought highly talented bakers on board several times, but he was constantly looking over their shoulders and criticizing their work, making them feel like they could never live up to his expectations. If you've ever been micromanaged, you know how frustrating and debilitating it is to have a supervisor check your every move, adding their critical comments, making demands, and even redoing your work—usually work that you have been doing competently for months, if not years. Joe's (literal) hands-on approach didn't make for happy bakers *or* better pastries, and it became a massive liability for the long-term survival of the business.

With Joe's retirement getting closer every week, the clock was ticking. To avoid shutting the bakery down, he wanted to try one more time to find a baker (or two) to carry on his work and serve the customers he'd had for so long. But first we had to uncover why his other trainees didn't work out, and that's where I came in.

Sure enough, after only a day on-site, I could see the missing element: secure relationships.

WHAT MAKES A RELATIONSHIP SECURE?

So, what are the ingredients of a secure relationship? Here's what they're not! They are not about liking each other, being friends, or going to movies together. They're also not about knowing all the ups, downs, and personal details of a teammate's life. In reality, secure relationships are ones in which each individual trusts that the others will reliably behave in ways that demonstrate the following:

- Acceptance and respect for individuals as they are, holding them in positive regard

- Belief in their ability and competence to perform work that meets expectations

- Care and concern for each person's success and well-being

When a relationship is secure, the other person can trust that you will deliberately take into account your impact on them before you make decisions or take actions. (To put this another way, you will represent in your mind their interests as well as your own when making decisions and taking actions.) And vice versa. One of the simplest ways of saying this? That you will "have each other's back."

Joe wasn't meeting even one of the three conditions of secure relationships—but I knew we could fix that. Let's look at the specific pitfalls in Joe's workplace of insecure relationships and what we coached him to do differently:

Joe's first pitfall → "The bakers today are lazy, sloppy, and unprofessional."

- Joe had such a strong confirmation bias that whenever a baker did something differently than he would have done it, he interpreted that as a lack of competence. He was looking for errors and evidence of a baker being unprofessional—and he found them! In fact, it felt to the new bakers as if every interaction was a test that they failed, and no baker had ever met Joe's high standards. An example of this: When new bakers showed up dressed in modern baking uniforms with splashes of color and no apron, Joe concluded that their education and experience must have been terrible—and it didn't matter that they had successfully worked in high-end bakeries and restaurants. And even though bakers readily conformed to his dress code (the traditional "chef's whites") when asked, it was as if they'd failed the first test and from then on Joe was just looking for evidence to confirm that they were novices not deserving of his professional respect.

- **Do Differently:** The solution here was to embrace that first ingredient of secure relationships and "accept and respect them as they are, holding them in positive regard." So I sat down with Joe during the hiring process and directed him to look at applicants' expertise and résumés—not their uniforms. I had him write down the (positive) reasons why he decided to hire a new baker, and I had him share that with the new baker on day one. And instead of putting a new baker right into the active production schedule, where Joe was sure to observe errors that would cause him to draw negative conclusions, we designed a specific training program, where Joe taught the principles and techniques that were important to him. He then baked alongside new bakers during an apprentice stage to evaluate their skills in action. By giving new hires the benefit of the doubt and specific support, Joe was much better able to discern who would best develop into a baker that he could rely on.

Joe's second pitfall → Demanding perfection and holding a grudge

- If a baker made a mistake, like using too much butter in the dough (is that even possible?) or giving the pastries too much time in the oven, it was held against them for a *long* time. From then on, they were required to "show their dough"—literally have Joe check the dough they had prepared—before forming it into pastries, even after a year on the job. They felt like they could never recover from mistakes. On top of that, Joe was incredible at making a batch of his dough yield an uncommonly high number of pastries, which the other bakers couldn't match— and they were constantly berated for this, even though their yield was extremely strong by industry standards. The result? Morale in the kitchen tanked.

- **Do Differently:** To fix this problem, I prescribed the second ingredient of secure relationships and encouraged Joe to believe in his staff's abilities and competence to perform their work. Instead of holding mistakes against his bakers forever, Joe would make them "show their dough" for only two weeks for a quality check, then trust them to continue on their own and to report to Joe their own evaluation of their dough. Also, for the bakers to build their trust with Joe, I had them agree to self-report mistakes and what they did to solve them, so that Joe could stop constantly looking over their shoulders. To address the yield issue, I decided to ground Joe's expectations by bringing him a report on how many pastries came from a batch of dough in other French bakeries. I also introduced him to a well-known baker so he could discuss it with another professional. This brought him back down to earth, and from then on, when he noticed something his bakers could do differently to maximize dough yield, he would explain the technique instead of unhelpfully berating them.

Joe's third pitfall → Criticizing or shaming someone in front of customers and other team members

- One of the worst things for Joe's staff was how quick he was to criticize his bakers in front of customers, saying things like, "These young bakers have no brains—I have to count out a dozen for them!" or "My bakers asked if they could use American butter . . . for French pastries! Good thing I'm the boss!"

- **Do Differently:** I discussed with Joe the impact of always cutting down his staff and the importance of slowing down and not responding in frustration. Joe agreed to walk away if he felt highly triggered. He also agreed to acknowledge what his bakers did well. He reported back that acknowledging the positive changed the dynamic and he was then better able to share his expertise with his bakers. And when he wanted to correct their technique, instead of piling on insults, he shared (for example) *why* European butter makes better pastries. With this shift, the staff could see that investing their energy into their role mattered.

One element that all this "do differently" guidance shared is that these were intentional choices made from Self-Leadership to deliberately create secure relationships. However, these new behaviors also helped create an overall work environment that was "psychologically safe," which goes hand in hand with and reinforces secure relationships.

Now that you've got an overview of what secure relationships look like, let's take a closer look at how psychological safety works and how to create it in *your* business.

PSYCHOLOGICAL SAFETY: AN ENVIRONMENT THAT EMPOWERS SECURE RELATIONSHIPS

Psychological safety has become a more well-known concept ever since Google discovered that it was the single consistent element of their highest-performing teams. The term indicates an environment where people believe they are safe to take interpersonal risks without being blamed, criticized, judged, rejected, embarrassed, abandoned, and so on. Taking an interpersonal risk includes behaviors such as telling the truth even if it's bad news, openly sharing opinions that sharply differ from others', and self-disclosing information that could create negative judgments or lead to being perceived poorly.

Once you understand this concept, it's easy to see why some teams consistently demonstrate self-protective behaviors, even when it's detrimental to achieving business results. No one wants to share bad news if they know they'll be blamed and judged, even if they caused the problem. Forget sharing an innovative idea if you anticipate being dismissed—or worse—having your boss snort to imply the idea is stupid, shaming you in front of everyone. In psychologically safe workplaces, people don't directly communicate—or give cues that imply—judgments, threat, or disrespect.

Another part of psychological safety is being able to count on being perceived as a capable and valued contributor. Team members can't perform when they are constantly worried about how they are stacking up and how their performance is being judged. Also, it's extremely difficult to perform when being compared to others on the team, which is why internal noncompetition is critical. In professional basketball, the players can trust that no team member will hog the ball, abandon the plays, and take every shot, even if that would generate more fame and glory for that individual. And yet, in business, it's common to have an environment where everyone must stay on high alert to protect themselves from being unfairly blamed, or having their credit stolen, or being passed over by a brownnoser.

Listen, in business it's inevitable that things go wrong, and conversations get heated when tension is high and a team member feels passionately about their perspective. It's natural in these moments to fall into habitual patterns of self-protection, which turn an environment unsafe and therefore unproductive. In those cases, it's important to repair the environment and restore the safety. But all too often, that doesn't happen, and instead these behaviors become the default.

Below, I'll give some examples of common things leaders say and do in challenging situations that sabotage the psychological safety we're trying to create. These habits can be difficult to avoid, but it's important to overcome them, and later in this chapter I'm going to show you how!

Communication Sabotage:

- Negative projections or exaggerations:
  - "I had to stay up all night to fix your work so that it didn't bomb with the client."
  - "If I didn't remind you to fix the web page, the whole launch would've failed!"

- Blame or shame instead of constructive feedback:
  - "This has to change; revise it, because it is awful."
  - "You blew this! How could you?!"

- "Clearly, you weren't paying attention."
- My personal favorite for all-in-one blame/shame, "You're better than this."

- Negative judgment of the person, instead of the work or the behavior:
  - "Anybody would've seen this!"
  - "I can't trust you."
  - "You just don't think."

- Dismissing or minimizing:
  - "I hear you saying this will take extra time, but it's so easy—it'll only take you ten minutes."
  - "You're always complaining about deadlines when there's plenty of time."
  - "If you actually prioritize, you'll easily get this all done."

- Avoiding or abandoning:
  - "I know you need to talk with me about [high-stakes project], but I'm too tired and will be out of the office for the next two weeks."
  - "We don't need to review the project progress; I'm sure you've got it." (When maybe you don't "got it.")

Hopefully you recognize some of these statements from interactions with your team, because that means you have the opportunity to learn and make changes to create more psychological safety that will greatly benefit your team's performance.

To illustrate the impacts a lack of psychological safety can have in an entrepreneurial business, I am going to share a story about Ana, the dancer CEO. Listen for the incremental shifts you can make that will step up the level of secure relationships on your team.

What Happens When It Isn't Psychologically Safe

When Ana, a dancer—and one of my superbly talented CEO clients—first began working with me, she really didn't understand how her behavior sabotaged the atmosphere of psychological safety for her team. She had been a professional ballerina, and she owned and ran a large dance academy. As a dancer she had endured very harsh, almost traumatic coaching, so when it came to working with dancers, she understood the importance of safety very well. She would say, "I want them to be able to muster their courage and try things, even when they're scared or when I am challenging them. So I make sure they know that I believe in them wholeheartedly and it's okay to make mistakes—that's how we learn." That was her first principle, and she demonstrated it day in and day out with her dancers.

However, she didn't extend this same consideration to her team of instructors and administrators. Whenever something didn't go as expected, she would berate them and accuse them of lacking commitment. It was hugely demoralizing, and the team quickly got to a place where they felt like no matter what they did, they couldn't please her. While I coached Ana, my team worked with her team members to understand the bigger picture of what wasn't working. When she brought us in as consultants, it quickly became clear that she was in immediate danger of losing her strongest instructors and administrators. Several employees told us that it was too painful to be criticized and seen as "never good enough," and that at this point, their strategy was to try and follow her exact instructions, no matter how unrealistic, and to stop asking questions. In fact, their strategy became "avoid talking to her at all costs," which isn't great when you're trying to run a business.

When psychological safety is low there are many negative impacts. The first casualty of this hypercritical environment was the flow of vital information. To stay below the radar, her team never revealed more than they had to and resisted sharing anything except undoubtedly good, super positive news. When one of the instructors learned that several of her students were leaving to attend a new studio that had just opened in town, she said nothing to the CEO for fear of getting blamed somehow. When the bookkeeper thought of a new way to structure their fees to bring in more revenue, she kept it to herself because in her experience, Ana only wanted to do things her own way and didn't like change. Not only was the CEO/owner driving blind because of all the information her team withheld, but the organization didn't get to benefit from any of the contributions they could make.

And, at the most basic level, people can't perform well when they know they're being thought of poorly. Sure enough, by the time we got there, morale had tanked, and Ana was close to facing a full-on mutiny.

Creating Safety in a Challenging Environment

It may seem like I'm painting a bleak picture here. But there's good news: Psychological safety can be restored, and secure relationships can be nurtured throughout daily interactions.

To help the dance school get back on track, we had to quickly create an environment in which Ana's team members felt safe to tell the truth, safe to raise concerns, and safe to talk about issues without getting blamed and criticized. At first, we couldn't include Ana in our meetings with the team, because her presence alone caused the group to automatically shut down. Instead, we worked with her team members to create a safe environment among themselves while at the same time encouraging them to *release judgments about their CEO—and thereby make it safer for her too*. We talked about how difficult it was to operate a dance school, and how unreasonable expectations from parents created constant pressure. We discussed how hard it was for all the students to want the "famous ballerina" (Ana) as their teacher, and how devastating it was for the other teachers to be seen as "less than" by dance parents and judgmental teens. And finally, we talked about how another dance school had come to the area and peeled off some of their most lucrative beginner students. After this conversation, it made sense to the team how stressful the business was for Ana and why she might have a tough time controlling her emotions and behavior. Developing compassion within the team for the CEO primed us to support her in changing her behavior.

Gaining this new, compassionate perspective toward the CEO was the most important (and the most challenging) part of the initial team meetings. No one changes when they're judged negatively and perceived poorly, so even when a CEO's behavior is responsible for the company's major issues, generating empathy and understanding for them is still the first step. This isn't a blank check for leaders to be awful; it's just necessary to regain the psychological safety and environment of respect that allows people to take responsibility for their own behavior and to change.

Additionally, it was important to stop the team members from complaining about and insulting the CEO behind her back. This behavior turns an environment not only unsafe but toxic for everyone. Think about it from a team member's point of view: If you're in an environment where people criticize others behind their backs, you know that they're capable of doing the same to you. Maybe you remember a time when you were in a group that was gossiping about a mutual friend—did you ever think, *Hmmm, I wonder what they say about me when I'm not around?* Or maybe you thought, *Note to self, do not ever tell these people about my personal life.* Can you see how psychological safety suffers when those kinds of criticisms, complaints, and judgments are omnipresent?

Once we got the dance school team off the ledge (no longer threatening to quit) and feeling safer, we then brought the CEO into the group to work with them to move the business forward. We started by reviewing and updating her business goals, making sure they were still relevant and important to her, such as growing enrollment by 35 percent for the next cycle. Then we talked about how the team could help achieve this enrollment goal, making the team an ally instead of an irritant that upset her every day. And finally, we discussed what the team needed to *perform.* Ana knew all about performance in the context of dancing on stage, but she had never perceived her team's work in that same way! This was a major insight for Ana, and she then became much more open to learning about how she could support her team to perform better when she saw them as business athletes and not mouths to feed.

Next, we created agreements and standards between her and the team for how they would interact with each other, especially when they were under pressure. For example, the whole team agreed that they (including the CEO) would not raise issues or give critical feedback in front of clients, or on the fly, when people were unprepared to hear it. Instead, they would raise issues and give feedback during team huddles or meetings, talking through issues to resolve them instead of creating a negative open loop. (You'll learn more about these interaction agreements and how to make and implement them in Agreement 5.) We also helped them put in place an agreement that if the tension got too high in a meeting or criticism or defensiveness set in, then someone would call for a "time-out" to pause the conversation and select a time—anywhere from five minutes to five days later—to pick up talks again. This pressure-release valve was incredibly useful, and it prevented meetings from spiraling out of control like they had in the past.

My team and I also taught the dance school staff specific dialogue techniques to give feedback, raise issues, and resolve problems. For example, any time someone was raising an issue or bringing up a problem, they agreed to provide ideas for solutions, even if the ideas were just tentative or loosely formed. With this new teamwork agreement in place, an instructor felt safe to raise the issue of the students who were leaving to attend the new dance school with the CEO and rest of the team, and to bring forward an idea that he had previously kept quiet about. He thought they could raise their company profile and attract new students by giving some community talks on youth performance culture and mental health. Ana loved the idea, and the community talks were green-lit. They were very well attended and really resonated with parents trying to understand their stressed-out kids. It was great to see the benefits of psychological safety expand so quickly for the dance academy!

Creating psychological safety in this organization was the single most important part of turning around the business. The CEO still criticized the team from time to time, but she learned to repair quickly, and over time she got better and better. The last time I checked in on them, her longtime instructors were considering buying the school as Ana prepared to retire. All in all, that's a pretty wonderful result!

Of course, the ideal would be to have secure relationships in your business from the outset and never have them shaken, but even if you've got an essentially safe environment, there will likely be times when you'll need to do some repair. We are human. When stakes are high, timelines are tight, and the pressure is on, it is easy to bump up against one another. Self-protection will show up from time to time, and when it does, it will erode the safety of our environment and our relationships.

When secure relationships do hit these unavoidable hurdles, the most important thing is to repair the relationship and restore the safety and security as soon as possible. I like to think of *apology* and *appreciation* as the essential tools of repair. Let's take a look at both.

APOLOGY: YOUR MOST EFFECTIVE REPAIR TOOL

A common misconception around apologizing is that an apology is an admission of guilt. It is NOT! In fact, an apology is not about you at all. It is how you acknowledge your impact on another person and let them know you care about them and their experience and are willing to do something about it, regardless of whether the negative impact was intentional (which it usually wasn't). I've created a simple formula for giving an effective apology, and it looks like this:

- Describe specifically WHAT YOU DID and/or how you behaved.

- Describe and apologize for the negative IMPACT it had on the other person (the negative consequences they experienced, from their point of view).

- Describe what you intend to DO DIFFERENTLY in the future.

- Describe what you'd like to do or contribute to relieve their suffering (if there is something you can do).

Here's an example of an apology a leader might make to a project manager: "I totally forgot to share with you that the deadline for Project XYZ was moved out by a week. I see that you worked on it all day to complete it, but by doing so you weren't able to finish the reports for the board meeting on Monday. I assume this means you'll need to work a half-day on Saturday, which could have been avoided if I had notified you yesterday. I am so very sorry! I feel especially bad that you've been working the hardest of the team members this week, so I realize how important and valuable the weekend time away from work is. Is there any way I can support you this weekend or on Monday? Also, the next time we have a critical deadline change, I'll post it and flag it in all the Project XYZ channels, and not just assume that the exec leaders will immediately communicate it."

EFFECTIVE APOLOGY

1. DESCRIBE SPECIFICALLY WHAT YOU DID AND/OR HOW YOU BEHAVED.

2. DESCRIBE AND APOLOGIZE FOR THE NEGATIVE IMPACT IT HAD ON THE OTHER PERSON
   (THE NEGATIVE CONSEQUENCES THEY EXPERIENCED, FROM THEIR POINT OF VIEW).

3. DESCRIBE WHAT YOU INTEND TO DO DIFFERENTLY IN THE FUTURE.

4. DESCRIBE WHAT YOU'D LIKE TO DO OR CONTRIBUTE TO RELIEVE
   THEIR SUFFERING (IF THERE IS SOMETHING YOU CAN DO).

Taking responsibility for your impact on others by apologizing can be a challenge if you're concerned that you'll get dragged in and blamed or criticized while doing it. In my example above, it might seem like the leader is at fault for not notifying the project manager and deserves to be blamed, in which case you may be tempted to ignore the whole thing. But at this point in the book, you know that blame comes from self-protection, that it isn't about you, and the way to not take it personally is to work the CCORE process.

Once you've done that and are back in Self-Leadership, that same energy can be harnessed and directed toward empathy and compassion. When you focus on putting yourself in the other person's shoes, you stop thinking about YOU (and whether *you* are right) and start thinking about solutions. And being sure to end with a "do differently next time" means that it is not an empty apology or a reflection on anyone's character, but rather an authentic intention to do better next time.

ACKNOWLEDGMENT: YOUR POWER TOOL

Acknowledgment is another important and easy way to both reinforce secure relationships and repair them when security is slipping. It is a seriously underutilized tool, and when it is implemented, the positive impacts will reverberate throughout the team. It's also the most effective way to quickly move the needle on building the positive company culture so many CEOs say they want for their organization. But one caution: For acknowledgment to be genuine, it must be thoughtful and specific. You can't just phone it in with "Oh, everybody's doing great. Good job." The generality of messages like that does nothing to show your team that their contribution is really seen and valued. In fact, overly general praise is often seen as inauthentic, throwaway comments.

Recently, I was on a coaching call with a leader whose team had been dealing with morale issues after a merger. Things were not improving despite her efforts, and she was flummoxed: "I have fun office contests for the team. I have inspirational posters on the wall. I have an employee-of-the-month chart and margarita nights. What more could I do?"

I asked, "Did you ever acknowledge them by sharing the details of something positive they did and specifically how it benefited you or helped achieve a better result? A simple example might be 'Leslie, the way you handled that upset parent yesterday was excellent! You didn't get defensive, and you suggested a great solution. You demonstrated our company values beautifully, and I'm grateful to have you on our team.'"

She laughed self-deprecatingly. "No, I did everything but that." And she committed to offering specific, positive acknowledgment at their next quarterly all-team meeting, and then incorporating it into her day-to-day routine. She happily reported back, "It made all the difference!"

Specifically acknowledging people on the team for their efforts, and the benefits those provided, immediately improved productivity and retention in her division. She couldn't change the reality of a messy merger, or the overall chaotic climate at the company, but she could make her team feel awesome by giving them praise that made them feel seen for their hard work and positive contributions.

Just like an effective apology, effective appreciation happens in several distinct steps:

- Explicitly acknowledge what the person did (their efforts and actions).

- Relate the positive IMPACT it had, describing the results it achieved, the difference it made (to you, the team, the customer, and/or the business), and how it made you feel.

- Say, "Thank you!"

Example: "Barbara, I want to take a moment to acknowledge you for waking up early (5:30 A.M.!) to make sure everything was properly set up for our live event. Knowing you were on top of things in the event room let me relax and mentally prepare for a full day of speaking, because I needn't worry about the setup and how our clients would be greeted. Because of your assistance, our event was a huge success. Thank you!"

EFFECTIVE APPRECIATION

1. EXPLICITLY ACKNOWLEDGE WHAT THE PERSON DID (THEIR EFFORTS AND ACTIONS).

2. RELATE THE POSITIVE IMPACT IT HAD, DESCRIBING THE RESULTS IT ACHIEVED,

   THE DIFFERENCE IT MADE, AND HOW IT MADE YOU FEEL.

3. SAY "THANK YOU!"

So don't hold back—practice effective appreciation! It fosters loyalty, dedication, and greater understanding when challenges hit. You know that nourishing culture you've been wanting to create, where people really thrive? This is one of the best ways to build it.

EXPANDING THE ZONE OF EMOTIONAL ENDURANCE

As human beings we don't have control of what happens, but we (almost) always have a choice in how we respond. As a leader, making choices from Self-Leadership ensures that you can navigate challenges and find the best way forward. It also enables you to create psychological safety and build secure working relationships. However, it does *not* mean that all your team members are going to feel good all the time.

When it comes to psychological safety, the most common misconception by far is thinking that it's about making people "comfortable." Let's be clear: Total safety and comfort in business isn't possible (or even desirable). Instead, business inherently faces challenge, loss, and problems. To achieve lasting success, companies need to endure the tough stuff and grow despite the difficulties—which means that people need to not just survive but thrive, even when they're experiencing stress, challenge, and change.

When we say that team members need psychological safety to do their best work, that doesn't mean they need to feel good, comfortable, or at ease all the time. Rather, we want our team members to feel psychologically safe *enough*—enough to endure the inevitable discomfort they'll experience and stay anchored in Self-Leadership so they can use their thinking brain to problem-solve, as well as step up to taking on greater responsibility and risk.

Trying new things is inherently uncomfortable. Often as humans we stick with behavior that's familiar, even if we suspect it will not get the best results, because at least we have relative certainty—we know we didn't die the last time we behaved that way. To be a part of a business that remains relevant, you need to know how to innovate with your team. Innovation sounds exciting, right? It is! But being effective at leading innovation means that you have to master your ability to spend a lot of time in discomfort, and make it safe for your team to be in discomfort right alongside you. I've made a model to illustrate this delicate balance between being totally at ease and being totally overwhelmed—a zone in which we're uncomfortable but still able to think clearly and take calculated risks, despite feeling fear and/or discomfort. This is how we learn and grow. Take a look at the graphic below to see how I think of it visually.

PANIC, PUNISHMENT, PLEASING, AND PARALYSIS ZONE

COMFORT AND DENIAL ZONE

The top zone is where you succumb to emotional reactivity: the panic, punishment, pleasing, and paralysis zone. Different people experience this differently. For some, extreme stress comes across as highly punishing; they think, *This is just too much, I can't take it, it's not worth it, I have to take a day off.* Others respond to extreme stress with panic, unable to be still or control their racing minds, which leads them to speak every irrational thought and every difficult feeling, including anger, out loud. They'll say things like "I can't believe this happened. I'm so upset! How did you mess this up?" while frantically putting notes and reminders in their phone. Still others become paralyzed, frozen in overwhelm or fear. They're often on the receiving end of someone yelling, "Gosh darn it—do something!" And some even go into appeasing behaviors, where they will say and do anything to reduce tension and avoid conflict, even if that involves lying, evasion, or manipulation. Such as "I'm sure I can get this solved before tomorrow"—when everyone who's in their right mind knows that's not possible.

The bottom zone represents comfort and (sometimes) denial. Unlike the top zone, this zone can actually have a productive use. We can't spend our entire lives with tension and stress present in every moment, so the comfort zone is where we recharge our batteries so we can face challenges later. This is the zone where we may busy ourselves with data entry or cleaning up our e-mail inbox, and it helps us cool down after a challenging workday (or week!). But you can indeed have too much of a good thing, and staying in this zone as a way to avoid facing issues (or deny they even exist) guarantees that there's no growth or learning going on. You're avoiding the stress of being challenged, sure, but you're also denying yourself opportunities for both you and the business to improve!

The middle zone is where you are at your most productive. In this zone, you are psychologically safe and secure enough to meet challenges, take deliberate risks, learn new things, and, yes, innovate—even though you're uncomfortable, doing things you haven't done before or stretching your capabilities beyond where you're confident in your own performance. You may even be experiencing pain, fear, frustration, or any number of emotions; however, these emotions don't control your behavior—you perform well even while experiencing some discomfort of negative emotions. And as you spend time in this zone, you'll function better and better in it. Imagine you're about to present a new idea, suggest a solution to a tricky problem, or have a potentially difficult conversation with a team member. You aren't 100 percent sure of the outcome and it's a bit nerve-racking, but you feel safe enough to give it a try. Once you make it through in one piece—even if the outcome isn't exactly what you hoped—you'll feel confident to do it (and other tough stuff!) again. Every time you reap the rewards of taking a risk, you grow your confidence and competence and "level up" your work.

I refer to this as *building your emotional endurance*—an element of Self-Leadership that we touched on in Agreement 1—and it is a key competency for team members and leaders alike. The main tool for building your emotional endurance is the CCORE Empowerment Process that you learned in that chapter. Your ability to keep yourself in your Secure Self in increasingly challenging situations is necessary as you move forward on your career path. You'll recall from Agreement 2 that we discussed how the range of acceptable behavior narrows on the journey from A to V. This means that more is expected in how the team functions as individuals and as a team. A team playing in a championship game has honed its skills and shows up with its best strategies top of mind. Its players are united in focus and clear on the outcome they are after. And any team member who doesn't show up with their best gets benched. In business, higher performance requires that we show up on the court in Self-Leadership, that we do our best teamwork by providing safety and having each other's back, and that we can handle discomfort and still perform. Self-protection cannot dominate the energy on a high-performance team.

When self-protection is present and driving the choices being made, not only will they not be the best choices, but your team's energy also gets unnecessarily drained. Dealing with the emotional upset and drama that often accompany self-protection zaps productivity, and team results take a huge hit. As a leader, the more Self-Leadership you demonstrate, the more safety you can create in your organization, and the more your team will step up to move the needle in this zone of discomfort, risk, and growth to move the company forward.

WHAT ARE YOUR SELF-PROTECTIVE TENDENCIES?

As I shared earlier, to reach a high level of leadership performance, you need to become aware of and address the more hidden, habitual ways that self-protection shows up. This requires taking a close look at the way you function under stress and pressure and a willingness to acknowledge your blind spots.

Business leaders react to stress and challenge in many different and sometimes surprising ways. Their reactions can seem rather random, especially if they differ greatly from how you might react or respond in a similar situation. However, individual reactions are usually quite predictable when we understand the typical patterns of how humans behave under stress.

When facing stressful or challenging situations, our automatic emotional reactions tend along two polar continuums. One axis plots how we most naturally react to challenging *situations*, where some people naturally decide and act swiftly, while others think deeply and strategize carefully. The other axis plots how we most naturally react when we're stressed with *people*, where some confront and engage assertively, while others go into avoiding and pleasing mode.

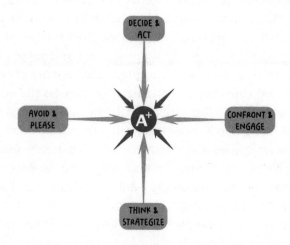

The default behaviors that we utilize when under stress and pressure are almost always a reactive overexpression of our natural strengths. For example, let's say you have a great strength in decisiveness, where under normal conditions you make relatively swift, confident decisions and move forward without second-guessing yourself. When a particularly stressful situation shows up, you will most likely have the strong urge to make decisions very fast and to move forward reactively, even if the most effective and logical action is to get more information and strategize before making a decision. Your strength then becomes a form of stealth self-protection. As you'll remember from Agreement 1, those are attributes that seem potentially positive on the surface but actually get in your way when used automatically in reaction to stressful situations.

What's important to know is that your self-protective defaults have a big impact on your interactions and relationships with others on your team. But as you gain awareness of your tendencies, you'll start to spot when you're slipping into self-protection and putting a painful distance between yourself and others on your team (who may be in the polar opposite self-protective mode). Then you have the opportunity to *lean in*, away from your self-protective default, so you can work productively with others.

Let's look at how your default behaviors can trip you up—and how to regain your balance—using the example of Thomas, who is a brilliant strategist and a very kind and supportive team leader. On the continuum of reacting to challenging situations, he leaned toward thinking and strategizing, and on the continuum of reacting to stress with other people, he was oriented to avoiding and pleasing. On a consulting call with me one day, he made the following confession: "Annie, I've been much more direct in asking for people to step up and take more responsibility, like you coached me. But last week, I did something that I'm kind of embarrassed to admit to you. In my management meeting, I asked for volunteers on a new project that crosses over several areas of the company. A few people volunteered right away for roles that they would be fantastic in. But then one of our newest managers, who is a bit overconfident for his experience level, and whom I've been having to correct often, volunteered to oversee the entire project. Immediately I thought in my head, *Oh no, not you! You aren't experienced enough in this industry, and you haven't even been at this company very long. If you're the project manager, I'll have to shadow your every move and will end up doing most of the project managing myself!* Then I thought, *But I can't hurt his feelings. After all,*

I did ask for volunteers, and he might feel insulted if I turn him down. As I looked at his eager and determined face, I said, 'Sure, you can be the project manager.' At the same time, I was thinking, *What have I just gotten myself into? Now I have an even bigger problem to fix because he can't handle this role.*"

Thomas's self-protective default in stressful situations with people, as I noted above, is to "avoid and please." With no time to think of a response to the new manager's request, his thinking stumbled. If he could have stayed in Self-Leadership and kept his rational brain engaged, he might have thought to say something like "Thanks so much—I appreciate you stepping right up! Let's connect right after the meeting and we can review the role together." Unfortunately, his emotional brain took over with thoughts of *I don't know how to respond! What if I insult him? I can't take that risk, so I'll just say, "Sure," and I'll figure out how to fix it later.* By contrast, a leader whose default behavior with people is at the polar opposite end of the continuum—"confront and engage"— would have likely blurted out, "Oh no, not *you*! I didn't mean someone so new could do it, sorry. I'll have Elsa do it." Neither of these responses works, and both would need relationship repair to clean things up.

After I worked with Thomas to help him understand what had happened, he did go back to the man, saying, "I asked for a volunteer and didn't think through that the role needs at least a year of company experience. I need to let you know that Elsa will lead the project, not you. I'm so sorry to have put you in that situation, and I want you to know that your skills are terrific, but this role needs the experience with our company to have any chance of leading the project successfully. But perhaps we could have you train with Elsa, so that you'd be ready to lead it next year. Would that interest you?" In the end it all turned out okay, and more important, it taught Thomas a valuable lesson about the weaknesses that accompany his natural leadership approach. He decided that the next time something like this happened and he caught himself defaulting to his self-protective "avoid and please," he would *pause* and say to the person, "Let's talk after the meeting" (or words to that effect). As time went on, he was able to be more assertive and "lean in" away from the worst inclinations of his natural self-protection tendency.

As we said at the start of this chapter, working with other humans requires being in relationship with them. And the *way* people relate to one another, the way they perceive one another, has an enormous impact on their performances—as individuals and as a team. I hope you're seeing now why it's so important to develop secure relationships and create psychological safety in the work environment. When these qualities are present, we're free to drop our self-protection and focus our efforts to innovate, take risks, meet challenges, and perform at our best. When they aren't, we will spend all our time thinking about ourselves, how we are being perceived, and if we're "safe" with our co-workers, instead of working together productively to achieve outcomes.

In the next chapter, we'll take a look at leveraging this base of secure relationships and psychological safety by using agreements to work highly effectively together.

Annie Says:

"The more psychological safety you generate, the more you can request people to perform outside their comfort zones. It requires courage to step up and take more ownership for delivering outcomes. That's why we need safety!"

○ ○ ○

SUCCESS STORY

Psychological Safety Is Essential for the Team to Contribute Ideas

Kyle Bradley, President—Performing Arts Instruction Company

THE SITUATION

I used to get flustered, often thinking, *I wish my team would step up and really think when bringing me ideas. Ones that would really make a difference in the business and not just waste my time.*

Every time my COO Sarah brought me new ideas, I reacted negatively and way too fast. I was constantly frustrated and had no idea how to get her to bring me ideas that were more fleshed out and useful. I knew I needed to find a way to slow down and take a breath before reacting or I would damage our relationship beyond repair. It wasn't that all her ideas were bad—it's just that they weren't well thought out. Many of her ideas were confusing and needed to be sorted out, leaving me with a puzzle to solve.

I realized that I reacted poorly when other team members brought ideas that I didn't think were workable, but it was particularly bad with Sarah. This was a problem because she was my COO—the person I trusted and relied on the most! She was really good at her job, so this was something I needed to figure out before she decided she no longer wanted to work with me.

WHAT I DID DIFFERENTLY WITH SECURE RELATIONSHIPS

First, I had to shift how I was relating to Sarah (and my team). As soon as they shared ideas, I began by acknowledging their commitment to the success of the company: "Hey, Sarah, thanks for thinking about what could improve this project—I really appreciate you looking to make us better!"

When I felt challenged, I knew I was prone to reacting with a critical comment, which would shut communication down. To counter that, I would anchor myself in the positive by reminding myself, *I know my team wants what's best and to help the company succeed.* This pause and internal acknowledgment helped me create and reestablish the safety needed for Sarah and other team members to come forward with any new ideas and solutions to current problems. I also learned to apologize quickly when I blew it, saying something along the lines of "Oh gosh, Sarah, I'm sorry for my comment—it was critical, undeserved, and put you in a defensive place. Let me back up and try again now, so I can also get it right next time." I've found that an apology that acknowledges my negative impact goes a long way to repair relationships and restore safety and goodwill.

THE DIFFERENCE IT MADE

Sarah's thinking and ideas got better and better because she knew it was safe to bring them, so she kept bringing more. She could also trust that I would take responsibility for my negative reactions, which made it extra clear to her that I did indeed WANT and value her ideas. This level of safety would not have happened had I not been able to take the pause needed to remember positive intent. I would have continued to damage the relationship, and Sarah might have quit or checked out and no longer cared about the quality of her work.

As Sarah's confidence grew and the team grew, we were able to get along and work side by side to create an environment that everyone wanted to be a part of because they felt valued.

AGREEMENT 4 TAKEAWAYS

We consider our impact on others, have their backs, and repair relationships promptly.

- Humans are hardwired to recognize even the smallest potential threats in situations with others. This can lead to reactive self-protection, which is counterproductive in the modern workplace.

- The antidote to acting out of self-protection, which damages relationships, is to provide "psychological safety"—an environment free of blame, judgment, and criticism, where your team is safe to raise issues and share ideas.

- An effective apology is about repairing a relationship and demonstrating that you care about another person's experience. It's not about determining fault.

- Effective acknowledgment and appreciation specifically describes the actions and behaviors of others and how that positively impacted you and the business.

- When stakes are high, timelines are tight, and the pressure is on, it is easy to bump up against one another. It is helpful to apply compassion and remember you are a united team going for big outcomes!

FOR YOUR REFLECTION

Take some time to think about what you've learned in this chapter. Write about what you're thinking in a notebook, on a device, or right on this page!

1) What one or two past situations (business or personal) come to mind that you recognize could have gone better based on what you know now?

_____

_____

_____

2) What insights did you gain about yourself from this chapter?

_____

_____

_____

3) What is one next action or interaction you intend to do differently moving forward?

_____

_____

_____

MAKING CONSCIOUS AGREEMENTS

We make collaborative, conscious agreements that we're confident we can keep.

The mechanism of effective teamwork

As we established in the Introduction, business is a team sport, and the way the team interacts with one another is through making and remaking a vast array of agreements. We also covered in the prior chapters how Self-Leadership and secure relationships are the foundation that effective agreements are made upon. Because without these, interactions will contain counterproductive, self-protective thoughts and behaviors that prevent people from making the best agreements they can to achieve results. For example, if I'm running late on a project and my boss is upset about it, I can easily agree to a new deadline that still doesn't give me enough time to perform well when I'm insecure about how my boss will perceive me. This will cause an even bigger problem later when I miss the deadline again.

So here's the thing: These types of agreements get made all day, every day, because they are so basic to business achievement. Agreeing upon (that is, committing to) deadlines is a fundamental component of working as a team to achieve results. The fact is, we are always making, adapting, or changing agreements, even if we're not aware of it! We generally know when we're making explicit agreements—meaning you and I have a two-way negotiation that ends with a clear agreement that each of us explicitly acknowledges. But there are many agreements that are assumed and/or implied. For example, let's say a customer service representative is newly expected to fill in a three-minute call sheet with specific details about each CS call. The customer service representatives and supervisors assume that all the other role expectations and duties stay as is. If the consequences of adding the new duty aren't specifically raised, then it's implied that everyone has agreed that the impact isn't enough to cause any other change that needs to be addressed. However, it's typical in a change like this that no one has thought through all the consequences, and that will become apparent when the representatives take longer to finish each call and therefore complete fewer calls than their stated targets. This becomes a performance miss that could have been anticipated with just a bit more thought and with team members remembering that they are responsible to renegotiate agreements that they can no longer keep.

This is why you and your team need *conscious* agreements: carefully thought-out but still malleable contracts in which intended outcomes are explicitly articulated and responsibilities are allocated with both the current circumstances and the big-picture goals in mind. And that's what this chapter is about: *the agreement to make conscious agreements*. In the pages ahead, I'll walk you through a process we call ACE Teamwork. You'll read about how to form conscious agreements, how to delegate effectively, and how to make group agreements that helpfully guide the way your team interacts and produces results.

AGREEMENTS ARE A PROCESS, NOT A PROMISE

In business, agreements are how we define who does what, when, and how. They're how we align expectations for what part each team member will do and how it will all work together. But those things change given the circumstances, and as such, agreements must be flexible to change as soon as either 1) we anticipate that the expectations (agreement) can't or won't be met or 2) the situation changes so that the original agreement doesn't achieve the desired result.

It's important for me to say that agreements are a process, not a promise. As I shared in the Introduction, this is sometimes difficult for entrepreneurs and leaders to understand, especially given that agreements are usually talked about as a contract or a matter of integrity—such as "Impeccable character is all about keeping your word." But in business, agreements are the process of setting intentions for what people will do in anticipated situations. Of course, everyone intends to keep their agreements; however, as the situations change, the agreements need to adjust. There is way too much change always happening in business to consider anything an unchangeable "promise."

You might imagine that if agreements remain flexible, no agreement will ever be final and team members will use that as an excuse, failing to act responsibly. In my experience, the opposite problem is more common. Leaders are extremely driven to achieve results, and they want to be seen as the high-integrity people that they are, so they can be overly attached to keeping agreements exactly as they're made. The trouble is that business requires us to flex and adjust as new information arises. We can stay committed to delivering the business outcome, but the path we take to get there may need to change along the way. Anchoring in the big-picture goals allows the team to make the best plan based on all the information at hand.

To show you what I mean, let me share a story from my own team. James was a college kid we brought in for a short new project. But, as is often true of new projects, it ended up being a lot more than we bargained for, and it only took a few months to see just how troublesome a project without ACE Agreements could be!

Our request to James was simple: "Grow our e-mail list to 7,000 e-mails by the time our book comes out, and don't spend too much." And sure enough, he successfully fulfilled our request, getting us on track for 7,000 e-mail leads within the budget—mission accomplished!

Well, not so fast. To make sure he was doing things right, we got James in touch with a business friend of mine and seasoned Facebook ads expert. Only a minute into their first call, he asked James, "What do you do with the leads? Do you follow up at all?" James, thinking that was someone else's issue, hadn't thought to ask. And my team was so busy working with clients that no one thought to discuss with him what kinds of leads we wanted and what we would do with them.

James had gone into the project focusing on quantity over quality. But as he worked with the expert, he realized that high-quality leads were super valuable because they'd spend more, so he realigned and changed his focus to quality leads. If he had been given more context at the beginning of the project, he would have known this sooner, saving precious time and money.

Let's take a closer look at the formula we used to come back into an aligned, effective agreement.

THE ACE AGREEMENT-MAKING PROCESS

Our process for forming conscious agreements is called ACE Teamwork, and it represents a shift away from top-down authority and control to unified, agreed-upon, team-driven results.

As illustrated in this model, there are three parts to making an effective agreement:

- **A stands for ALIGNMENT:** Seeing eye to eye on intended outcomes and the purpose behind them.

- **C stands for CONSCIOUS AGREEMENT:** Where team members actively negotiate, taking all the impacts they recognize into account, and agree on the actions they'll take to achieve the intended outcomes.

- **E stands for EFFECTIVE ACTION:** Where team members take the most effective action to achieve the result, which is almost always the one outlined in the agreement (go time!).

As you'll see in the graphic below, each element of ACE Teamwork builds on the others in a cycle that repeats as the team passes the ball up and down the court. This is *the* essential playbook of high-performing teams!

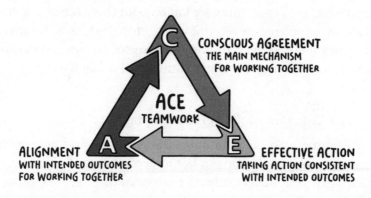

The A in ACE: Alignment (to intended outcomes)

In business, all decisions, agreements, and actions are ultimately meant to achieve desired results. Having a shared understanding of what a successful outcome looks like and why it matters is not only important at the level of the company's biggest goals; it's just as important for individual agreements. It's helpful to think of goal achievement as executing many individual agreements to achieve the "mini" outcomes that will all add up to the big goals.

What James experienced in his Facebook lead-generation project was in reality a classic example of "not getting clear on the desired outcome." We hadn't given James all the important context for WHY he was doing Facebook ads. We had skipped over how the ads were meant to find people who would ideally be interested in enrolling in our yearlong leadership development program and mastermind. Instead, we gave him an arbitrary goal of 7,000 e-mails, without sharing who we really wanted on the e-mail list!

To resolve this, we took a step back and put an ACE Agreement in place, and our first step was to establish the desired outcome and make sure it was aligned to our greater goals—that it would contribute to and support those goals. We met with James to show him that we ultimately wanted people to *enroll in our leadership development programs.* Then we educated him about who our ideal clients were, plus everything we knew about them (demographics, industries, experience level, ambitions, etc.). And lastly, we shared our program enrollment and revenue targets, so that James could put together an advertising lead funnel that made sense.

The C in ACE: Conscious Agreement-Making

As humans, we assume many expectations and agreements every day, often relying on our last understanding of a situation—which may not match others' understanding. For example, I worked with a retailer whose staff took inventory by staying late after closing on the last day of each month. After a couple of months, they assumed (correctly) that this would continue going forward. The store owner assumed (incorrectly) that staffing the late shifts would be like staffing any other day, until suddenly it was impossible to get staff scheduled for inventory days! So the owner figured out what was needed and then set an expectation (after getting the team's input) that each member would attend four inventory days a year (every third month, rotating). The team easily agreed because the business couldn't operate without inventory management. This is a super simple example, but I'm using it to point out what makes this agreement "conscious": that everyone involved understands the request, sees why it's needed, and works together to get it solved in a way that shares the responsibility and works for the business. The owner wasn't making an arbitrary demand that would cause team members to resist and avoid complying.

In business, there are some agreements that can be reasonably assumed, like everyone knowing to show up on time for client meetings, or not to send e-mails late at night and expect an immediate reply from co-workers. However, assuming agreements in business often leaves too much to chance in an already unpredictable environment. When it's not clear who does what, why, and when, it leads to chaos, confusion, and failure. It's essentially like driving blind, because you can't reliably anticipate what others will do. Explicitly negotiating and articulating agreements—meaning saying it all out loud and discussing until an agreement is reached—needs to be the standard. What is the agreement needed to get the work done? What's my part and what's yours? By explicitly negotiating a conscious agreement, you create the space for questions, clarifications, and stronger alignment—all of which lead to better results.

In the example of James's project, to further set him up for success, once we were aligned on the project's true goal (getting high-quality leads that would later enroll in a yearlong leadership development program), we made an explicit agreement that specified James's new responsibilities. No longer would he just be an island of one dealing with Facebook ads; the rest of the team had a part to play in keeping him up to date on how the program enrollments were progressing and anything else that could impact how he approached the Facebook ads, such as when we got clearer about what types of leaders and companies benefited the most from our program. He also had to know what his e-mail leads would see in their inbox after they opted in to the list, so he and another team member agreed on a regular meeting time to review what e-mails were being sent out and how often. Now that James had a seat at the table, not only was he more informed and better supported, but he was also able to contribute to our critical thinking from what he learned about our potential clients on Facebook.

The E in ACE: Effective Action

At first glance, this step may seem obvious. Effective action is simply taking consistent, productive steps to achieve the outcome we're aligned on by following the conscious agreement we've made.

However, it gets a bit more complicated when things don't go according to plan. Sometimes a situation changes, making the specifics of an agreement obsolete. In that case, a team member is trusted to make a choice that's in accordance with the *alignment to the intended outcome* (from the first step of ACE), but maybe *not with the exact agreement.* People will sometimes have to make judgment calls on their own, and that's why they need to know what the specific goal is, which they determined in the alignment step. If they know what a project is supposed to achieve, they'll change course and get it there!

Once James had a clear understanding that we wanted leads with a high potential of enrolling in our program, his performance instantly improved. He was able to target audiences that were interested in business and leadership topics similar to ours, and he focused on quality over quantity of leads. He also made a big pivot, in which he decided to direct leads to a private Facebook community in addition to getting e-mails, because he knew that getting people engaged in a group would generate more enrollments. It worked, and after bringing in several thousand leads, our Facebook group ballooned to include hundreds of engaged CEOs and department heads forming a community of entrepreneurial leaders. And we learned a valuable lesson: It doesn't matter whether the project driver is a 19-year-old intern or a veteran in your company, alignment and conscious agreements are what make for effective action, not heavy-handed commands from up on high.

So now that we've covered the steps involved in making an ACE Agreement, let's look at one of the most common types of conscious agreements you'll likely be making in your business. It's time to learn how to delegate!

DELEGATION–BECAUSE YOU CAN'T DO IT ALL

If you've been a business leader for more than a few months, chances are you've been encouraged to delegate often. You can't do everything yourself, and delegation will get things off your plate so that you can focus on the strategic and higher-level responsibilities in your role. Delegation is meant to leverage your team and increase your productivity, which makes perfect sense, right? That's a big part of why companies have teams! It's such a core productivity principle that you've probably heard common sayings like "Do it, delete it, or delegate it," or "Focus on your strengths, delegate your weaknesses," or my personal favorite, "Never put off to tomorrow what you can delegate today."

But if you've ever delegated *anything*, you know that it can totally backfire. Because when a delegation goes wrong, not only do you need to step in and complete the tasks, but you also end up having to fix the impacts of not having things go right the first time. Also, when a delegation goes badly, it can mean that you have a team member with a performance problem, which is a significant issue and an extra problem to address—who has time for all that? Having been involved with a high number of messy and failed delegations in my career, I understand how many leaders struggle and end up thinking that it's easier, faster, and more effective to just do most things themselves.

Delegation is commonly thought of as a one-way demand, but it usually fails when it's set up that way, as it discourages and disempowers the team member who must commit to achieving the result. Delegation is most effective as a bilateral agreement. In fact, delegation is the most common type of agreement made in day-to-day business. Simply put, it describes the process of one person requesting that another person take on a new or expanded responsibility to achieve an outcome.

The most effective way to approach delegation is as a team development tool, because in the big picture, delegation is the most common way that team members learn new tasks or skills and gain experience in taking on more responsibility. Delegation isn't about giving your crappy work to others—it's about raising up your team's ability (over time) to do more with less of your input and oversight by coaching, mentoring, and supporting them to take on new responsibilities. When delegation is about development, you avoid the internal conflict of thinking it's faster and better to do it yourself versus delegating it; for others to learn, they have to do.

You may think that you already know how to delegate, but I want to encourage you to engage your beginner's mind. Because delegation may *seem* easy, but there are specific steps that most people never learned to do properly. You may be missing a step or two, handicapping your team instead of setting them up to easily succeed.

Delegate Outcomes, Not Tasks

The number one trap of delegation is delegating *tasks*. Directing someone merely to do a series of steps is ineffective because they don't know what those steps should produce or why they matter—thus the person can only do *exactly* what you tell them. The solution is to delegate *outcomes* and give *context* instead. When you delegate outcomes, you're making people responsible for the finished product. This naturally prompts you to give them the information they need and the agency to plan their own steps toward the goal and adjust if needed. Without the outcome and context, they won't be able to solve problems on their own and will have to come back for help—unless they don't even realize they have a problem, which is even worse! Here's a client example, which I have permission to share without changing any details, that clearly shows why delegating outcomes matters.

One of our international clients has a business that teaches people how to sell products and services online. Each year they produce several large, multiday live events for thousands of attendees. If you've ever produced a live event, you know that there's more detailed coordination and effort involved than most people could possibly imagine. But this client was quite exceptional at producing live events and had systems and processes that made sure events ran like well-oiled machines. In fact, they had produced about a half dozen events that were almost flawless, so they were extremely confident in their expertise.

However, while most parts of each successive event were the same as previous ones, this time they were doing something new. The CEO, Carlos, had planned a surprise giveaway for the 7,000-plus attendees. The big reveal was going to be at the end of the first day, when he would say, from the stage, "Now everyone look under your seat!"—where they would find an envelope with valuable surprise materials inside. The envelopes were given to one of the event leaders, who gathered the event team and said, "Tape one envelope under each chair." The team did exactly that on all 7,000 seats, which took hours.

A few minutes before the doors were to open for the participants, Carlos walked out on stage, looked out at the seats in this huge auditorium, and saw the pristine white envelopes all over the place! They weren't taped far enough under the seats to be hidden! Carlos panicked a bit, saying loudly, "This is not going to work! The attendees will see the envelopes and open them right away!" Then he put his hands on both sides of his head, exasperated, and said to the leaders with him, "We need the outcome, not the task! Annie warned us about this! I can see that we told them what to do instead of sharing the result we wanted, which was to surprise our audience—and now *everyone* will see the envelopes, ruining our plan!"

The team had merely followed the simple instruction they were given to tape the envelopes under the seats—*instead* of being told the desired outcome and purpose of what they were doing. The communication should have sounded something like this: "We are doing a big surprise reveal at the end of the day, when we will give each attendee some valuable materials contained in an envelope hidden under their chairs. These envelopes need to be attached under the seats where they cannot be seen at all. Then we'll announce for the attendees to look under their seats, find the envelopes, and open them up to find their gift inside."

Because there wasn't an effective delegation, the CEO and the team faced a crisis minutes before the event's scheduled start time. They had to hold off on opening the doors for 20 minutes while every available person in the entire building scrambled to rapidly re-tape 7,000 envelopes. This was a learning experience they would never forget!

In the company's overall growth journey, this was a one-time situation that was solved without major negative consequences. But their next challenge came almost immediately—out of nowhere—and was something huge that turned their live events upside down.

The Delegation Script

When the COVID-19 pandemic hit, this same company had to shift its next event from people attending live (in person) to attending virtually (watching live people over a video stream from home). At first glance, it might seem like an easy shift to make—all you need to do is provide a webinar link, right?

Wrong. This was a high-stakes and massively complex shift! This event was where they sold their annual membership program, which was a big part of their annual revenue. It was an enormous undertaking that required a complete event restructuring under a tight timeline to produce a three-day virtual, multi-speaker event that could attract and hold attendees—while also inspiring them to buy a high-end program! The pressure was on. They had to plan and delegate super accurately, as there was no time to fix errors, so I had some serious training to do. One of the most challenging and critical parts of the change involved getting people to register and then actually show up for a virtual event! As a registrant, it's easier to blow off a virtual event because it doesn't require the advance planning and commitment to travel, so the perceived negative consequences for missing it are smaller.

There were lots of moving parts to be thought through and delegated, but for this example we will focus on how we delegated the marketing part that drove the critical attendance goal. We had Carlos's team closely adhere to our delegation process, called ACE

Delegation, which has six steps—and it was important that they didn't skip any. This gave them the best chance of getting the marketing done right the first time!

ACE Delegation Script

1. *WHAT* – The intended outcome looks like:

2. *WHY* – The purpose and benefits are:

3. *HOW* – What do you (the person performing the work) need to be successful?

4. *WHAT IF* – What challenges might you encounter? How will you respond to those?

5. *FOLLOW UP* – How will you monitor and/or follow up on progress? How will you respond to significant challenges and urgent issues?

6. *FINISH* – How will I (the person delegating work) know when the work is complete and what results were achieved?

1. The intended outcome looks like _____

The first step was to outline the *WHAT*: the measurable goals that the marketing pivot should achieve. Carlos's team quickly determined that to reach their original goal of 4,000 program purchases (this goal was unchanged), they'd need to increase the virtual audience size and the number of preregistrations, to account for anticipated lower conversion rates and event show-up rates.

They increased the attendee goal from 7,000 to 9,000, and the preregistrations from 10,000 to 12,000. Other details in a successful outcome included maintaining leads that were high-quality and qualified, and gaining an increased engagement level before and during the event in the virtual community (meaning the attendees expressed even more excitement to attend the virtual event than an in-person event). Summarizing the intended outcome sounded like this:

> The intended outcome from the new marketing campaigns is to achieve 12,000 qualified, high-quality leads that are super excited and actively engaged in the virtual community (more than last year) to attend the virtual event, so that 9,000 attendees show up to generate 4,000 program purchases by the end of the event.

Next, we moved on to step 2, where we looked at an even fuller picture of the project and what the company wanted the new marketing campaigns to achieve.

2. The purpose and benefits are _____

The second step was to define the *WHY behind the goals*. This meant examining how achieving the defined outcome would contribute to the company's greater goals—specifically, what it would provide or what it would make possible for the company. I identify the purpose and benefits by asking myself, "If we totally succeed in achieving the outcome, what else do we make possible for ourselves to achieve? What else is positive in the bigger picture of the business?"

The most important purpose in this case was to drive the live-to-virtual pivot so that the company maintained strong revenue—meaning they didn't *lose* major revenue, which would impair their financial health and create a cascade of difficult consequences. (This purpose might seem obvious, but it's not; I had other clients completely cancel events at the time because they were much less important to the business finances.) Another purpose for Carlos's company was to learn about virtual events and add this to their operational competencies, because this virtual event was likely the first of many that would be needed in the future. In hindsight this became very true as the impacts of COVID on event attendance lasted a long time and may have permanently shifted consumer preferences.

3. How will you (the person performing the work) approach this, and what do you need to be successful?

Next up was the *HOW*, including the types of resources needed (such as people, time, money, equipment, or materials) and types of support needed (such as direct training, special access, expert help, mentoring, or new processes or systems). The *how* might also include other considerations for making the project possible, such as changing prior commitments, moving other deadlines, and handing off existing work to other team members.

Now it was the marketing team's turn to think about what they'd need to produce the outcomes, share their thoughts, and collaborate with Carlos about them. They made a simple outline of the "big rocks" of the project to help them anticipate what they'd need. Then, with Carlos, they first talked about how they'd need support to quickly come up with the best strategies to get people excited about and show up to a virtual event, since they'd never done this before. They asked Carlos if he had recommendations for people to talk with who had strong experience in virtual events, as the marketing team members weren't confident in coming up with strategy all on their own. (He did recommend some resources.) They also asked if they could hire some freelance copywriters to help turn things around quickly, and finally, they asked if Carlos would be available to review draft materials on a faster timeline than normal. They emphasized this would be important because they anticipated needing more rounds of editing than usual.

Carlos and the marketing team worked through these points with relative ease. But what would happen if the plan didn't go as expected, if problems came up or if things got off track?

4. What challenges might you encounter, and how will you respond?

Step 4 concerns the *WHAT IF'S*—because in business we know that things almost never go exactly as planned, and sometimes they go nothing like we planned! So it's especially helpful to think ahead and anticipate the challenges that we can, while at the same time getting clear on what we'll do about the unexpected problems and obstacles that might arise. Anticipating challenges up front is a game changer, because most of the time we can do something to either avoid or minimize them, or we can at least plan the most effective response. This prevents unneeded crises, which increases team performance, like, a millionfold!

In this situation, the marketing team surfaced a risk that could destroy their performance if it went badly, which was that social media sites could suspend their ad accounts for the smallest missteps in wording. Normally this wasn't an issue because they were using ads that had already run for months with no problems. But in this case the ads would be new, and if several of them were flagged in a short time, the whole account could be suspended, which could take weeks to resolve (and they didn't have weeks to spare). After raising this challenge, the team put together a more strict and stringent internal review process, which might have prevented a total collapse in the project as none of their ads got flagged.

For unanticipated obstacles or urgent problems, they articulated a simple recovery plan. When they encountered a significant new issue that couldn't wait for the next project meeting to address it, they'd immediately report it in their project messaging channel. In that report, they'd say what the problem and impacts were and how they were planning to address them (if they knew)—and if the issue was URGENT, they'd write that as the first word in the message. They'd also indicate if they wanted a group call or video meeting to work out a solution, if the situation had significant stakes or impacted and involved many team members.

I consider steps 3 and 4 the "engagement steps" because the recipient of the delegation has to proactively think about doing the tasks and also anticipate what might get in the way of having success with this new responsibility. When we ask someone what they'll do or what challenges they might encounter, that person has to imagine themselves *actually doing* the project or tasks, including thinking about the steps involved and what might be impacted in all the other responsibilities they already have on their plates. These steps get the people who will actually do the work immediately and immersively engaged, driving them toward success at the very beginning of a delegation.

5. How will we monitor and/or follow up on progress?

In this step, the person delegating and the person(s) doing the work agree on times to connect and discuss progress (such as meeting weekly until the deadline), along with a clear method for communicating urgent issues.

It might make sense to meet daily for an urgent project with a short timeline, or to meet for half an hour every other week to discuss a more hands-off, monthlong project. Or it could even be written updates with a check-in during department meetings. You'll figure out what schedule and mechanism work for all involved. The important thing is that the person who has delegated the responsibility to others gets proactive, consistent updates. Connecting regularly is meant to clear up any uncertainties, confusion, or obstacles, so as the delegator you don't get stuck thinking, *Oh geez . . . I wonder how project X is doing. Is it moving forward on pace? Are there issues I don't know about? Am I supposed to be doing something that I don't realize?* Tracking down and policing others to get updates or to learn about challenges takes up way too much precious time and mental space. You've got your own outcomes to proactively think about and deliver!

For Carlos's live-to-virtual project, the marketing team 1) changed the Monday weekly meeting agenda to begin with this project and 2) added a Wednesday and Friday morning huddle (20 minutes each). They also created a daily snapshot report, which they sent to Carlos and the other senior leaders, about how the leads, registrations, and community engagement numbers were progressing. I want to point out that this daily snapshot report was not created "for Carlos"; this was something the team needed to monitor and guide their own work!

As a quick aside: When a leader is requesting a new report and it's perceived by the team as unneeded and inconvenient, that's worth exploring more deeply to understand the purpose and context of the request. It's extremely rare that leaders ask for business information that only they themselves need, because everyone is going for the same outcomes. Chances are the team needs the exact same information, but they aren't grasping why it matters. So exploring this type of request is a great way for team members to learn more about the strategic big picture and how their part fits into it.

6. How will I (the person delegating work) know when the work is complete and what results were achieved?

This step addresses the *FINISH*! Here, the person (or persons) doing the work takes responsibility for letting the delegator know when the work is complete; the delegator in turn acknowledges and appreciates the team member or members who made it happen.

In this example, the marketing team was reporting progress and results to Carlos each day, which takes care of this point. However, at the end they prepared a one-page summary of what was achieved that went not only to Carlos but also to his virtual event program team, who were working with the registrants that came from the marketing department's hard work!

The final result: Although this was Carlos's first virtual enrollment event, it was a smashing success, with registrations and enrollments beating expectations. He also reported zero "hidden-not-so-hidden" envelope crises, acknowledging that outcome-focused delegation played a huge role in the success of this major, unexpected project.

That's it. These are the six steps of delegation. I created this as a script so that you can share it with your team. Once everyone learns to delegate effectively, you will see that things most often get done right the first time and with much less frustration than ever before.

ACE DELEGATION SCRIPT - 6 STEPS

1. THE INTENDED OUTCOME LOOKS LIKE:

2. THE PURPOSE AND BENEFITS ARE:

3. WHAT DO YOU (THE PERSON PERFORMING THE WORK) NEED TO BE SUCCESSFUL?

4. WHAT CHALLENGES MIGHT YOU ENCOUNTER? HOW WILL YOU REPOND TO THOSE?

5. HOW WILL YOU MONITOR AND/OR FOLLOW UP ON PROGRESS?
   HOW WILL YOU RESPOND TO SIGNIFICANT CHALLENGES AND URGENT ISSUES?

6. HOW WILL I (THE PERSON DELEGATING WORK) KNOW WHEN THE WORK IS
   COMPLETE AND WHAT RESULTS WERE ACHIEVED?

There is one caveat, and that is that delegation is a two-way street! It might seem like delegation is a way to off-load your responsibilities, but that's not true at all. Even though someone else is committing to deliver an outcome, the delegator has the overarching responsibility to ensure that the delegation is set to succeed. That means instead of thinking about how they themselves will achieve the results, the delegator is thinking, *How can I support this other person to succeed? What will they need for information, resources, guidance, problem-solving support, etc.? Are there any obstacles they need to know about, or that I need to help clear for them? Do they really understand the scope of this responsibility, so that they can plan accordingly without getting shocked halfway through when they recognize they underestimated? Am I accurately assessing their skill set, experience, and competence to determine they are indeed capable of delivering the result on their own? If not, what do I need to do to help bridge any shortfalls?* The point here is that the delegator still has a high level of responsibility, but the delegator's part changes from delivering the outcome to supporting, empowering, and enabling the new person to achieve it.

Effective delegation requires people to actively engage and negotiate a solid agreement. And though there is no formula that guarantees results, this delegation process empowers and guides team members to bring their best thinking to their pieces of the puzzle. The person delegating and the person on the receiving end of the delegation have a shared responsibility to create an agreement that has the best chance of achieving the result! If the person receiving the delegation has any questions related to any of the steps outlined in the delegation script, it's expected that they will speak up and get clarity. For example, the recipient might say, "Hey, I understand the big picture here, but I'm unclear on how we will follow up and monitor progress. How do you see that working?" Or "Could we circle back and talk more about the *why*?" This kind of interchange, where the person taking on the new responsibility essentially "back-leads" the six steps, is what we call *recipient-led delegation*.

Active participation and responsibility on both sides lets teams avoid major slipups since they are not relying solely on one person's ability to communicate perfectly. Say, for example, a member on Carlos's marketing team had conflicting priorities; they had committed to prepare materials for the event itself, but they now also needed to prepare new ad campaigns. With the two-sided responsibility of delegation, it would be expected that this team member would raise the issue of how best to manage the limited resources, even if the delegator didn't ask if they had any conficts. When recipients take initiative, then participate in and guide the delegation process, they have a better understanding of what to do and how to do it.

BOUNDARIES VERSUS AGREEMENTS

Making explicit, collaborative agreements is a huge time and energy saver because these agreements not only bring multiple perspectives and critical thinking to the table, they also minimize misunderstandings, conflicts, and feelings of being excluded or disrespected by the team. But what about the situations where the collaboration isn't working to come to an agreement? And what happens when an agreement repeatedly isn't kept? An example might be when someone agrees to work three hours on a Saturday but ends up working six hours—and this happens many weekends in a row. Is this the time to set a boundary? So that after three hours you stop working, as long as the consequences of stopping aren't dire?

The idea of having boundaries and keeping them has become more popular in the workplace as a response to overworking and to prevent burnout. There certainly are times when a team member should not agree to a request or follow through with actions that would cause significant harm, violate laws, or cross moral standards of conduct. In these cases, a team member would probably give a strong, nonnegotiable refusal, thereby effectively implementing a boundary.

However, when people invoke boundaries as a way to serve themselves at the expense of other team members, then it becomes counterproductive. A situation common in entrepreneurial companies is when one team member violates a company norm—a behavior so common that it becomes an implied expectation. For example, imagine that one team member holds their working hours to 40 per week and refuses to work weekends, when everyone else who works at a similar level and with a similar type of responsibility routinely works around 50 hours and sometimes weekends to achieve the needed company results. No explicit expectations have been set, but it's clearly the norm in the organization for team members to work extra to meet important deadlines and to serve high-stakes clients. So when this one team member refuses to work extra, citing the fact that they're only obligated to work 40 hours, the others have to work more to make up for it. In those cases, the boundary is perceived as an unfair way for one person to get what he or she wants, without regard to the negative impact on the others involved in the situation. This breaks down trust and damages relationships.

Also, utilizing a boundary to avoid a challenging negotiation is certain to backfire. For example, say someone regularly performs extra duties outside of their formal role, but those duties become increasingly difficult and time-consuming until one day the team member says, "I'm no longer doing the extra duties because they're not in my role description." Technically this statement is valid, but when someone accepts ongoing duties and responsibilities, an agreement is implied, and others come to rely upon it. So then when the person comes back with the boundary, stating, "It's not in my job description," it's perceived as breaking an agreement without regard to how it affects the other team members. This is a form of self-protection because using the boundary is a convenient way to avoid the tension and uncertainty of a renegotiation. What the boundary holder doesn't usually realize is that breaking the trust of the other team member(s) leads to the team no longer having that person's back or considering their success and well-being, if the relationships aren't repaired.

A more effective way of addressing an uncomfortable situation like this is first to move *out* of self-protection the way we discussed in Agreement 1: Pause and work the CCORE Empowerment Process to regain a sense of confidence and empowerment within yourself—to come back into Self-Leadership. From this perspective, you are better able to clarify what you truly need, then articulate it and approach others in such a way that others' needs and perspectives can be considered to create a new agreement. Agreements are meant to satisfy and work for everyone involved. That means renegotiation is in order when circumstances or needs change.

If, after reading all this, you truly feel that you need to hold a boundary because it's your only option to meet your needs, here is how I recommend you approach it so that you minimize damage to your relationship(s):

- State the situation and how you'll meet your need: In this situation of _____ *I'm going to/not going to* _____

- State your reason—the positive impact you're seeking for yourself and the other parties involved: *I'm taking this position because* _____

- State anything you can contribute, within your boundary, that will support the other parties (if there is anything): *However, I will* _____

For example, let's say you've been helping customer service by taking customer calls the last two weekends (after full workweeks). Then you encounter an especially difficult week, and by Thursday you're exhausted. Customer service asks you on Friday to work the weekend, and at that point you know two things: 1) Customer service is desperate since they're asking for your help for a third weekend in a row, and 2) you can't possibly work this weekend because you're bone-tired. You could say, "Hell no, I'm not working a third weekend! I can't believe you even asked!" (An emotional response from self-protection.)

Or you could say, "I'm so sorry, but I can't work this weekend. Because I'm so exhausted, I know that I couldn't talk with customers coherently, and I need to recover so that I can be productive next week to meet my big project deadline. However, if it would help, I'll ask others in my department if they're interested in taking a shift." (A thoughtfully chosen response from Self-Leadership.)

Different from setting a boundary, which creates a winner and a loser, an agreement seeks to bring both parties together for mutual benefit. It increases safety, keeping secure relationships intact, creating clarity and a path to resolution. When you start by making a conscious agreement, you have a good base in place from which to renegotiate if you try it out and something different is needed. Even when making an agreement with yourself, having flexibility allows the best path forward.

Agreements are the most versatile tool in your leadership toolbox. They are how the work gets done most effectively. Because of that, I want to talk about one more aspect of conscious agreement-making with your team: making agreements as a group.

GROUP AGREEMENTS

Group agreements are super common in business, even if we don't actually call them agreements. Explicit group agreements include things like "standards of conduct" or "ground rules." Implicit group agreements include common expectations and behavioral norms, such as not listening to music on your headphones during team meetings, or not conducting band practice in the office—unless your office is a music studio!

In general, group agreements usually reflect broad expectations about behavior that apply the same way to everyone, often presented as rules or nonnegotiable expectations. These are things like "Be on time to meetings" or "Respect upset customers by listening intently, avoid interrupting or talking over them, and focus on solving their core issue." But what about group agreements that don't apply the same way to everyone? Or when expectations differ depending on roles, or when exceptions are needed? What about when an agreement should be applied only in some situations and not others? Or when certain conditions can change the agreement? Most leaders and teams have not learned how to handle these types of situations, so that when everyone can't agree on a universal rule, then no agreement happens at all, which causes performance to break down. Without an agreement, no one knows what's expected of them individually.

This is when a tool I call the ACE Interaction Agreement comes into play. Interaction agreements are situational, conditional agreements that account for differences in individual behaviors and expectations. They're used when a one-size-fits-all approach just won't work.

For example, a thorny issue for many teams involves how to establish appropriate responsiveness protocols for internal e-mails and messages (not ones that include clients). Think about the times you've sent an e-mail or message to another team member and received a reply either many days later or not at all. Maybe there wasn't a big impact when it happened, and you didn't think much of it. Or maybe this negatively impacted your work performance, causing you to miss a deadline, or worse. Perhaps the issue is still ongoing, and you're now dedicating hours of extra effort to get responses that you know would take only minutes if the other people would just take a moment to look at the message!

Most people can totally relate to this, and yet when the team tries to make agreements about internal responsiveness, it rarely works. Some companies try to set a rule, such as "Everyone must reply to internal messages within 24 hours." Total compliance usually lasts less than a week before people start breaking the rule. Then, when they realize that nothing happens—that there aren't any real consequences—compliance tends to fall off a cliff. Eventually the people who were consistently complying feel like fools for continuing to dedicate effort to something that barely anyone considers worthy. This wouldn't be a problem except that some people really, truly need the responsiveness to perform well and achieve the company goals. Which is why the rule was created in the first place!

At this point, most leaders are thinking about what incentives and punishments can be put in place to make everyone comply with the rule. However, not only is this a tragic waste of resources (creating and enforcing carrot-and-stick programs takes precious time and energy that are already scarce), but it doesn't even work! Punishing people for failing to return an internal message—to a degree that gained compliance—would be terribly counterproductive, causing people to overdedicate their brainpower and focus to returning those messages out of fear, not because other teammates needed the responses.

So how can you negotiate an agreement that everyone will honor, without hiring a full-time enforcer? Or how can you form an agreement that will meet the needs of a few people without negatively impacting the rest? This is where the ACE Interaction Agreement comes into play.

ACE Interaction Agreement

You start with forming the main intention of the agreement—that is, what you want team members to do differently and what success looks like. In this example, it might sound like the following:

> *We, the team members of XYZ Corp., will respond to internal team requests and questions within 48 hours, unless the sender specifies another timeline.*

This sentence sounds like the "rule," but we're not stopping here. Next, we're going to consider the situations, conditions, exceptions, and clarifications needed to make this agreement work for everyone.

Conditions and Clarifications

The questions we need to ask here are the following:

- "What would YOU need to meet the intentions of this agreement?"
- "What would make this practical for you?"
- "What situations might you struggle with to meet the agreement?"
- "What could we do differently in those situations?"
- "What would make this agreement feel psychologically safe for you?"
- "How could we recover when the agreement gets broken?"

This is where people think about their *own* needs and individual situations, and we come up with a list of conditions and clarifications. That list might look something like this.

As a member of the team, I also agree that:

- *If anyone needs a response sooner than 48 hours, they need to specify that in the subject line. If I'm unable to respond within the timeline, I will answer the requester (within the 48 hours) that I'm working on it, and I'll share when they can expect the full response.*

- *If you don't need a response in 48 hours, please say so in the subject line by indicating the last day I can get it to you, such as "Respond by July 30."*

- *If I'm unavailable to reply within 48 hours, I will either set up an autoresponder or respond right away with the timing you can expect.*

- *If there's a conflict between the project management schedule and the request, I will ask the requester to update the project management schedule, as it's the master we follow.*

- *If I don't respond within the 48 hours, please send the request to me again with "Second Request" in the subject line.*

Then we ask if each individual can agree to all the conditions. I find it's super rare that anyone can't, but it's always been resolvable when it comes up.

Agreement Recovery

Lastly, we think about what to do when the agreement gets broken, how we'll address that, and what we'll do to get ourselves back on track. We call this recovery, and in this agreement, it could look like this:

- *When someone breaks the agreement, we will confront them without negative judgment, shame, or criticism, and instead focus on solving the issue and impact.*

- *If someone is regularly breaking this agreement and causing a negative impact for a team member, that member will first confront the person directly to resolve the issue.*

- *If the issue above isn't resolved and the negative impact continues, then it will be put on the cross-functional leadership meeting agenda and addressed during a meeting.*

- *We will review this agreement annually at minimum, to make any needed modifications to increase its effectiveness.*

At the end of creating the above agreement, we confirm with each individual that they do indeed agree, and then we celebrate our amazing teamwork!

You might be wondering if these ACE Interaction Agreements actually work. Yes, they work exceedingly well, because they address and resolve the root causes of why people don't comply, and they comprehensively clarify the "why" behind the agreement, so that people understand what's at stake and how others are impacted. These two things provide the natural motivation for team members to make adjustments to keep their agreements.

I can't overemphasize the importance of *making adjustments*. You must renegotiate agreements when you see that you can no longer achieve the outcome without a significant shift. That is the superpower of agreements: They are clear yet flexible in the face of change. In the next chapter, we'll take a closer look at how to renegotiate skillfully when change happens.

Annie Says:

"Agreements in business are a process, not a promise!"

O O O

SUCCESS STORY
It Takes Calm Collaboration to Make Good Agreements
Lucas Allen, COO—
Eight-Unit BBQ Restaurant Chain

THE SITUATION

I was so frustrated that I could barely keep from blowing up. I said to my leadership team, as nicely as I could muster, "We've been talking about improving our quality control system for meal preparation for months—what's taking so long?"

I had actually been talking about this for closer to a year—ever since we started tracking how some restaurant units had more complaints about the food quality, while others rarely had any. We hadn't found any obvious reason why.

My leaders knew we needed to resolve this issue, but they just didn't ever get to it. I was feeling more and more at risk that we'd get a bad reputation for inconsistency in our restaurants, which could easily cause our sales to drop. Adding insult to injury, one of our bankers told me that in her last two meals, her ribs were tough. That feedback was especially upsetting to me. At one point, I even told my leaders, "Just hire a restaurant consultant to come in and put in place the best quality control processes." But they rejected that idea, because they were "too busy" to work with and supervise a new consultant. They continued to put me off, saying, "We'll address it as soon as we can." To me, that meant they'd probably never get to it.

WHAT I DID DIFFERENTLY WITH CONSCIOUS AGREEMENTS

First, I had to address my own feelings of resentment and disappointment toward my team and stop blaming myself for allowing the customer complaints to go on for so long. I was ruminating on this issue, and it was spiking my anxiety. So, I got myself centered, and then I made a "fact list" of everything I knew about the situation—and everything I didn't. I then organized the monthly complaint data by comparing it to customers served, along with other information about the restaurants themselves, including the leaders and teams.

When I looked at the facts in a bigger-picture format, I realized that I was overreacting. We needed to address the issue, but none of the restaurants had complaint levels that were audacious. While my team might be underestimating the urgency of this, I was honestly overestimating the urgency.

Realizing this, I was able to interact with my leaders from a more compassionate and level-headed place. We FIRST defined the outcome we were going for, which was to consistently meet a minimum quality standard based on customer expectations. Once we were clear on the outcome, we had a discussion about what might be going on and how we could clearly assess the situation. I was certain we needed better quality control, but the team thought the main issue could be related to old kitchen equipment in some of the restaurants. And one team member had a theory that our meat supplier might be cheating on quality. We quickly created an assessment project, which our Director of Operations led, to gather more facts and give us a clearer picture of the issue. We all agreed to a 60-day timeline to complete the assessment.

THE DIFFERENCE IT MADE

When I was able to calm down and approach the leaders from a place of Self-Leadership, the whole situation changed. Instead of being avoidant and defensive, they got curious about the problem and figuring out what to do about it. I had doubted that my team would be able to take on the responsibility of addressing this, and they proved me wrong. Once we negotiated a clear and well-aligned agreement, not only did they keep it, but they finished the assessment in 40 days instead of 60.

And you know what we ultimately learned? The complaints about food quality involved a few different issues, but the biggest one was the following: The restaurants with smaller kitchens and less oven space sometimes had to speed up their meat cooking, or they couldn't serve all the customers on a very busy night. But raising the temperature, even slightly, to speed up our slow-roasted meats impacted the tenderness and taste. The kitchen staff thought the solution was working just fine, especially because they only needed to deploy it once in a while, but boy, customers who dined on those nights noticed the difference. This was a big "aha" moment for me and would require more than just a quality control process to fix!

Looking back, I can so easily see how my anxiety and upset was causing me to make incorrect assumptions, escalate the issue, and press for a "half-baked" solution that wasn't going to solve the heart of the problem. It made such a huge difference to work with my team from a calm, centered, curious place because then we came up with excellent solutions and effective agreements—ones that were kept! This experience raised my confidence in both myself and my team, which was such a welcome turnaround from where we started.

AGREEMENT 5 TAKEAWAYS

We make collaborative, conscious agreements that we're confident we can keep.

- Agreements are where the rubber hits the road in business. They are the main mechanism of teamwork. We are always making agreements, even if we're not aware of it!

- Agreements are a process, not a promise. As situations change, so must the agreements. There is way too much change always happening in business to consider anything an unchangeable "promise."

- Delegate outcomes rather than tasks.

- Delegation is a two-way process with mutual responsibility. When everyone involved is responsible to generate a good agreement, it takes the pressure off any one person to get it right.

- Group agreements take things out of the realm of the implied and assumed, where individual interpretation can cause challenges, to clear agreements that work for everyone.

- Making clear, conscious, effective agreements is a foundational skill. It's worth practicing to achieve mastery.

FOR YOUR REFLECTION

Take some time to think about what you've learned in this chapter. Write about what you're thinking in a notebook, on a device, or right on this page!

1) What one or two past situations (business or personal) come to mind that you recognize could have gone better based on what you know now?

_____

_____

_____

2) What insights did you gain about yourself from this chapter?

_____

_____

_____

3) What is one next action or interaction you intend to do differently moving forward?

_____

_____

_____

AGREEMENT 6

RECOGNIZING AND RESPONDING TO CHANGE

We recognize change, anticipate impacts, and proactively adapt our agreements.

The formula for succeeding in an ever-changing reality

In the previous chapter, we talked about making agreements that are clear and outcome-focused and—crucially—that work for everyone involved. But no matter how well you've aligned everyone on the goals and consciously thought through all the details and impacts of your agreements, things don't always go as planned. In fact, sometimes it can feel like they *rarely* go as planned!

This makes sense—the external business environment is incredibly unpredictable as major technologies change, industries shift, customer expectations rise, new competitors appear, and economies go up and down. The company internal environment isn't much better, as results sometimes disappoint, people overestimate their time and resources, team members make mistakes, internal technology breaks down, and products don't work as expected. A lot can go wrong, and it would be great if you could predict the future and fix everything before it happened, but then you'd probably be day-trading right now instead of reading this book!

RECOGNIZING CHANGE

To get performance and outcomes back on track, you first must recognize when you've gone off track. You know things are off track when achieving the intended outcome isn't possible without a meaningful or significant change to the current plan, expectations, or agreements. Now, that sounds pretty simple! However, surfacing problems isn't easy for humans, as the people on your team must face negative emotions and create tension by engaging in conversation and volunteering *information that usually is NOT good news*. And to do that, they need to feel it's safe to speak up without getting blamed, criticized, judged, or dismissed. For example, if you come into the conference room looking for someone to blame because you're not getting enough program registrations, the person managing the promotion will have the urge to hide what's really going on and share, for example, that Facebook suspended their ad account (especially when it's in front of the whole team and the CEO!). And when people fear speaking up transparently because it makes them vulnerable to anger, judgment, or disrespect from others, you won't get the information you need to fully understand the situation and make effective adjustments. So, this is an area where psychological safety is particularly important. (Turn back to Agreement 4 if you need a refresher on this crucial component of the People Part.)

Psychological safety is also crucial when fielding possible solutions to the adverse impact. Throwing ideas out there feels risky: Your co-workers (or even your boss!) might judge or embarrass you, and everyone is tense because, well, things aren't going that great. But it's essential that everyone's ideas get shared and heard so the team gains all the differing and important perspectives to confront the problem they're facing—as a team. One common pitfall for individual leaders is to jump in and try to fix all the problems themselves, even the complex ones. This can be especially tempting when doing the work yourself is the simplest and fastest solution. And occasionally this is the most effective solution. However, if you get in the habit of fixing problems for a team that's capable of learning how to do it themselves, you'll stay trapped in the vicious cycle of putting out fires and then getting burned out (no pun intended!). Teams learn through doing and problem-solving, which involves renegotiation and is all about using your company's collective brains (not just yours) to solve problems and get back on track.

Before we get into the nuts and bolts of renegotiating agreements, I want to bring you back to another essential component of the People Part. Determining that things are off track is pretty easy, but doing something about it is harder, especially when we think we're partially or fully at fault. So before you move forward to address any gap, make sure you are coming from a place of Self-Leadership! You should walk into any negotiation free of self-protection, so take a pause and flush out any frustration or fear.

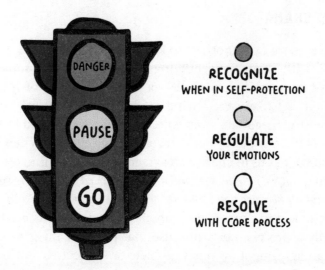

RECOGNIZE
WHEN IN SELF-PROTECTION

REGULATE
YOUR EMOTIONS

RESOLVE
WITH CCORE PROCESS

The easiest way to do this is by anchoring yourself in your overall positive intention and the desired business outcome. Business outcomes are not about who you like or dislike or who's at fault; they are about achieving a goal. So when you sit down to address an issue, anchor yourself in the desired outcomes to ensure productive negotiation and a respectful back-and-forth. (Turn back to Agreement 1 if you want a recap of the importance of Self-Leadership and a proven process for getting there and staying there—or check out the graphic reminder on page 169.)

We have two words to help articulate the consequences that these changes create for a company: *gap* and *impact*. Think of a gap as the difference between where you thought you would be and where you end up, like trying to get 200 registrations for an upcoming conference but getting only 50. That's a gap of 150 registrations, which comes with all sorts of impacts! We solve for these by surfacing resulting issues and renegotiating our agreements accordingly. Being able to make timely adjustments is essential to the success of your business, and in this chapter I'll share what you need to know to navigate change and achieve results for the many times things don't go as planned.

"WHAT CHANGED?"

Because we expect others to keep their commitments with us, and we with them, renegotiating an agreement can sometimes feel like an admission of guilt—or worse, a breach of integrity. We often feel like we're letting others down when we take the initiative to renegotiate, even when the issue was caused by something completely out of our control. And vice versa: When someone approaches us to change an agreement, we may find ourselves thinking, *But we had an agreement! Now I'll need to scrap my valuable work, and all because you couldn't keep your side of the bargain.*

We talked in Agreement 5 about how agreements are fundamentally a process, *not* a promise that puts our integrity at risk when an agreement becomes obsolete or ineffective. But how do you take that approach in a real situation where an agreement needs to shift and emotions are running high? I wasn't always sure myself how to surface gaps and renegotiate without causing major pain all around—until I learned an important lesson from my husband, David.

Compared to him, I'm slow to make decisions and I often change my mind. He recently joked that a new Amazon warehouse (the size of three football fields) being built near our home was just for my returns—even I had to laugh. Most of the time this isn't a problem for us, but when we were remodeling our home, it almost tore us apart. After spending weeks carefully exploring options, I would make a decision on something like a light fixture or a paint color. But then when it was being put in place, I'd realize I didn't like it. This type of thing is disastrous in a remodel, of course. The day I decided the bathroom tile—already half installed—wasn't right, my husband reached the limit of his patience (and I'm sure our contractor did too). With the most pained expression I'd ever seen on him, he said, "I thought you had decided! We spent hours together in Tile City, and we agreed on this tile because you said you loved it! It goes with everything else you already chose! *What changed?!*"

I was about to tell him all the reasons that I didn't like the tile when it was installed—but something about his question made me pause. At that moment, I realized this wasn't really about the tile, or even the time and money it would take to redo it. It was about *changing a deal*—a deal in which my husband had invested considerably with his time and patience, and that we had clearly agreed on.

Let's take a closer look at that question he asked: *What changed?* We naturally understand that agreements, especially at work, are situational and have lots of interdependencies. However, we also understand that we make agreements so that we can depend on one another to take the actions we're expecting and relying upon. Since both these things are true, it makes sense that the way to respectfully and most effectively renegotiate an agreement is to start by looking at how the situation has changed. This is how people move past the knee-jerk "We had a deal!" response. Whether the "change" is a struggling supplier who can't deliver on time, a new ad campaign that didn't perform well, or a terrible weather forecast before the outdoor event, all involved parties need to know what made the old agreement obsolete. Then they can start to think about what will work instead.

In the case of my tile crisis, several things had changed. We had put in a new window in the midst of the renovations—after we planned the bathroom—and the light coming through created a glare we hadn't anticipated; then the tile pattern had a lot more white tiles in it than the manufacturer represented, and all the extra light made the room's colors wash out. Adding the window had a ripple effect that I first noticed when the tile was laid down. Once I explained all of this, my husband recognized that I wasn't glibly "changing the deal" because I just wanted my way and didn't respect him or his time, but instead that a series of things had happened that I couldn't anticipate that impacted my original decisions in a negative way.

But before I explained all that, I had to do some on-the-spot relationship repair. David was mad—understandably—and I felt a lot of compassion for him, that he was making sacrifices for *me*, to make *me* happy, only to have me complain and seemingly disrespect him. And that's a feeling I know well, because I've been in similar situations in my own life. So even though he was upset with me, I could empathize with him, which allowed me to apologize sincerely. I started by apologizing for complaining about the tile without considering our deal, a deal that he was both invested in and counting on to alleviate the stress and uncertainty of the remodel. I also thanked him for taking his time and considerable energy to supervise the contractors for a remodel that *I* rather than *he* wanted, when he would rather be working on his own business.

After David and I calmed down, we sat down to renegotiate our tile agreement together. My explanation of what had changed, together with my relationship repair, put us on the same page for productive problem-solving, and in the end, we got a gorgeous bathroom.

Now here's what you need to know about articulating "what changed." It's super simple—when addressing the people impacted by the situation, explain the following:

- Here's what changed *with the situation*: Identify unexpected external changes (such as a butter shortage or spike in flour prices for a baker) or internal company changes or unexpected events (such as a department leader resigning or new software not working right).

- Here's what's changed *with my work, my project, or my performance*: Explain the gap between the expected versus the current status by identifying misses, like making a mistake and there not being enough time to fix it before the deadline or adding a needed (but time-consuming) last-minute change that pushes back the project finish date.

CLOSING GAPS WITH THE "GAPA" FORMULA

Once we've recognized what has changed in a situation, the next step is to look at, and deal with, how it's affecting us—the gap it has created and why it matters. This is the *impact* of the change, and the impact is what we're looking to turn around by renegotiating agreements. While we might not be able to do anything about the specific conditions that have changed, we can hopefully cushion the blow or even navigate around it to get to our desired outcome.

The process I use for closing a gap has four steps, to which I've given the acronym **GAPA**. Before you start, be sure to introduce the conversation by stating your intention for it and why you're having it in the first place—that is, *what has changed* in the situation to make the conversation necessary. Then go on to GAPA:

- **G:** Describe the **GAP** (the difference between expected performance and current or anticipated performance) and the **IMPACT** on the desired outcome.

- **A:** Request and suggest potential **ADJUSTMENTS** and solutions—remembering that we're looking to resolve the impact, not the gap itself.

- **P:** Consider all the **PERSPECTIVES** and discuss alternatives to make the most effective decisions.

- **A:** Finally, form a new or modified **AGREEMENT** on the chosen solution(s) and map out the next steps in the new plan.

Now let's walk through the steps with an example from a talent agency client of mine. This company had been in business for over 50 years and was highly successful. However, the talent agency business is extremely competitive and has only become more so in the last decade. Not only do the desirable actors and artists have tons of choice for which agency they choose to represent them, but the accomplished agents themselves are constantly targets of poaching attempts by all the top-tier firms. To sustain success as a talent agency, the firm must sign and retain, long-term, both the talent and the agents.

Talent agencies are in the image business, and agents care immensely about the look and feel of their office environment. They want their clients and prospective clients to be highly impressed with ultra-posh offices, taking that as a success signal and increasing their confidence in the firm. The agents also want fancy offices for both status and pleasure—if you spend most of your life in the office, as many agents do, it helps to have gorgeous art and a fabulous sofa to occasionally sleep on. Even though I know the importance of all this, I was still surprised about how serious and contentious an internal negotiation had become about an upcoming office remodel and redecoration. The firm's agents and the partners had previously agreed on an overall budget for the project, but when the construction estimates and designer specifications came in, the agents were underwhelmed and felt strongly that the office upgrade would be a waste of time and resources if the budget wasn't increased. Predictably, the partners didn't agree that raising the budget was needed.

I worked with the agents to effectively raise and work through this issue with the partners, and this is how it went, step by step.

Intention of the conversation and what changed:

The agents formed their intention for the conversation: They wanted to review the remodel plan and budget with the partners to resolve the issue they had identified, namely that the new plan wouldn't accomplish the image upgrade they needed. "What changed?" was simple—the cost estimates came in higher than expected, so the remodel design, finishes, furniture, and artwork were downgraded or cut to meet the budget.

G: Describing the GAP and the IMPACT

When we're seeing a gap, the first things we need to determine are 1) what *is* the gap and 2) why the gap matters: What impact could the gap potentially have on the outcome? To assess the impact, we not only recognize the current status of the situation, but we also hypothetically play forward to see what is likely to happen if things continue as they are. For example, if our customer service response time continues to increase because of the current technology glitch, what are the consequences now and how will they grow or change if we don't do something? This helps us see the full scope of the impact, what's really at stake, and helps motivate people to think through what they most need to resolve.

In the case of my talent agency client, the gap was pretty easy to articulate: The agents anticipated that the remodel would fall short of their expectations if the budget wasn't increased.

The impact is always important to articulate clearly: To the agents, the new plans for the remodel would not produce an impressive enough office for them to get a significant boost in signing and retaining top talent—which was the main goal of the remodel. That was the impact we were solving for—increased signing and retaining talent. Making the offices extra fancy was not the goal in and of itself.

The agents met with the partners to share their opinion. The partners, meanwhile, felt that the remodel plans and budget would work just fine. At first glance, this situation seemed like it might end in a stalemate, where the differences of opinion couldn't be resolved—after all, who's to say what type of design and what level of luxury décor would effectively convey the successful, high-end image they wanted? Isn't that type of thing extremely subjective and based on individual tastes? Also, how can you seriously measure the impact and value of improving your company's image? It's not likely your clients will say, "Wow, I love the new lobby—that does it for me! Let me sign the contract immediately!" Considering all this, how the heck can you make a good business decision for how much to invest in an office remodel?

Thus the agents knew they had to present an effective business case to move the needle toward their desired outcome. They smartly conducted both a professional design survey of their main competitors' office environments and a related psychological "image" survey, and plotted themselves against both. This helped them more concretely identify where they needed to be and what type of design and décor improvements were needed to get there. It became clear that they really did need to invest more, about 33 percent more than they had budgeted, in the remodel.

A: Suggesting possible ADJUSTMENTS

This step is where we think up solutions and put them on the table! We want plenty of ideas to work with, and we want to stretch our creative thinking. Remember, we're solving for the IMPACT (not the gap), and in this case the impact is that an insufficient remodel won't generate the image uplift that the company needs to improve the signing and retention of top talent.

During the meeting with the agents and partners, there was a lively discussion that yielded many potential solutions, including:

- Raise the remodel budget by putting a freeze on staff raises for a year
- Push the remodel out one year to enable a larger budget
- Inquire with another designer for ideas that could accomplish the design goals for less money
- Do the remodel in phases and prioritize the expensive purchases (such as lobby first, wall art last)
- Ask the landlord for tenant improvement money, to increase the budget, in exchange for increasing the rent during the remainder of the lease

P: Consider the different PERSPECTIVES

In this step, we debate the solutions we've come up with and pick one or more that we will implement. This part is all about fully exploring the options to assess the positives and the negatives, the benefits and the risks, and the ways we'll mitigate the risks and recover from any setbacks.

In our agency's case, after reviewing the options, the agents and partners decided to use a combination of the solutions that had been proposed. They quickly decided against a wage freeze, as they had to stay competitive with the other firms, and also against pushing the remodel out, which could actually harm the company since the remodel was overdue. They decided on a combination of the last three ideas. First, they'd bring in another designer to innovate for higher style at a lower cost. Then they'd schedule the remodel in two phases: lobby, reception, conference rooms, and elevators this year, staff offices next year. And finally, they'd ask the landlord to contribute to the remodel in exchange for a rent increase.

A: Create and confirm the new AGREEMENT

This step is about confirming the new agreement and starting to plan the implementation. The agents and partners came to a solid agreement on the budget and formed the basic timeline and milestones of the project. They also agreed that the CFO would supervise the remodel project closely and produce written reports, and that the leaders would review the progress at their biweekly management meetings.

GAPA

G: DESCRIBE THE **GAP** (THE DIFFERENCE BETWEEN EXPECTED PERFORMANCE AND CURRENT OR ANTICIPATED PERFORMANCE) AND THE **IMPACT** ON THE DESIRED OUTCOME.

A: REQUEST AND SUGGEST POTENTIAL **ADJUSTMENT** AND SOLUTIONS—REMEMBERING THAT WE'RE LOOKING TO RESOLVE THE IMPACT, NOT THE GAP ITSELF.

P: CONSIDER ALL THE **PERSPECTIVES** AND DISCUSS ALTERNATIVES TO MAKE THE MOST EFFECTIVE DECISIONS.

A: FINALLY, FORM A NEW OR MODIFIED **AGREEMENT** ON THE CHOSEN SOLUTIONS(S) AND MAP OUT THE NEXT STEPS IN THE NEW PLAN.

Active Listening = Active Problem-Solving

I'm sure you can see by now that the GAPA process is very much a collective undertaking. As such, it presents a great opportunity for team members to demonstrate their respect and belief in one another through their attentive listening and considered responses—and their problem-solving is the better for it.

Here are a few hot tips on how to use active listening when you're negotiating an agreement:

- During the phase where you're suggesting adjustments and sharing perspectives on them, don't interrupt the person who is speaking; instead, give them adequate space to explain their vantage point and the important context behind their proposed solutions.

- Ask them to slow down if they're going too fast. Stress can cause people to feel pressured and speed up, but slowing things down and hearing all the critical thinking involved is the way to find the best solutions.

- Use perception checking to make sure you understand clearly what they are trying to communicate. This not only helps you clarify your perceptions of their proposed solutions or concerns, it also helps them hear if they are making their points as they've intended. Paraphrase what they've just said; for example, "If I am understanding correctly, the biggest impact to our customers is X and that is why you are thinking the optimal solutions are Y and Z. Did I get that right?"

- Demonstrate active listening by using supportive phrases of understanding, like "That makes sense to me," or "I really hear you," or "I can see how you came to that conclusion."

- Once you have shared your perspectives and start approaching the winning solution, you can use active listening to double-check your proposed plan and be confident that it will achieve the needed outcome. Rearticulate what's been said to confirm that you're all on the same page, and if you get anything wrong, your team members are there to correct and address confusion on the spot. This might sound something like "I believe we've agreed to move the project back by one month, and that we're going to redo the video shoot this week. Is that right?"

- At the close of your GAPA conversation, be sure to acknowledge and appreciate the team members who took part. Everyone's time, attention, and thinking efforts are super valuable resources and should be treated as such!

WHEN THE GAP IS ABOUT INDIVIDUAL PERFORMANCE

So far we've been talking about recognizing change and rene-gotiating agreements in situations that, in most cases, are caused by a mix of external and internal factors—meaning the problem or change wasn't centered on one individual's performance. Some-times, though, you find yourself confronting a gap at the more personal level, where an individual's performance falls short of expectations. What do you do if there's a chasm between a team member's current performance and where it needs to be? You can use GAPA in this type of situation too. Let's take a look at how to have a productive conversation, one that results in actual perfor-mance improvement when someone's work is missing the mark and threatening or preventing the effective achievement of results. Before you confront the person, it's super important to deperson-alize the situation by anchoring yourself in the business outcome. This helps boost the psychological safety by removing the focus from "what went wrong" and replacing it with achieving the com-mon goal. This way the discussion becomes a problem-solving exercise instead of a personal attack.

After getting clear on the business goal that's at risk, surface the problem by identifying the gap and articulating the adverse business impact. This could sound like "Okay, so today is Wednes-day and your draft of the report isn't done yet. I was planning to review and finalize it over the next two days and submit it to the printer on Friday. Here's the situation now: If we don't finish by Monday, the printer won't guarantee that we'll have the report in time for our conference. However, it looks like the only way to submit on Monday is if I work during the weekend. Unfortunately, I have prior plans, so I can work only a couple of hours, and I don't think that will be enough time. So how might we work together to get this done? Is there anything we could do differently to get this across the finish line on time? Here are some possible solutions I see: 1) You and I could review it together for the next 90 minutes and see which parts you could revise over the next two days, then we could meet again on Friday to coordinate the weekend; 2) we could see if Mary would work with you on the difficult parts today so that you could be ready with the draft tomorrow. What ideas do you have?"

Even though the other person may be feeling tension and some pressure, it is much easier for them to stay engaged and in productive problem-solving mode than it would be if you took a critical, contemptuous, or demanding approach. Here, you are clearly a teammate working to find solutions. If, on the other hand, you come in with "Well, the project is behind because you never turn in your work on time," positive progress is impossible. The team member would sense a threat and their fight-or-flight reaction would take over and prevent them from engaging in effective problem-solving. Instead, they might go into full defense mode, where they would rationalize, make up stories, or even outright lie about the situation in a desperate attempt to improve how they're being perceived.

But here's the truth: Nobody intentionally misses a deadline thinking, *I just want my teammate to work all weekend*. Things happen, usually unexpectedly, causing the team member to lose control of the timeline. It usually takes teamwork to sort out all the factors, as well as to put in place new "do differently" agreements and actions that will circumvent similar problems in the future.

Let's pick up our example again, this time with collaboration at the forefront. The leader might say something like, "So, what adjustments can we make to meet the timeline? What do you think we could do differently to get this back on track?" Then the leader and the team member would share their perspectives. Their first agreement would be to resolve the project issue: "To get it back on track, we'll put down all our other work for today and work together to finish the report." The second would be aimed at future success: "If you think you're going to miss a deadline in the future, tell me as soon as you recognize that could happen. That way we can try to get ahead of any challenges and make a backup plan."

You can see how this type of situation can turn damaging and volatile—or can be handled so that everyone keeps their cool and makes a new agreement.

Things Aren't Always What They Seem

In leadership conversations, it's essential to keep an open mind. As you work to close a specific gap, you may discover the gap is something completely different than you expected. For example, you might begin giving performance feedback to a team member who seemingly isn't meeting expectations only to find out it's more a misunderstanding than a performance problem. I was recently working with a COO who was planning a live event and was frustrated that she couldn't get the estimated number of attendees from her event project manager, despite asking constantly. This had been going on for many months, and the COO was preparing to have a GAPA conversation about the live-event manager's neglect of reporting critical data.

The GAP above is the missed expectation on delivering anticipated attendance data; the IMPACT of the missing numbers was that the COO couldn't plan the rest of the event—including what size room to book, how to organize the audience flow and event timing, or even how much food to order. This seems like an obvious case of the project manager dropping the ball on reporting numbers, but the truth was a bit more complicated than that.

As the GAPA conversation got underway, it quickly came forward that 1) the event manager's responsibilities had unexpectedly increased, because he had to integrate new software the company adopted for selling event tickets; 2) though the software was effective for selling tickets, the data wasn't working properly due to an issue with the payment gateway; and 3) the ticket sales were well above original expectations!

The event manager had dedicated his time to the software integration, as he felt that was the most pressing need given that the ticket sales were not in danger, but the payment recording and tracking might be. So while there was a problematic lack of communication between him and the COO, the actual work performance was *not* the issue here, as the manager was making good choices in prioritizing his work. In truth, once the COO understood what was really occurring, she was grateful that the event manager pivoted his focus to an issue that had the potential to gravely impact customer experience and revenue. This misunderstanding, in the end, strengthened their professional relationship and built mutual respect, because they learned they could rely on each other to make good decisions for the business.

In business, the situation is almost always more complex than one co-worker simply ruining another one's day by not meeting their agreement. In sports, it always irks me when a tied game comes down to the very last play and a player under intense pressure misses the goal—and then gets blamed for the loss. I always think, *Wait a minute, why was he put in that position anyway? Certainly, the entire team was a part of that end result; no single player caused them to be in the position where one goal mattered so much!* Equally, in business, when people don't keep agreements and an outcome is affected, there's almost always more to the story than meets the eye. This is why it pays to be more *curious* than you are *critical*. Bringing down the hammer immediately makes the situation worse, as people become avoidant and protective. So stay open-minded and be *cautious* with how (and how often!) you challenge anyone's performance.

Using Authority When the Gap Won't Close

As I hope you know by now, top-down authority no longer works as an operating model to run a sustainably successful business. That said, there are still times that call for the use of authority. In fact, the different leadership conversations I've taught you do use varying levels of authority. Delegation is very much a two-way conversation, because we want mutual accountability for achieving the outcomes. In a GAPA conversation, one person's role may determine that they have the authority to make a final call, but GAPA is very much a conversation in which all the context, perspectives, and critical thinking has space to be heard. In both these types of conversations, we're moving information up, down, and across the Business Operating Triangle.

It's a different story when you find yourself confronting repeated gaps with damaging impacts that are tied to a specific team member's poor performance, and attempts to close the gaps with new agreements have failed. Then it becomes clear that collaboration isn't working and a different approach is needed, one where an authority makes the decisions about change. These conversations are *not* typical negotiations. They call for the leader to use the full authority of their role to address the issue. Sometimes they represent the last opportunity for the team member to change; at other times, they become a way to shift a team member's role, or to let the team member go.

When it is time to use your authority, you can do it in a way that leaves the relationship in a respectful place. In these situations, preparation and choosing the right time and place is critical, but most important is your clarity about the directives you're about to give, why it's the right decision for the business, and what's negotiable versus what is not. I've worked with clients who were so nice and gentle when they terminated someone that the person didn't realize they'd been fired. The same goes for feedback conversations—a well-intentioned wish to be kind, coupled with a leader's discomfort around addressing a challenging subject, can make it difficult to communicate clearly, which can then leave a team member without the solid redirect they need to be successful. Underneath the discomfort is usually fear—fear that the other person will feel hurt, or become angry, or defensive, or attacking, or even hold a grudge or bad-mouth you later. This fear can trigger our self-protective behaviors, such as trying to play down the problem ("Don't worry, it's not that big a deal"), or avoiding sharing the truth ("It's just as much my fault as yours") or being overly positive ("I'm sure this won't happen again").

These are examples of kindness that are actually stealth self-protection, which is guaranteed to backfire. Instead, the leader driving the conversation needs to be sure to anchor in Self-Leadership.

This is especially important because the conversation is likely to be a painful wake-up call for the team member on the receiving end and can easily trigger *them* into emotional reactivity. Sometimes they've been in denial about the seriousness of the performance issue you're about to address. Or they might have a rigid opinion that their way is the right way and be unable to see that it no longer works in the current business situation.

Authority That Is Clear and Caring

To set you up for success with these challenging conversations, I've created a script I call the ACE Authority Framework. I will walk you through it in the pages ahead, with some notes on the differences between a last-chance wake-up call and a letting-go conversation.

1. "I want to talk to you about _____ . My positive intention for this conversation is . . ."

For this first step, you are framing the topic and the intention (why this conversation is happening). Be clear and direct but keep it simple. It's helpful to let people know they will have a chance to respond after you share a few things. This way you can get through the heart of the conversation without interruption.

In a wake-up call feedback conversation, sharing your positive intention at the start can be a great relief (because they will hear your intention to get things back on track and let go of the fear of being fired). This allows them to breathe and improves their ability to listen.

In a letting-go conversation, I often tell leaders to know this positive intention for themselves but not necessarily articulate it out loud. This might sound like saying, "I want to talk to you about your role," but not specifying "because I'm letting you go." That information you'll convey in step 2. When you're in the conversation, you can anchor in your intention to help this person get to their best future possible, while knowing that you have made the right decision for everyone involved. This way, you will be less vulnerable to becoming emotional in reaction to their likely emotions.

2. "I've made a decision . . ."

This is a statement of fact, clear and concise, without blame, judgment, or criticism. Whether the decision is to remove the team member from a project or terminate their employment, the decision is made and there won't be a reversal, no matter how much they may feel they want a do-over. Your decisiveness here is critical.

3. "The new expectations are / What's going to happen is . . ."

This is an articulation of how things will go from here, including specific "do differently" behaviors and actions. It may be a set of steps that will occur to support immediate change in their role performance, or the steps that come next in the termination process.

4. "The purpose of this change is . . ."

For a role-performance adjustment, this is an explanation of the main outcome you're going for—and how this change is tied to achieving business outcomes, right up at the top of the triangle. You're articulating the "big why," the reason the change has to happen—now.

In the case of letting someone go, less is more. Simply stating, "This is no longer a fit," is generally the best approach, keeping it clean and keeping the relationship in as good a place as possible. Sometimes in these situations, leaders or CEOs feel strongly compelled to express the full list of the member's failings to them. Don't do this! It's already difficult for the other person to maintain their composure—no need to throw fuel on a fire you're trying to put out. At this point the decision is made, so there really is no upside to rehashing anything. Just be done.

5. "I intend/want . . ."

This is a connection back to the core of the People Part: the relationship. Here, you're expressing the positive outcomes you want for the team member, and sometimes for yourself, for the two of you together, and/or for the situation as a whole. Ultimately, when a team member is not performing up to par, we are addressing it because we cannot miss our business goals, *not* because their performance reflects on them as a person. With compassion and connection, you can say, "I want the best for you and I believe you will be much more successful in a different situation that's a better fit," and leave them with the feeling that you mean it, even if the conversation is about parting ways.

6. "You have a choice, and I respect whatever you choose . . ."

When you're talking to a team member about a need to up-level their role performance, even though this is not a negotiation, the team member still does have a choice. They have the option of choosing to align with the new direction and improve their performance, or they can recognize that they don't want to do what is required and would prefer to leave. If they no longer want to stay on the team, respect their choice. At the end of the day, their decision will save everyone from a more painful and disruptive process.

When you are letting someone go, sometimes that day needs to be their last. Other times you may offer them the option to stay on for a period of transition. Demonstrating respect for the team member's choice in this difficult moment can go a long way in mending any relationship damage.

7. "I'm doing/owning/contributing . . ."

This step is about offering any support or positive contributions you can toward a better future for the team member.

In a wake-up call conversation, this is where you acknowledge the part you're playing in the solution and the commitments you will make toward it. Performance feedback that's meant to gain a crucial change needs strong support from whoever is supervising and guiding the team member. You may decide, for example, that for the next month you will huddle with them for 15 minutes at the start of their day to review their priorities.

If this is an ending of employment, you can still express what you're willing to do to support them. This can be things like providing a good reference for the skills you feel they excel in, involving them in deciding what to tell the rest of the team, sharing ideas you have for what types of roles may be a better fit for them, and so on. Don't offer anything you can't or won't actually do. That may seem obvious, but it's worth noting, because when you feel discomfort, the urge to offer something, anything, to ease the pain is super strong.

8. "I'm listening . . ."

Now that you've laid out what is happening and they are clear on their choices, convey that this is their opportunity to respond—and that you genuinely want to hear them and support them in making the change. If they become upset, do your best not to engage with it. Focus your energy on active listening and providing a space for them to feel heard.

In the case of termination, try to keep things short and succinct. Listen, but if the tension is rising and their emotions are increasing, bring the conversation to a close.

In either type of conversation, you can offer to reconnect with them in a day or so if they have follow-up questions.

I hope you're seeing what a powerful tool agreements—and renegotiating them—offer you for navigating rapidly changing business conditions and circumstances you can't control. Happily, there are some aspects of your business reality that *are* solidly within your control—like the the culture you create within your company. In the next chapter, we'll look at what it means to build a culture that incorporates all the aspects of the People Part and sets your business up for long-term success.

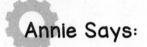

Annie Says:

"You must renegotiate if the outcome cannot be reached with the current plan."

○ ○ ○

SUCCESS STORY
Renegotiating Until the Result is On Track
Brandy Warner, CEO—
Online Specialty Gift Retailer

THE SITUATION

"Argh—I wish this wasn't happening," I said to my HR leader. "It's the last thing I have the time or emotional strength to deal with right now." We were in the middle of our busy holiday season, and our HR leader shared with me that the customer service staff was struggling and complaining about their leader, the director of customer service (CS). When I asked the CS director about their complaints, he said it was just "ridiculous drama." His team was resisting necessary requests he made of them. He also pressed me hard, demanding, "Who made the complaints? It's my right to know!" (Though it actually wasn't.)

This wasn't the first time I'd heard complaints about this leader—in fact, it wasn't even the 10th time. It seemed that every month I'd have someone on the team complaining about how he was behaving. It felt like Groundhog Day for me. Each time the complaints came forward, the situation got more intense, and now it was starting to really disrupt not only me, but my other leaders as well.

When the director of CS first came on board, the complaints were about him being very strict and exacting, holding team members to high standards. At the time, I was happy to have a strong leader taking control of an area that was in chaos, so I dismissed the complaints. The truth was the performance in customer service improved greatly when he took over. Ticket response times improved, issues got resolved faster, and our customer service scores went up.

Things became problematic when the tension between the director and his team never went down—instead, conflict plagued the department. The team lodged constant complaints against their supervisor using words like *disrespectful, passive-aggressive, micro-managing,* and *manipulative.* I had a strong feeling that the situation would only get worse, not better, but I had more pressing considerations and was thinking that now was not the right time to let this person go. I also wondered if maybe I was handling the situation all wrong, and that perhaps the CS leader wasn't getting the support, guidance, and development he needed and deserved. After all, he totally turned the whole department around when he got here, so how bad could he possibly be? I felt overwhelmed with guilt at the thought of firing him.

WHAT I DID DIFFERENTLY WITH RECOGNIZING CHANGE

Normally I'd just try to figure a situation like this out by myself, but instead I talked with both Annie and my executive team to get more perspective and ground my own thoughts. Here are the steps I took to work through this:

I thought about what had changed in the customer service department since this leader joined the team. Two big things were clear. First, the CS area was using more technology now, which the leader wasn't embracing. He felt it was blocking the visibility he needed on his team's performance. I believe this discomfort with technology triggered him to become more controlling with his team than when they were using manual processes. Second, customer service was being used as a "farm team" and the leader was being asked to develop and transfer his top talent into other areas in the company. Developing people wasn't a natural strength of this leader, and it was a new part of the role—one that we didn't anticipate needing when we hired him.

To determine the best solution, I first identified the GAP and the IMPACT of the situation. The GAP was that the CS leader couldn't maintain a stable, effective relationship with his team. The IMPACT was that it led to ongoing conflict and negativity, which was terrible for retaining talent and was a major disruption to me and the other leaders (because we had to address the complaints and restabilize the department over and over).

I considered what it would really take for this leader to be successful given the changes to the situation and the company's needs. Not only would his leadership and relationship skills need improvement, but he'd also need to learn the new technology *and* how to develop people. I concluded that the negative impact of this leader's lack of skills was too big a gap and that the chances of him developing fast enough in multiple areas were too low.

Now I had clarity on what would ultimately serve the business best. I decided to let the CS leader go. I explained to him that because of our super-fast growth, the role had shifted in a way that wasn't a good fit for him. I pointed out that he excelled in taking a department from chaos to running smoothly by putting basic processes and structure in place, and many companies needed that. I provided a letter of recommendation focused on his strengths and achievements, let him know how much I appreciated his contributions to our company, and offered a good severance package. I was proud that we were able to keep our relationship good even though we were parting ways.

THE DIFFERENCE IT MADE

While it was an incredibly difficult conversation, I was so relieved afterward, and the leader was too—not feeling successful in his role had been taking a big emotional toll on him. Letting him go was absolutely the right decision, and while we had challenges with the transition, we eventually found a CS leader who was a fantastic fit!

I think one of the biggest takeaways was noticing how much my feelings of guilt hampered my ability to confront the situation. By reaching out for help (from Annie and team) and following the structure for a performance conversation, I was able to process the situation objectively. This led to me making a confident decision that ultimately served the business best.

AGREEMENT 6 TAKEAWAYS

We recognize change, anticipate impacts, and proactively adapt our agreements.

- Recognizing when things go off track is key! You know you are off track when achieving the intended outcome isn't possible without a significant change.

- Start with what changed. The way to respectfully and most effectively renegotiate an agreement is to start by looking at how the situation has changed.

- Remember GAP + IMPACT! The gap is the difference between where you thought you would be and where you actually are. The impact is why that gap matters. We solve for IMPACTS.

- When in doubt, go back to the outcome. Anchoring a discussion in desired outcomes makes it psychologically safe and not personal.

- Perform active listening by slowing down, using perception checking (to fully understand another's point of view), and making supportive, affirming statements.

- When using your authority to insist on change, you can maintain a respectful relationship by communicating clearly and demonstrating care for the other person's well-being. Refer to the ACE Authority Framework script in this chapter.

FOR YOUR REFLECTION

Take some time to think about what you've learned in this chapter. Write about what you're thinking in a notebook, on a device, or right on this page!

1) What one or two past situations (business or personal) come to mind that you recognize could have gone better based on what you know now?

2) What insights did you gain about yourself from this chapter?

3) What is one next action or interaction you intend to do differently moving forward?

AGREEMENT 7

CREATING YOUR COMPANY CULTURE

We make best practices habitual to achieve our highest performance potential.

The collective behaviors for sustainable success

So far, we've looked at six important agreements that define the critical behaviors, the People Part, of a high-performance team. These agreements can each be thought of as a "best practice" for company leadership and teamwork. You've probably noticed that many of these agreements work in tandem, like clarity about your company's desired outcomes and clarity about everyone's roles. When you put these agreements all together, you have more than a set of best practices—you have a company *culture* within which everyone can do their best work and show up as their best selves.

So it makes sense that the last agreement we're going to learn is about exactly that—a culture based in the principles of the People Part that supports excellence in every facet of your business. This is how you develop a motivated team turning out quality products and services in a fulfilling environment, inspired by like-minded peers.

Does that sound like something you'd want for your business? I thought so!

But before we get to what that culture consists of, we first need to take a quick look at what culture isn't.

It isn't something you can conjure out of the air by wishing for it, or something you can force by mandating it. Let's say you're dreaming of an amazing "work hard, play hard" ethos (in which highly committed people enthusiastically drive for results while also having the life balance they desire) and thinking, *Man, I really want that for my company.* Unfortunately, you won't get there by issuing orders or making demands ("Okay, everyone, you need to work harder! But it's okay because you'll play harder too!").

What's more, a company culture isn't just about values you share; these are important, but not nearly enough to generate high performance. Maybe you've heard inspirational pep talks or seen feel-good slogans like "Only a crew with strong values can weather the storm," or "Decision-making is easy when you know your values." But values rarely drive our behavior moment to moment in the tension-filled course of business, because a person's values aren't on display when he or she is thinking or acting from self-protection. We can draw on our values to inspire one another, but we can't use them as yardsticks to evaluate each other—especially to call out a team member's negative behavior as "poor values." We don't think about our values when we are reacting emotionally, because we don't think at all during those times! Demonstrating our values by acting with the intention to do so, while under stress and challenge, is a skill we need to learn and a habit we must build. It's the *actions* your team collectively takes day after day, regardless of the circumstances, that add up to a high-performance work culture of the kind I want for you.

In this chapter we're going to drill down on implementing the essential best practices to create the culture you want. We'll look at the habits and behaviors that drive both growth and excellence, plus how to structure team meetings to support them. Finally, we'll talk about how a strong company culture sets you up to bring in new A Players who can become A+ Leaders and expand your high-performance team.

THE HABITUAL BEHAVIORS THAT MAKE UP CULTURE

Everything you've learned in the book so far—Self-Leadership and secure relationships, the Business Operating Triangle, role clarity and agreements—comes into play when we're talking about the way a team interacts and the habits and behaviors that make up the fabric of each day's work. Many of the best practices that make up an effective culture are combinations of multiple behaviors that we demonstrate all at once. But we need to clearly define those behaviors and essentially give some instruction for how to demonstrate each best practice, so that team members can learn and practice them until they become habits. We've identified four best practices that every organization needs to cultivate in their habits and culture.

#1: Inviting Engagement and Candid Dialogue

The two strategies I teach to foster open, engaged, and highly collaborative communication are:

- Soliciting engagement through asking for opinions
- Talking tentatively

Often when my team comes into an organization, we find that they have been operating in a paradigm in which the CEO does most of the talking and critical thinking, while fielding very little information or input from the team. As we saw in Agreement 1, the cost of this is high, because leaders are prone to making poor decisions when they lack the critical information and perspectives possessed by their people on the ground. This habit of CEOs is common because when they start a business, they are the ones who, for example, understand their clients most—since they work with them directly! But when the business grows, and the CEO's role moves into growth and strategy and away from client interactions, they may find it hard to accept that they no longer know the clients or their situations as well as they used to. In fact, it's usually the client delivery team and salespeople who have the most current and relevant information and insights, so the CEO should invite opinions from them!

Inviting engagement and soliciting relevant opinions works best when it's a habit that becomes part of the culture. You might have heard someone say, or even thought to yourself, *I wish we had a more open, collaborative, and inclusive culture. I almost never get to contribute my ideas or share important feedback that would benefit the company! I guess no one cares what I think.* In fact, the other people usually care a lot about relevant input, but other assumptions and habits get in the way. They might think they don't have the time to ask, or they just might not be in the habit of asking. Or they might assume that if someone has something relevant to say, they will. However, over the years I've learned that people in the workplace, as a group, generally stay quiet and don't volunteer extra information unless they're asked. In fact, to be respectful to others, most people feel it's not their place to speak until asked.

To create an open, collaborative, inclusive culture, you've got to habitually invite input and opinions whenever you've got multiple stakeholders involved in a project or issue. I have trained myself to always be asking, "What do you think?" Because I'm always asking, they don't wonder whether I want their opinion—of course I do! Their input and opinions are extraordinarily valuable and necessary for our success. Team members who work with me now often anticipate this question and offer their opinions even before I ask.

There is a second dialogue behavior that goes hand in hand with the question "What do you think?" that actively cultivates an environment in which people feel free to share what's really on their minds. It's called "talking tentatively." Here's how it works: Let's say that I'm negotiating to solve a problem with my team about the schedule for a high-stakes project. I have a solid opinion about it, but I also want their opinions and input before I make a final decision, because I might be missing something or perceiving the situation incorrectly. I know (from tons of experience) that if I share my opinion in an authoritative, definitive way, it sounds like I've made the decision, and therefore the dialogue and input from the team will come to a screeching halt. No one wants to challenge the boss's decision once it's made. And if I ask for thoughts at that point, it sounds like a rhetorical question and leaves people wondering if it's a test of their compliance.

Instead, whenever I'm working with the team to solve issues, plan, or make decisions, I'm always talking tentatively. Using tentative language implies that my ideas and opinions aren't fixed and final. It will likely sound something like this: "I'm thinking we should move project A forward and delay project B until second quarter. What do you think?" If I present my ideas as a directive or a demand, I shut down the collaboration, as team members resign themselves to doing what I say, whether they think it'll work or not. But if I say, "I'm thinking . . . What do you think?" this lets the team know that I'm receptive to feedback and open to change. It creates space for others to ask questions and bring challenges forward. It also allows you to test ideas, theories, and alternative solutions without signaling a clear bias. Whatever plans and agreements result are better set up to succeed.

Some more examples of tentative talk include:

- "Given these facts, I'm considering this (plan, solution, etc.) . . ."

- "I've considered (context), which is why I'm intending to . . ."

- "The story I've told myself about this situation is . . ."

- "The meaning I've made of this information is . . ."

- "I'm not certain of this, but here's how I see it . . ."

Here's an example of tentative talking in action. One year during my interim turnaround work as an executive of a small education company, their physical (in-person) course enrollment was smaller than it had been during any previous year. Understandably, team members were pretty anxious about it. Many (if not most) CEOs would naturally jump in and immediately do all the problem-solving themselves, and then share with the team something like: "This year's student enrollment missed expectations by a significant amount. The impact is that we won't cover our minimum costs without extra revenue before the end of the year. So we're going to speed up the online course timeline and launch it in 4 months (instead of 10 months) to bring in the revenue to cover that shortfall." This type of communication not only sends the team into a panic ("How are we going to do all that?"), but it also tells them that their opinions don't matter! They're stuck with the CEO's decision even though it was made without their input. If I had taken this approach (which I didn't), my team probably would have either hidden the real issues from me or used them as an excuse in their own minds to not even try. Instead, I slowed down to investigate a bit further and uncovered some major issues, such as lagging video production and how marketing was already behind schedule—both of which caused the team to doubt that we could successfully shift the timeline.

Instead, I shared the new information (remember from Agreement 6? "Here's what's changed!") and started a discussion in which I invited everyone to participate. I said, "Hey, enrollments missed our target and that impacts revenue. Here's how much the revenue is estimated to fall short of the costs we need to cover (the gap and the impact). Here are some immediate actions we can take to help increase revenue (such as offering alumni to audit the course for a lower fee), but that will cover one-third of the shortfall at most. So I'm also thinking the online course is the next big revenue-producing opportunity in our plans and could bring in revenue earlier. Now, I do recognize that we've carefully planned for launching the new online course ten months from now, but given the new revenue urgency, maybe we should consider reevaluating to see if it would be possible to launch earlier. What do you all think? Could this even be possible?" This made it much safer for the team to discuss different options and brainstorm for how we could shift resources and what additional support we could employ.

If I had used an approach of "I already made a decision and here it is . . . ," it would have led to poor decision-making all around and maybe even big resignations from the company's top talent. A Players are not going to stay if you don't care about their input, and they won't tolerate being put in a position to fail.

#2: Cross-Functional Communication and Inclusivity

Talking tentatively is a great communication technique for both leaders and team members. It's about *how* we say what we say to others. In building the habits of a strong company culture, we also need to consider *who* we're saying it to—meaning who needs to hear it and who needs to be included in the communication. In other words, we need to get good at inclusive and cross-functional communication.

Inclusive and cross-functional communication is being mindful of who, including which areas of the business, will be impacted or will need to know the information being communicated. Building this habit requires all team members to hold themselves accountable for keeping in good communication about changes, being sure to think through the ripple effect and impacts on other team members and departments. A team member shouldn't just be thinking, *How does this new initiative or change impact me and the people I supervise?* Rather, they should be thinking, *How does this change impact not only my team, but also the other areas of the business? Does this shift take us off track from achieving other goals? If so, what should we do about it?*

The best medium for cross-functional communication varies depending on the team. I've seen successful teams utilize team meetings (in person or via video), project management systems, and messaging platforms (such as Slack or WhatsApp) to do their cross-functional communicating. They also utilize recovery-plan agreements that include things like texting or phoning when a situation is urgent. Whatever form the communication takes, it's not something that works perfectly all the time, because some situations are extra complex or uniquely surprising. And that's okay! When a team has good cross-functional communication, they acknowledge a miss when it happens, work together to recover from any negative consequences, and identify the "do differently" actions for next time.

#3: Proactively Surfacing and Solving Problems

Problems left unaddressed get worse over time, which is why it's crucial for a team to spot potential problems as early as possible, even *before* they land. Team members can develop the habit of thinking ahead and anticipating challenges so that they can proactively surface and solve them. This gives the best chance to solve issues early and with the fewest negative consequences. This habit is most effective when solutions are also suggested at the same time. Otherwise, surfacing a problem can be perceived as a way to shift or escape responsibility—to imply, "It's your problem now that I've told you about it."

When a solution isn't simple or obvious, it's important to at least share your thoughts, even if your ideas are developing—or if you've already rejected them. This shows that you've given the issue your attention and that you're trying to solve it. It also helps others rapidly gain important context and allows them to build on your thinking with their added knowledge and perspective.

Team members often don't realize that entrepreneurs and leaders *want* to be brought potential solutions. If a team comes to a CEO and says only, "We have a problem with this project. What should we do?" it will lower the CEO's confidence in the team, as none of their critical thinking is demonstrated with that question. But if the same team says to the CEO, "Hey, so we have a problem and we've started to reorganize the project *this* way to address it, and we want to share it with you and see if we're on the right track," the CEO is going to be much more receptive and helpful. Not only does this habit build the leader's confidence in the team, but it radically speeds up the process of problem-solving and leads to significantly better solutions. And that leads to the big bonus: The CEO gets out of the weeds and has time to focus on the big picture, which is what we need for the business's long-term success. Can you see it?

Remember, your critical thinking is your most valuable company contribution! Don't leave it out. The best leaders share the problem, the situation, relevant context, and ideas for possible solutions. And that's not all: They also maintain responsibility for seeing through the solution, unless the responsibility is clearly assumed by someone else. They're committed to getting the issue resolved. When a team has the habit of surfacing and solving problems early, the whole organization is more successful.

Here's how the ads manager for one of our clients brought an issue to their COO: "Hey, last week Facebook increased their advertising costs across the board. It looks like it might be between twenty and thirty percent, depending on the type of advertising. I think this could increase our costs for our big promotion next month by thirty thousand dollars. I don't know if we can mitigate these costs yet, but I've been thinking about how we might be able to eliminate one of the eight weeks of advertising. Do you have time in the next few days to discuss this with me and the director of social media?" This led to a super effective discussion and solution!

You can probably tell that cultivating this habit within a team requires a solid level of psychological safety to be in place. But with all you've learned about the People Part, you know how to create safety!

#4: Filling the Bubble

There's one more habit that I'm excited to tell you about, because it profoundly improves how you and your team members communicate. First, picture a conversation bubble like you'd see in a comic strip (or in the graphic on page 204). This "bubble" is how I describe the space where dialogue takes place between two (or more) individuals about their mutual work interests. You can think of it as a "context bubble."

There is limited space and time available in this bubble, and it's all too easy for one person to fill it up all on their own. Particularly between CEOs or leaders and their direct reports, the norm can be for the most senior leader to do all the talking, filling the bubble with only their thoughts and opinions. This often looks like the senior leader launching into a monologue, avoiding any inquiries, giving one-sided opinions, making demands, or even complaining about what they don't like. The other leader is left with no space to share anything, so they don't.

What we want is to fill the bubble in a *balanced* way so that it contains the many perspectives and full picture that everyone needs to share. For this to happen, the team member with less authority needs to proactively "fill their supervising leader's bubble." This means the team member should come fully prepared to a meeting with their leader and should talk first. They'll usually start a conversation with what's changed or going differently than expected, and what they're anticipating, planning, doing, thinking, etc. The supervising leader will naturally have less to say, because the team member has already brought forward what's most important. When the team member drives the conversation and delivers the latest and most relevant information, the supervising leader can focus on answering questions and giving guidance. If there's a situation in which a leader needs to take charge and direct others, they should still include the input from the others involved to get the best outcome.

Once this concept becomes a habit, a leader or team member who is having difficulty getting words in with their superior might even say in good humor, "Okay, now I need to fill the bubble!" Or in reverse, a COO might say to a department leader, "I need you to fill my bubble, it's been two weeks!" and that leader immediately knows the COO wants them to take more responsibility to keep them apprised of what they're working on. The phrase "fill my bubble" makes for accurate and quick communication between leaders and team members.

When you and your team understand this simple concept, it's a game changer for both the person speaking and the person listening. Not only does it save time by structuring a conversation in terms of who talks and what to cover, but it also causes people to self-regulate their communication so that they allow everyone space to fill their portion of the bubble and thereby gain all the important facts and perspectives. This method is especially effective between two people aiming to make their communication as efficient and effective as possible. And it can be done face-to-face or through written reports, team meetings, e-mail, or even WhatsApp or Slack.

This behavioral tool has been life-changing for many clients, including Elizabeth, the COO of a publishing company. Elizabeth was the type of leader who truly did not want to micromanage people, police them, or interrupt them. But when she wasn't getting the information she needed to stay apprised of business progress, she felt she had to do exactly that. She told me, "I hate chasing down my leaders to ask them, 'How are things going?' Not only does it feel like I'm interrupting their important work, but the question feels a bit disrespectful, like I should just assume everything is going well and I shouldn't need to ask. But I can't do my job when I don't know where things stand, especially because things change so darn fast. I want to do this differently. How can I approach my leaders in a better way? I don't want them to feel like I'm micromanaging and don't trust them."

This was a significant issue, as a great deal of her day was spent running around trying to get information and updates from her six executive leaders. Everyone was frustrated by this approach. Elizabeth met with her executive leaders and made a request: that they take the responsibility to proactively bring her information, keep her updated, and "fill her bubble." They happily agreed, as now they could plan their days and avoid being interrupted when they were totally focused on something else. The bubble reverses responsibility. It was no longer up to Elizabeth to hunt down her leaders for the information she needed; instead, they took the initiative to think about and communicate what they believed she needed to know. And it has been highly effective! Not only has this change saved Elizabeth significant time; even more importantly, she has freed up a big portion of critical-thinking space in her brain. She now gets what she needs and doesn't have to strategize for how to micromanage respectfully (which isn't possible). Her leaders tell her what she needs to know much faster and more effectively than she could ever ask for it.

ACE MEETINGS

Okay, so now you know the most crucial habits for great teamwork. And they're all easy to apply in a one-to-one conversation or in a small group. But what about larger group discussions and interactions? What do you do when you're working on goals that are big and complex, ones that need input, involvement, and accountability from many different leaders and team members? This is when team meetings come into play.

I heard you groan. *I know, I know.* Team meetings can be the most frustrating and time-wasting parts of the day. There's even a book called *Death by Meeting*! They have a bad reputation because when they aren't productive, they waste many people's time and energy, cause conflict and chaos, or spike resentment and apathy. I've worked with many frustrated executives who at one time or another tried to either ban or severely limit meetings. One company disallowed meetings with more than six people because those meetings seemed to bring out the absolute worst in the team, draining productivity and tanking morale. However, every one of those executives had to reinstate the meetings because they serve a unique purpose that is almost impossible to accomplish any other way. Team meetings are the main mechanism in business for groups to collaborate, innovate, problem-solve, and make decisions that need input and agreement from multiple people and areas, while also maintaining unity and alignment.

Fortunately, I'm going to show you how you can totally overhaul your team meetings, transforming them into a cornerstone of productivity for your organization. With the right structure and preparation, meetings are the catalyst for confronting challenges, removing obstacles, and getting things done. Using this approach, meetings will become something you look forward to!

There's no denying that a poorly run, overly long meeting can tank everyone's energy. However, in an effective meeting, the productivity per head goes up exponentially. You'll get more out of six people putting their critical thinking together than you would from those six people doing everything separately on their own, without the shared perspectives.

I strongly believe that team meetings are terribly underleveraged in most organizations, and by doing a few things differently, you can radically improve your team productivity and results. To do this, we start with (you guessed it) getting clear on a meeting's purpose and intended outcome. That way you'll avoid scheduling the kinds of extraneous meetings that make people want to abandon the conference room altogether.

So let's look at the kinds of meetings that you and your team *should* be having.

Three Types of Meetings

Identifying the types of meetings your business needs is step one in transforming them. The meeting type indicates the broad purpose and tells the team where to bring what information, problems, ideas, decisions, etc. The following three categories of meetings will cover the vast majority of meeting needs:

1. Business performance meetings

2. Team huddles

3. Special-purpose meetings

The first type of meeting is absolutely essential for every business. These meetings are where leaders, team members, and stakeholders—in fact, any group that is responsible for achieving goals, such as a leadership team, a functional department, or a project team—monitor business performance and drive goal achievement. Every business needs to have at least one weekly or biweekly meeting with the company executives or senior leaders (the people with the most responsibility) in which they track the business's progress, address any changes, surface problems, make decisions, review strategy, adjust plans, allocate resources, and ultimately take responsibility—as a group—for achieving the expected business results. Since these meetings are about achieving results, they are often needed in multiple areas of the company (such as department meetings), or for cross-functioning (such as cross-functional leadership meetings with department heads), or for projects (such as major project team meetings).

The second type of meeting is the team huddle, which usually includes 3 to 12 people. Huddles occur anywhere from twice a day to once a month. They're like a huddle during a game, or a time-out on a sports field, when the team comes together to quickly discuss what's happening on the field and plan their immediate next moves. Typically 10 or 15 minutes long, but not longer than 30 minutes, these huddles are where members share briefly about what was just accomplished, what immediate problems need solving, any changes to the project or plan, and what members are aiming to complete next. Huddles are effective because a few minutes in a group with everyone together can quickly close loops and align the entire team on the latest info. This is way more efficient than trying to interact by chatting back and forth in an e-mail stream, where you don't have everyone's attention and participation at the same time—if you get their attention at all! Also, just like a game huddle, a team huddle not only quickly aligns team members on next steps, it also provides an excellent connection point where team members support and motivate each other to become even more effective and unified in achieving their goals.

The last type of meeting is the special-purpose team meeting, which is exactly what it sounds like. These are one-time meetings, or a limited series of meetings, that address a special need *not* covered by business performance meetings or team huddles: They include everything from "working sessions" (in which a handful of collaborators do tasks together to get specific work completed) to "team training" (to teach new skills, processes, or systems) to "town halls" (in which leaders address all the team members in an organization together, usually to give a big-picture business progress report, or to reveal new plans or major changes). One of the most important special-purpose meetings is the strategic or annual planning meeting, which refers to a meeting held at least once a year (and ideally updated each quarter!) to establish the big goals and strategy for the year. This is where you clarify your financial and strategic goals (including identifying new products and services, or making major changes), review and allocate resources, and plot out the year's biggest projects. You'll typically also identify internal changes for leadership, team, and infrastructure, including things like hiring and training, or implementing new systems and processes needed to achieve the overall business goals. (You can turn back to Agreement 2 if you want a refresher on strategic planning and goals.)

Phew, that was a lot of meetings! But they deserve our attention because they are where your leaders and your team members come together to do their best and most collaborative thinking, align to outcomes, and maximize productivity. Honestly, I can't think of anything more important to a business than that, and I guarantee that you can't achieve it all over just e-mail and Slack.

So now that we know which meetings our business might need, we'll move on to the practical tools we can use to make them über-productive and avoid wasting people's time and energy.

Old Faithful: The Meeting Agenda That Never Fails

Without any guidance, a meeting can sometimes feel like a group of people sitting around a conference table staring at each other (or worse, talking without going anywhere). So I've developed the "Meeting Agenda That Never Fails" to guide meetings toward results! With a little tailoring for your organization, the Meeting Agenda That Never Fails will guide any team meeting that is focused on business performance, namely monitoring and driving execution to achieve goals.

Let's list the components of this agenda:

- Monitor milestones for top priorities, acknowledge achievements and wins, and identify where milestones are due: Time = 10%

- Problem-solving—surface and resolve challenges, obstacles, and unresolved conflicts

- Major and cross-functional decision-making: Total time for #2 and #3 = 65%

- Recap meeting, document decisions: Time = 10%

- Clarify next action steps: Time = 5%

- Align communication and coordination to execute outside the meeting: Time = 5%

- Evaluate meeting effectiveness and share appreciation: Time = 5%

Now let's take a look at each:

- The first step includes **sharing major accomplishments and wins** since the last meeting— this gets each meeting off to a positive start and helps members maintain an effective mindset. Then we **monitor top priorities**—this is where we share the big-picture status, acknowledge progress on our active and priority projects, and identify the milestones we've met. We also talk about the important deadlines coming up, changes we encountered, and the challenges we've spotted—the things that are off track. This first agenda item is about gathering the overall status for how we're doing in achieving our goals and identifying what we need to address.

- Next is **problem-solving**—this is all about closing the gaps we just identified. It's also where we surface other meaningful challenges and obstacles that may get in the way or prevent us from achieving our goals. Meetings are *the* place to do this so that we, as a team, work out how to vault over the hurdles we inevitably encounter!

- Which leads to **major and cross-functional decision-making**—or, more specifically, the kind of decision-making that needs multiple people's input. These are where we need to understand all the impacts, usually affecting multiple functions or projects, so that we make final decisions that work for everyone. This is how we avoid the all-too-common scenario in which a few people make a decision they believe will work, they start to implement it, and *then* they encounter a vital piece of information that requires them to go back and redo it all. These unknown or unintended consequences are a frustrating waste of time and energy, and no one wants to rewind a project. Because problem-solving and major decision-making are so critical, they typically constitute 65 to 70 percent of our meeting time. If you are spending 65 percent of your meeting time on other items, say, on monitoring milestones, you are missing the main value of the meeting!

- The next step of the Meeting Agenda That Never Fails is über-important but often forgotten: **Recapping the meeting, confirming decisions.** When we miss this step, team members easily forget what we talked about versus what we actually decided, which may mean they'll take the wrong action or assume someone else has the ball. So in this step we go back and confirm the decisions that came out of the problem-solving. We also want to note what questions we didn't answer and when they should be addressed, like that one finance question that we agreed we'd put first at the *next* meeting. That's also a type of decision, right? We're not solving it now, but we're deciding to solve it next time.

- The next item follows naturally: **Clarifying next steps and upcoming actions**. This is when we say out loud, one by one, what our own next actions will be to make sure that everyone involved clearly understands their parts. This helps everyone confirm the alignment, and we can make corrections as needed if we have any discrepancies.

- Next is **aligning communication and coordination for execution outside the meeting**. This step is critical because it's how decisions made *inside* the meeting get shared clearly with people *outside* the meeting. It helps confirm what the people on our teams will communicate to others—what they will actually say!

- Now, the very last step in our team meeting agenda is to **evaluate the meeting's effectiveness and share appreciations**. In school we got feedback on how we were doing and what to do better. My teachers used to leave comments on every paragraph of my essays telling me whether I clearly communicated the ideas. And isn't that the point of meetings too? It's also the perfect place for leaders to express appreciation for team members who have contributed above expectations to the team and the company.

> **TEAM MEETING AGENDA THAT NEVER FAILS**
>
> 1. MONITOR MILESTONES FOR TOP PRIORITIES, ACKNOWLEDGE ACHIEVEMENTS AND WINS, AND IDENTIFY WHERE MILESTONES ARE DUE: TIME = 10%
>
> 2. PROBLEM-SOLVING—SURFACE AND RESOLVE CHALLENGES, OBSTACLES, AND UNRESOLVED CONFLICTS
>
> 3. MAJOR AND CROSS-FUNCTIONAL DECISION-MAKING: TOTAL TIME FOR #2 AND #3 = 65%
>
> 4. RECAP MEETING AND DOCUMENT DECISIONS: TIME = 10%
>
> 5. CLARIFY NEXT ACTION STEPS: TIME = 5%
>
> 6. ALIGN COMMUNICATION AND COORDINATION TO EXECUTE OUTSIDE THE MEETING: TIME = 5%
>
> 7. EVALUATE MEETING EFFECTIVENESS AND SHARE APPRECIATION: TIME = 5%

The clarification, alignment, and unified actions generated by the Meeting Agenda That Never Fails (recapped in the script above) are an integral part of what drives great results for your business.

CREATING A CULTURE THAT ATTRACTS A PLAYERS

The point of a high-performance work culture is to support great team performance and achieve fabulous business results. There's also a huge secondary benefit: attracting new high-performance people to join you—the people we call A Players. Whether you're bringing in a COO or adding an IT assistant, it's the culture that gets winners to join and stay with your company.

Often, when companies think about hiring, they first think: *Where do I look? Where can I get the best people and the best team?* As if A Players are a product, like shoes, that you can buy at the store. If you can't find the right shoes in one store, you'll walk down the street to another one! Surely if we can't find that perfect pair, we must be shopping in the wrong place.

You are not looking in the wrong store! A winning team isn't plucked off the shelf, no assembly required—it's developed.

Unfortunately, there isn't a store for A Players where we can compare our options, read the reviews, and return the product if we aren't satisfied. In any case, hiring isn't really about seeking people out, it's about bringing people in. And the way we do that is by fostering a culture that people truly want to work in!

Here's another way to look at it: You are not shopping for A Players; A Players are shopping for *you*! Remember, A Players have a lot of choices, and they are *very* savvy shoppers. They're going to ask around, gather information, and check out what it's really like to work for you before they join your company. And they're going to use their network to get the inside scoop on what's really going on there.

What A Players Want

So what *do* A Players want beyond competitive and fair compensation? One of the main things is to perceive that they are assets to your organization, the way a professional athlete is to a pro sports team, and to be treated accordingly. This means investing meaningfully in their learning and career development, helping them to grow and supporting them to build more skills that will serve them well in your company and down the road. This includes everything from internal coaching and training, to outside professional programs, to formal education that can result in degrees or licenses. A Players want to excel and are willing to put in the work needed to take on more responsibility and contribute at ever-higher levels.

I must point out that you can't accomplish effective team member development without effective leaders. In fact, according to Gallup's "State of the American Workplace" report (2017), a whopping 75 percent of what makes an A Player most effective, fulfilled, and satisfied with their role and their company involves their leaders and managers. Those leaders and managers provide direction, feedback, support, training, and mentorship, while also advocating for their direct report's development, recommending them for new opportunities, and promoting their skills and talents to others. For most A Players, their success depends markedly on the quality of their bosses.

A Players also want to be part of a "winning team" and to know that their efforts are contributing to the company's success. They struggle when stuck in companies that aren't achieving their goals, and they are prone to leave if they don't experience solid improvement.

There's one more must-have for A Players, and in the years since I entered the entrepreneurial business world, I've seen its pull increase *dramatically*: A Players want to work for a company that stands for a purpose greater than the owner's status and financial enrichment. This means you should clearly communicate the purpose and your intended positive impacts so that A Players know *exactly* what they're going for and what it looks like when it's done. Your business needs to be transparent in its vision and the plan for achieving it. Then the right A Players will know they have found a good match for their skill set and their *own* sense of purpose.

Better Together

There's one key element that underlies everything we're talking about here, and that is *how you perceive your team*. On one level, of course, your team is the means by which you achieve results—the way you make your desired outcomes into reality. However, your team is not a group of minions whose only purpose is to do things for you. They are whole humans with gifts, talents, and expertise, looking to express the best of themselves and be part of something great.

On a high-performance team, people bring out the best in one another—and this includes not only your full-time leaders and team members but also your contractors and even your vendors, everyone who plays a part in delivering your big outcomes. They bring out the best in one another and together take the most effective actions to achieve your business vision. I can't emphasize the *together* part enough. It's the heart of the People Part.

We saw at the very start of this book that the model of top-down authority is no longer the way to make a business successful and sustainable. It no longer works for attracting the best people either. The best people have a great deal of choice in where they work. And since they spend a significant portion of their lives working, they care more and more about their experience being fulfilling, allowing them to grow and connect with others while contributing value in ways that matter to them. When you implement the seven agreements I've presented in this book—when you truly tap the power of the People Part—you will build a culture that attracts the best people naturally, because your team is where they want to be.

Annie Says:

"To have the culture you desire, you have to build good leadership habits!"

○ ○ ○

SUCCESS STORY
Decision Tracking Makes Everyone Perform Better
Derek Ito, CEO—Sales Training Company

THE SITUATION

At one point I was so frustrated that I let the entire leadership team have it. I said, "I thought we had already decided to change our client onboarding process for our new program, but when I talked to the delivery team, they hadn't heard anything about it. How could that be? We've already sold the program and dozens of clients need onboarding in three weeks, and yet they haven't started planning! Please, someone explain to me how the heck this could have happened!"

I knew we had been moving fast, but this wasn't the first, or even the tenth, time in the last few months that a major decision had fallen through the communication cracks. But this time it happened during a high-stakes situation—one that wasn't easy to recover. I had tried to make sure that each leader was posting important decisions directly into the relevant Slack channels, but somehow it just wasn't working.

I knew that our business was becoming increasingly complex: More projects were being added, and we needed to organize and document our decisions much more accurately. But our team had been resisting using a project management system—they wanted to do everything in Slack. Slack is great for staying connected and communicating simple things in groups, but it doesn't work for capturing and organizing important information (like decisions!) within projects.

So here's the thing: This incident made us recognize that we needed a reliable system for communicating decisions—decisions that often changed suddenly. We couldn't keep using Slack for everything or wait for a more convenient time to implement a real project management tool. It was crucial to start using one right away to track all decisions so that things wouldn't get missed.

WHAT I DID DIFFERENTLY WITH CULTURE BUILDING

My team leaders and I got together to discuss the best way to make decisions and how to best deliver those decisions to the rest of the team. We agreed that we had to clearly define where and how all of the communication happened to set ourselves up for success. We knew that if we didn't make team agreements around our tools and interactions, we would continue to risk making repeated, preventable (and sloppy) mistakes that could damage our company reputation. None of us wanted that.

We landed on an agreement to never make important decisions inside Slack. We knew that this was a key step to making sure no important details ever got missed again. Our new agreement was to wait (when possible) for our next leadership meeting or jump on a quick huddle to come to a decision, and then make sure it was captured in our project management system so that every team member could easily find the information. We even made one of our current leaders the overall project coordinator to keep us on track as we made these changes. Then we'd communicate to the team in Slack that the new decisions and details were available in the project management software where they wouldn't be missed.

THE DIFFERENCE IT MADE

I felt so much relief knowing that we had a new mechanism for making and tracking decisions and that we were finally inside a dedicated project management system. There has been more trust and a feeling of safety on my leadership team now that we have a clear agreement on how decisions are made. There have also been fewer mistakes overall, and I've felt more confidence in the team to deliver quality results. And because all decisions live in one place and teamwork happens there, it is so easy for me to check in on where everything stands at any given time. No more waking up in the middle of the night wondering if a decision was carried through. This has noticeably boosted team morale and improved our company culture!

AGREEMENT 7 TAKEAWAYS

- Step one in any business, leadership, or team situation is to start in Self-Leadership.

- It's the consistent behaviors and actions your team collectively takes day after day, even in challenging circumstances, that add up to a high-performance work culture.

- Remember these four must-have best practices:

  - Inviting Engagement and Candid Dialogue—two core communication strategies that foster openness and collaboration are soliciting opinions and talking tentatively.

  - Cross-Functional Communication and Inclusivity—asking ourselves "who is impacted and must be included."

  - Proactively Surfacing and Solving Problems—anticipating impacts and addressing them as soon as possible.

  - Filling the Bubble—leaders and team members "fill the communication bubble" by proactively sharing their latest and most relevant information, along with their thinking, so that executives can focus on asking questions and giving guidance.

- Meetings are where team members come together to become a "professional think tank," doing their best collaboration and most effective decision-making.

- A Players want their achievements to be recognized, but even more, they want their work to meaningfully contribute to the company's success.

FOR YOUR REFLECTION

Take some time to think about what you've learned in this chapter. Write about what you're thinking in a notebook, on a device, or right on this page!

1) What one or two past situations (business or personal) come to mind that you recognize could have gone better based on what you know now?

_____

_____

_____

2) What insights did you gain about yourself from this chapter?

_____

_____

_____

3) What is one next action or interaction you intend to do differently moving forward?

_____

_____

_____

YOUR NEW PART

**How you interact with your team is key to success.
Business is not a solo sport—it is a team sport!**

Your leadership matters. That well-known Gallup poll I mentioned a few pages earlier states that 75 percent of workers who voluntarily left their jobs did so because of their bosses, not because of the position itself. Let me make sure that lands: People don't quit jobs, they quit bosses. The good news is that you're in control of both your reputation as a leader *and* the way you actually lead.

I want you to experience yourself as a highly respected, successful leader—one who leads team members who truly thrive and share with others how lucky they are to work with you. I want your team to accomplish more results with less frustration, overwhelm, and burnout. Through making and keeping these seven agreements, you can transform the "people parts" of your role from difficult and draining to highly satisfying and productive.

You now have the tools to implement these agreements to do things differently. When you strengthen your own Self-Leadership and increase your emotional endurance, your team will automatically begin to perform better as your critical thinking, relationships, and communication improve. When your team members no longer need to cope with your and others' self-protective behaviors, they can drop their own and truly focus on achieving outcomes. This is the fundamental truth that runs through all seven agreements—that as humans, we can learn to regulate our emotions so that we reside in our higher selves to collaborate, cooperate, and combine together our best thinking and creativity.

In this way, we can produce outcomes that are way beyond what anyone could possibly imagine, let alone accomplish by ourselves.

Listen, leadership is a journey. When team interaction isn't going well, it's painful for everyone involved. But if you implement the teaching in this book, that pain can lift and you will find yourself enjoying parts of your business you used to dread. You will look forward to meetings because you can't wait to collaborate with your team. You will listen intently, eager to hear their well-thought-through ideas and how they plan to implement them. You will find yourself becoming a mentor and coach to your team, no longer needing to solve their problems or police their work, because they take the type of ownership normally only seen from actual owners.

Your leadership role is your vehicle to personally and professionally grow, develop, and contribute meaningfully to your organization. It's how you achieve what matters most to you. I believe you will fall in love with being a leader, so that the People Part of your role becomes the most fulfilling and exhilarating part.

❁ ❁ ❁

These are my desires for you as a leader, but what I most want you to take away from *The People Part* is something even simpler.

Business is a team sport, not so different from professional sports in many ways, where the team members are by far the most important and valuable part of the organization. Your people may not yet seem like much of an asset in your business—you might still perceive them as a necessary (big) expense. But the long-term, sustainable success of your business depends on shifting your mindset so that you can confidently invest in your team as your greatest asset, because it's through them that you will achieve both the business's potential and the life you desire.

That last part is especially important, because the teaching in this book applies not only to your business life but to your personal life as well. The improvements in my relationships with my husband, kids, and friends have been profound ever since I learned to take responsibility for my own Self-Leadership and well-being. I carried a tremendous amount of anxiety, judgment, and self-criticism as a younger person, which prevented me from being emotionally available and truly present with my family and friends. I wish I had known earlier that I could learn to regulate my emotions—and that it was the key to my satisfaction and fulfillment in both my work and my life.

It's not easy being human—given our differences and our hardwired survival instincts, sometimes I'm amazed that we get along at all! But to go back to what I said right at the start of this book, if you find yourself thinking that people are the problem, keep in mind that they're also the solution. And now you have the tools to connect intentionally, positively, and effectively with all the people in your world.

Business success, like life, is always unfolding; it is an ongoing process that requires continual development and learning. This *is* leadership. This is *your* new part. You are doing it. Keep going!

Warmly,
Annie

This graphic represents everything you've learned in this book. I've placed it here to remind you how it all fits together. It is meant to demonstrate the absolute importance of the People Part—the foundation your business is built upon.

The People Part starts with your individual leadership development and ability to show up in Self-Leadership. From Self-Leadership you are able to build secure relationships with your team. And together you do ACE teamwork, the kind of effective teamwork that delivers results.

ACE teamwork connects the People Part to the Business Part, because it's how the work gets done.

The Business Part triangle shows how the business operates. It represents structure, systems, team development, the thinking needed at every level, and how the functional tasks, projects, and annual goals all add up to your business having the positive impact you came together as a team to achieve. The Business Part needs The People Part working well in order to thrive!

YOUR PEOPLE PART PLAN

How to Use the People Part
Tools with Your Team

In the pages ahead, you'll find exercises to help you apply each of the seven agreements you've learned about in this book. These exercises are meant to meet you at your level of team development right now, whatever that is. You can also revisit these strategies in different ways as your business continues to evolve.

You can start in whatever way works for you!

You might want to start by working through all the exercises yourself, so you can see the level of clarity you have about the seven agreements and the tools you've learned.

Or you can start right in with your team, by creating a monthly meeting to teach them one of the agreements in this book and then setting aside time to work on the exercises together.

Depending on the size of your business, you may choose to apply this work across your whole team (easier for smaller organizations) or start with your leadership team and then bring it to others (a good approach for larger organizations).

Remember, leadership development is an ongoing journey, and you now have the tools to build sustainable success. This is leadership. You are doing it right now. Keep going!

AGREEMENT 1: SELF-LEADERSHIP

Use the Power of the Pause!

For the next workweek, make it a point to hit Pause when you feel your reactive side revving up. At the end of each day, write (on paper or digitally) about one "pause" that you've taken that day. It could be about when you "paused" during a fast-moving message chain with a co-worker to consider your next reply, or took a beat to allow your team to figure out a challenge. Or it could be just a deep breath to reset after some negative self-talk. Whatever you choose, write about:

- The situation—what specifically triggered your reactive side?

- Your experience of "pausing"—how did it make you feel?

- Did you do anything differently because you'd paused?

- How did it turn out?

AGREEMENT 2: DEFINED OUTCOMES

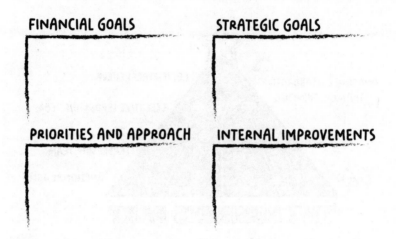

FINANCIAL GOALS

STRATEGIC GOALS

PRIORITIES AND APPROACH

INTERNAL IMPROVEMENTS

Strategic Planning on the Back of a Napkin

Do you know your company's goals for this year? What does your "back of the napkin" look like?

First, take 15 minutes and sketch this out for yourself.

Then ask yourself: How did it go? Maybe you discovered that you know more than you thought you did. Or maybe you're less than certain about some big things and need to talk to a senior leader to get more clarity.

No matter what your role is in the business—whether you're the CEO or a member of a functional team—you can learn from doing this exercise.

AGREEMENT 3: ROLE CLARITY

ONGOING COLLABORATIVE
STRATEGIC THINKING

CEO/ENTREPRENEUR

EXECUTIVE LEADERSHIP TEAM

CROSS-FUNCTIONAL
LEADERSHIP TEAM

FUNCTIONAL ROLES

THE BUSINESS PART

Map Out Your Structure

Spend some time thinking about the following questions—and taking notes!

- How is your business currently organized?
- What functional areas do you have?
- What are the roles within those functions?

If you're an entrepreneur leading a small but growing business, this exercise can be the first step toward creating an organizational structure to help you grow.

If you're the CEO of a company at a later stage of business development, this map can help you get a fix on how your organizational structure is working.

And if you're leading a team within a larger organization, you can use this exercise to get a fresh perspective on the roles within your team.

AGREEMENT 4: SECURE RELATIONSHIPS

EFFECTIVE APPRECIATION

1. EXPLICITLY ACKNOWLEDGE WHAT THE PERSON DID (THEIR EFFORTS AND ACTIONS).

2. RELATE THE POSITIVE IMPACT IT HAD, DESCRIBING THE RESULTS IT ACHIEVED,

   THE DIFFERENCE IT MADE, AND HOW IT MADE YOU FEEL.

3. SAY "THANK YOU!"

EFFECTIVE APOLOGY

1. DESCRIBE SPECIFICALLY WHAT YOU DID AND/OR HOW YOU BEHAVED.

2. DESCRIBE AND APOLOGIZE FOR THE NEGATIVE IMPACT IT HAD ON THE OTHER PERSON

   (THE NEGATIVE CONSEQUENCES THEY EXPERIENCED, FROM THEIR POINT OF VIEW).

3. DESCRIBE WHAT YOU INTEND TO DO DIFFERENTLY IN THE FUTURE.

4. DESCRIBE WHAT YOU'D LIKE TO DO OR CONTRIBUTE TO RELIEVE

   THEIR SUFFERING (IF THERE IS SOMETHING YOU CAN DO).

Practice Appreciation and Apology

For the next workweek, use the formula for Appreciation that we outlined in Agreement 4 to acknowledge the positive impact of at least one person a day. Also, use the formula for Apology to acknowledge the negative impact of something you did. (Hint: You can use the scripts on this page as cheat sheets!)

At the end of the week, look back: How did it go? What did you observe as you acknowledged, appreciated, or apologized to your team members? And how can you make effective acknowledgment a part of your ongoing approach with your team?

AGREEMENT 5: CONSCIOUS AGREEMENTS

ACE DELEGATION SCRIPT - 6 STEPS

1. THE INTENDED OUTCOME LOOKS LIKE:

2. THE PURPOSE AND BENEFITS ARE:

3. WHAT DO YOU (THE PERSON PERFORMING THE WORK) NEED TO BE SUCCESSFUL?

4. WHAT CHALLENGES MIGHT YOU ENCOUNTER? HOW WILL YOU REPOND TO THOSE?

5. HOW WILL YOU MONITOR AND/OR FOLLOW UP ON PROGRESS?
   HOW WILL YOU RESPOND TO SIGNIFICANT CHALLENGES AND URGENT ISSUES?

6. HOW WILL I (THE PERSON DELEGATING WORK) KNOW WHEN THE WORK IS
   COMPLETE AND WHAT RESULTS WERE ACHIEVED?

Practice Effective Delegation

In the coming workweek, choose one new task you need to delegate (not something that's already part of your team's routine). Then:

- Prepare for the delegation conversation by following the steps in Agreement 5 (and in the script on this page).

- Schedule a meeting with the team member and follow your script to delegate.

- Ask yourself: How did it go? Was the delegation smooth and easy, or did you come away with a "do differently" for next time?

- Practice, practice, practice until you no longer need the script and proper delegation becomes a habit.

AGREEMENT 6: RECOGNIZE CHANGE AND RENEGOTIATE

GAPA

G: DESCRIBE THE **GAP** (THE DIFFERENCE BETWEEN EXPECTED PERFORMANCE AND CURRENT OR ANTICIPATED PERFORMANCE) AND THE **IMPACT** ON THE DESIRED OUTCOME.

A: REQUEST AND SUGGEST POTENTIAL **ADJUSTMENT** AND SOLUTIONS—REMEMBERING THAT WE'RE LOOKING TO RESOLVE THE IMPACT, NOT THE GAP ITSELF.

P: CONSIDER ALL THE **PERSPECTIVES** AND DISCUSS ALTERNATIVES TO MAKE THE MOST EFFECTIVE DECISIONS.

A: FINALLY, FORM A NEW OR MODIFIED **AGREEMENT** ON THE CHOSEN SOLUTIONS(S) AND MAP OUT THE NEXT STEPS IN THE NEW PLAN.

Practice Successful Renegotiation

In the coming workweek, identify something that is going differently than planned or falling short of expectations—something you need to have a GAPA conversation about. Then:

- Using the GAPA script in the chapter as a guide, prepare for the conversation.

- Schedule a meeting with the team member and follow your script to address the gap and the impact.

- Ask yourself: How did it go? Did you and the team member arrive at a new agreement and next steps in the new plan? Did you come away with any "do differentlys" for next time?

- Practice, practice, practice until you no longer need the script and effective renegotiation becomes a habit.

AGREEMENT 7: CULTURE THAT DRIVES EXCELLENCE

Cultivate Good Collaboration and Meeting Habits

In your next team meeting, make it a point to use this approach:

- For each agenda item, have your team members speak first, sharing their ideas and the thinking behind them. (This is how they "fill your bubble"!)

- Ask curious questions and practice active listening.

- Collaborate with your team, being mindful to add to their thinking.

- Ask yourself: How did it go? Even better, ask your team how they think it went!

YOUR LEADERSHIP TOOLBOX

You now understand the true importance of the People Part and know the fundamental tools of leadership that will serve you day in and day out. You have learned how to develop and strengthen your own Self-Leadership and build up your emotional endurance. You have learned the importance of agreements as the main mechanism of teamwork. And you know how to make the kind of team agreements that will create a thriving culture.

What's more, you have the tools to communicate effectively, repair relationships as needed, and paint the picture of your vision and goals in such a way that they can be achieved by a team, which will give you more space to grow and excel.

In the pages ahead, I've gathered the graphics you've seen throughout the book that represent the most important tools you have at your disposal now. The more you use and master these tools, the more you will develop as a leader. So don't let your leadership toolbox gather dust!

The People Part is the foundation of your business!

ACE Teamwork connects the People Part to the Business Part—
it's how the work gets done.

BLAME AVOID JUDGE DEFEND
DENY RESIST HIDE
RATIONALIZE
OVERWHELM

SELF-PROTECTION

Self-protection is our default human hard-wiring. It's great for saving us from immediate physical danger, but not so great for the challenges we typically face in business.

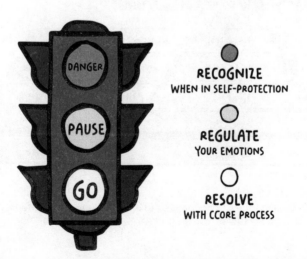

DANGER

PAUSE

GO

RECOGNIZE
WHEN IN SELF-PROTECTION

REGULATE
YOUR EMOTIONS

RESOLVE
WITH CCORE PROCESS

When you're in self-protection, the first step is to recognize you're there.

Take a pause to regulate your emotions . . .

. . . then use the CCORE process to bring you into Self-Leadership.

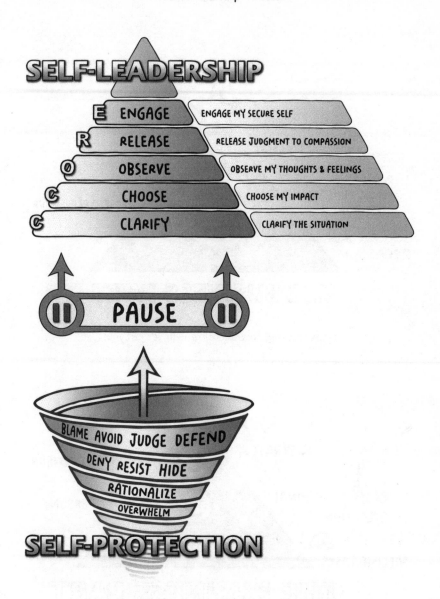

The goal is to spend less and less time in self-protection, because your good critical thinking is only available to you in Self-Leadership.

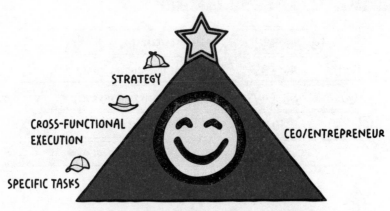

In the first stage of business growth, it's just you!

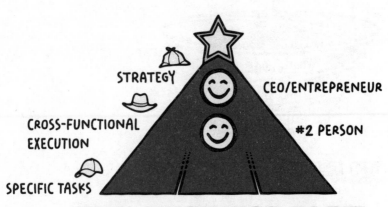

In the second stage of business growth, a strong right-hand person takes on key responsibilities.

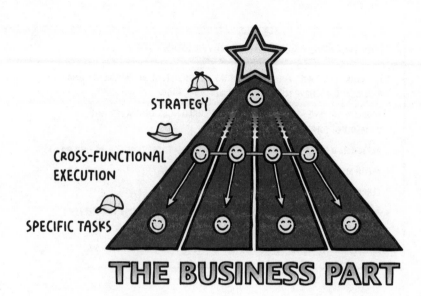

The third stage of business growth has clear functional areas, with leaders who do cross-functional planning and execution.

As your business grows even more, you'll be ready to put an executive leadership team in place.

TEAM MEETING AGENDA THAT NEVER FAILS

1. MONITOR MILESTONES FOR TOP PRIORITIES, ACKNOWLEDGE ACHIEVEMENTS AND WINS, AND IDENTIFY WHERE MILESTONES ARE DUE: TIME = 10%

2. PROBLEM-SOLVING—SURFACE AND RESOLVE CHALLENGES, OBSTACLES, AND UNRESOLVED CONFLICTS

3. MAJOR AND CROSS-FUNCTIONAL DECISION-MAKING: TOTAL TIME FOR #2 AND #3 = 65%

4. RECAP MEETING AND DOCUMENT DECISIONS: TIME = 10%

5. CLARIFY NEXT ACTION STEPS: TIME = 5%

6. ALIGN COMMUNICATION AND COORDINATION TO EXECUTE OUTSIDE THE MEETING: TIME = 5%

7. EVALUATE MEETING EFFECTIVENESS AND SHARE APPRECIATION: TIME = 5%

Anything you need to accomplish with your team will go more smoothly if you have a practice of using the meeting agenda that never fails.

A PLAYER	ACE TEAM MEMBER	A⁺ LEADER	MASTERY
☆ Strong skills & experience	☆ Demonstrates Self-Leadership	☆ Higher level of responsibility for achieving results	
☆ Independently completes functional tasks	☆ Effectively interacts with others to achieve results	☆ Guides and develops team for more effective and improved performance	
	☆ Able to perform under stress	☆ Future-focused change agent	

Hiring A Players is just the beginning. New hires need to develop until they lead with their expertise in the way that serves your organization best. And Leadership Mastery is an ongoing journey of elevating your People Part skills to even higher levels—so you can go pro!

LEADERSHIP CONVERSATIONS CHEAT SHEET

Leadership conversations are an everyday part of your role, no matter what your business is or how large a team you're working with. After reading this book, you have some powerful tools at your disposal to conduct a leadership conversation effectively!

On these pages, I'll give you a quick-reference guide to recap the key components of a successful conversation. Whether you need to deliver performance feedback, adjust project timelines or expectations, or repair a working relationship, this can serve as a mental checklist (or even a physical cheat sheet) to ensure your thinking is prepared and you're ready to raise and resolve the issue at hand.

By getting familiar with all these components, you'll continually up-level your ability to have effective conversations—the kind that help things go better from here.

LEADERSHIP CONVERSATION COMPONENTS

1. **Self-Check**

   - Check in with yourself: Are you in Self-Leadership?
   - If not, PAUSE, regulate your emotions, and apply the CCORE process.
   - Prepare for the conversation.

2. **Positive Intention**

- Say to the team member, "I want to talk to you about _____ . Is now a good time?"

- State your positive intention for the conversation—the overall outcome you are going for or what you want to address.

- Paint the picture, giving context to bring the team member into your thinking.

- Be sure to include "what's changed"!

- Use "what's changed" as an anchor point to keep coming back to if the conversation goes off track.

- Share the stakes and your vulnerability to add safety (if needed).

3. **The Issue and the IMPACT**

- As simply and directly as possible, state the issue and how it impacts the business outcome.

- Is there a gap? If so, explain it.

- Look more closely at what's changed. Has something changed in the bigger picture? Or has your thinking changed? Explain this.

- Has there been a new development that may impact the outcome? Explain it.

- Stay neutral and objective. Stick to the facts—drop the stories!

4. **Possible Solutions**

- Ask others what possible solutions they see or what they're thinking.

- Share possible solutions you see or what you're thinking. Suggest some "do differentlys."

- Remember to talk tentatively!

- When putting forward solutions, share the critical thinking behind them.

- Keep it action-based and focus on solving issues (not debating the issues).

5. Safe, Productive Negotiation

- In your dialogue, allow space for everyone to contribute, and keep your own focus on listening.

- Be curious about the other person's perspective; ask for input and opinions on solutions.

- Make sure they are following your thinking by asking them to recap what they heard.

- Look for common ground and build upon that; stay anchored in business outcomes.

- Keep talking tentatively!

6. New Agreement and/or Next Steps

- Confirm any decisions, agreements, and/or next steps with all involved, and document them as needed.

- Establish follow-up: when, where, who, how.

- Establish recovery: what to do if things diverge from the new plan.

- If a solution or new agreement isn't achieved, determine next steps to move the issue forward toward a solution.

- Many issues need multiple conversations to generate an agreement—be patient!

MORE PEOPLE PART RESOURCES

Visit thepeoplepartbook.com/resources to find:

Strategic planning guidance

Training support

Ways to work with Annie

Other exclusive gifts and resources
for readers of The People Part

And more!

INDEX

NOTE: Page references in *italics* refer to figures.

A

A Players, attracting, 213–216, *214*
Acceptable behaviors, leveling up and, 50, 126
Accomplishments, sharing, 210, 213
ACE Teamwork
    ACE agreement-making process, 138–142, *139*
    ACE (Alignment, Conscious Agreement, Effective Action), defined, 138–139, *139*
    ACE Delegation Script, 146–154, *147*
    ACE Interaction Agreement, 158–162
    ACE meetings, 206–213, *210*
    A+ Leaders/A Players, 94–96, *96*, 213–216, *214*
    Alignment to intended outcomes, 138, 139–140
    Conscious Agreement-Making, 138, 140–141
    delegation as bilateral agreement for, 139, 143–144
    Effective Action, 142
    See also Communication
Acknowledgment, 120–123, *121, 122*
Action plans, clarifying, 212
Active listening, 178–179, 188–189
Adjustment, requesting, 174, 176–177.
    See also GAPA formula
Agency, 4
Agendas for meetings, 209–213, *210*
Agreements
    as best practices, 195
    boundaries vs., 154–157
    delegation as bilateral agreement, 143–144
    forming/modifying, 174, 178–179

    recovery in ACE Interaction Agreement, 161–162
    See also Conscious Agreements (Agreement 5); Culture That Drives Excellence (Agreement 7); Goals (Agreement 2); High-Trust Relationships (Agreement 4); Recognize Change and Renegotiate (Agreement 6); Role Clarity (Agreement 3); Self-Leadership (Agreement 1)
Annie Hyman Pratt Consulting, xxvii
Apologizing, 119–120, *120*
Appreciation
    acknowledgment of, 120–123, *121, 122*
    showing, 212
Approach ("How" step in ACE Delegation Script), 147, *147*, 149
Avoiding, 12–13, 129–130. *See also* Self-protection

B

Blame
    apologizing and, 120
    creating safe environment vs., 168–170 (*See also* Culture That Drives Excellence (Agreement 7))
    defensiveness and, 14–15
    deflection of responsibility, 19–21
Boundaries vs. agreements, 154–157
Brain
    amygdala, 6
    hypothalamus, 6
    prefrontal cortex, 4, 23
    sympathetic nervous system, 6, 9
Brown, Brené, 15
Business environment
    changes to, xvii–xix

creating safe environment, 111–118, *118*, 168–170 (*See also* Psychological safety)

purpose sought by A Players, 215

as situational, 18

See also Culture That Drives Excellence (Agreement 7)

Business Operating Triangle

business structure as foundation of success, 78–80

communicating within, 88–89

Define and Assign (Stage 2), 84–85, *85*

defined, 80, *81*

defining business structure, 80–82, *81*, *82*

Establishing Executive Leaders (Stage 4), 87–88, *88*

Establishing Functional Leaders (Stage 3), *86*, 86–87

functional tasks of, 81–82

I Can Do It (Stage 1), *83*, 83–84

translating up/down/across, 82, *82*, 89, 93

Business Part and People Part, *224*

Business performance meetings, 207–209

C

CCORE (Clarify, Choose, Observe, Release, Engage) Empowerment Process, 25–34

apologizing and, 120

building emotional endurance, 125–126

Choose impact (step 2), 28, *28*

Clarify situation (step 1), 27, *27*

discomfort and, 36–37

Engage my secure self (step 5), 34, *34*

five-step process, overview, *25*, 25–27, *26*

Observe thoughts and feelings (step 3), 28–29, *29*

putting it all together, 34–36

Release judgment to compassion (step 4), 29–33, *30*

CEOs. *See* Entrepreneurs and CEOs

Certainty, Wizard Test for, 30–31

Challenges ("What If" step in ACE Delegation Script), 147, *147*, 149–151

Change. *See* Recognize Change and Renegotiate (Agreement 6)

Choose impact (step 2, CCORE), 28, *28*

Clarification

about action plans, 212

in ACE Interaction Agreement, 160–161

Clarify situation (step 1, CCORE), 27, *27*

clarity and concreteness of goals, 58–59, 70

Client-facing projects, prioritizing, 63, *63*, 65–66

Coffee Bean & Tea Leaf

early history of, xxvi, xxxi–xxxv

goals of, 43–44, 46–48

rapid growth of, 1–3, 7–8

Communication

about role clarity, 88–89, 93

aligning coordination outside meetings, 212

articulating "what changed" in agreement, 172–173

cross-functional and inclusive, 201

"filling the bubble," 203–206, *204*

platforms for, 158–159, 201

sabotaging, 112–113

See also Culture That Drives Excellence

Compassion, Release judgment to (step 4, CCORE), 29–33, *30*

Complaining, 14

Completion ("Finish" step in ACE Delegation Script), 147, *147*, 152

Conscious Agreements (Agreement 5), 135–166

ACE agreement-making process, 138–142, *139*

boundaries vs. agreements, 154–157

delegation and, 143–154, *147*

expectations in high-trust relationships, 108–109

group agreements, 158–162

as mechanism of effective teamwork, 135–136

Practice Effective Delegation (exercise), 232, *232*

as process vs. promise, 136–138, 170

reflection about, 166
success story, 163–164
takeaways, 165
"Context bubble," filling, 203–206, *204*
Control, self-blame and, 16–17
COOs (chief operating officers), role
    clarity and, 87–88, *88*
Critical thinking
    executive actions for, 4
    overview, 1–3
    for proactively surfacing and solving
    problems, 202–203
    See also Self-Leadership
Criticism vs. secure relationships,
    110–111
Cross-functional leadership teams, 87,
    89. *See also* Role Clarity
Culture That Drives Excellence (Agree-
    ment 7), 195–200
    ACE meetings and, 206–213, *210*
    to attract A Players, 213–216, *214*
    cross-functional and inclusive com-
    munication, 201
    Cultivate Good Collaboration and
    Meeting Habits (exercise), 234, *234*
    defined, 195–196
    "filling the (communication) bub-
    ble," 203–206, *204*
    inviting engagement and candid
    dialogue, 197–200
    proactively surfacing and solving
    problems, 202–203
    reflection about, 220
    success story, 217–218
    takeaways, 219

D

Decision-making
    cross-functional, 211
    recapping decisions, 211–212
    See also Self-Leadership
Define and Assign (Stage 2, Business
    Operating Triangle), 84–85, *85*
Defined Outcomes. *See* Goals
Delegation, 143–154
    ACE Delegation Script, *147*,
    146–154
    as bilateral agreement, 143–144
    business as team sport and, xxi–xxii

Practice Effective Delegation (Con-
    scious Agreements, Agreement 5),
    232, *232*
    recipient-led, 154
Denial, 13
Discomfort, learning from, 36–37

E

Emotional endurance zone, 123–126,
    124, 221. *See also* Self-Leadership
Emotional reaction, 6–8
Employees
    firing, 187
    hiring, 84
    quitting jobs vs. quitting bosses, 221
    See also Teamwork
Empowerment. *See* CCORE (Clarify,
    Choose, Observe, Release, Engage)
    Empowerment Process
Engagement
    asking for opinions, 197
    engagement steps in delegation, 151
Engage my secure self (step 5, CCORE),
    34, *34*
    inviting engagement and candid
    dialogue, 197
    See also CCORE (Clarify, Choose,
    Observe, Release, Engage) Empower-
    ment Process; Communication
Entrepreneurs and CEOs
    employees' quitting jobs vs. quitting
    bosses, 221
    entrepreneurs as CEOs, 96–97
    inviting engagement and candid
    dialogue, 197
    perception of team by, 216
    poor behavior of, 116 (*See also* High-
    Trust Relationships)
    proactively surfacing for problem
    solving, 202–203
    role clarification as responsibility
    for, 92 (*See also* Role Clarity)
    See also Culture That Drives
    Excellence
Establishing Executive Leaders (Stage
    4, Business Operating Triangle),
    87–88, *88*
Establishing Functional Leaders (Stage
    3, Business Operating Triangle), *86*,
    86–87

Evaluation. *See* Self-Leadership (Agreement 1); individual performance gaps

Exercises, 227–234
Cultivate Good Collaboration and Meeting Habits (Agreement 7), 234, *234*
Map Out Your Structure (Agreement 3), 230, *230*
overview, 227
Practice Appreciation and Apology (Agreement 4), 231, *231*
Practice Effective Delegation (Agreement 5), 232, *232*
Practice Successful Renegotiation (Agreement 6), 233, *233*
Sketch Out the Back of the Napkin (Agreement 2), 229, *229*
Use the Power of the Pause (Agreement 1), 228, *228*

Expectations
clarifying, 91–92
in high-trust relationships, 108–109
See also Conscious Agreements

External drivers, goals and, 59

F

Fight-or-flight response, 6–8
"Filling the (communication) bubble," 203–206, *204*
Financial goals, 63, *63*, 63–64
"Finish" step in ACE Delegation Script, 147, *147*, 152
Firing (termination), 187
Follow Up step (ACE Delegation Script), 147, *147*, 151–152
Functional Leaders, Establishing (Stage 3, Business Operating Triangle), *86*, 86–87
Functional tasks, creating, 81–82

G

Gallup Organization, 215, 221
GAPA formula, 173–179
considering Perspectives, 177
defined, 173–174, *174*
describing Gap and impact, 173, 174–176

forming/modifying agreements, 174, 178–179
for impact, 173
intention of conversation about change, 175
suggesting Adjustments, 176–177

Goals (Agreement 2), 43–75
alignment of (*See* ACE Teamwork)
business growth from A to V, *45*, 45–54, *48, 49, 52, 53* (*See also* Vision [V] state)
as foundation of team achievement, 43–44
measurability of, 58–59
missed goals, 69–70
reflection about, 75
Strategic Planning on the Back of a Napkin (exercise), 229, *229*
success story, 72–73
takeaways, 74
translating goals to tasks up/down/across, 82, *82*, 89, 93
Visionary Master Plan for, 44, 54–71 (*See also* Visionary Master Plan; Visionary Master Plan (VMP))

Gossip, 14
Group agreements, 158–162

H

Habit, 5
High-Trust Relationships (Agreement 4), 103–134
acknowledging and, 120–123, *121, 122*
apologizing and, 119–120, *120*
boundaries vs. agreements, 154–157
emotional endurance zone and, 123–126, *124*
Practice Acknowledgment and Appreciation (exercise), 231, *231*
for productive team interaction, 103–105
psychological safety for, 111–118, *118*, 168–170
reflection about, 134
secure relationships and importance to, 105–111
self-protection and, 126–130, *127*
success story, 131–132
takeaways, 133

Hiring, role clarity and, 84
"How" step in ACE Delegation Script,
147, *147*, 149
How's This Working for Me? Test,
32–33
Huddles, 207–209
Human behavior, 4–9
Hyman, Mona, xvi–xviii

I

I Can Do It (Stage 1, Business Operating Triangle), *83*, 83–84
Impact
of change, 173, 175–176 (*See also*
GAPA formula)
Choose impact (step 2, CCORE), 28,
28
problem-solving for, 176–177
Individual performance gaps, 180–189
authority as clear and caring for,
185–189
identifying gap, 180–182
keeping open mind about, 182–183
need for authority in, 183–185
Individuals, perspective of
active listening and problem-solving, 179
change and considering Perspective
of others, 174, 177 (*See also* GAPA
formula)
goals of A Players, 94–96, *96*, 213–
216, *214*
psychological safety and, 111–118,
118
role clarity and, 89–90
Intention
in ACE Interaction Agreement, 160
conversation about change to agreement and, 175
human behavior of, 4–5, 8–9
intended outcome ("What" step in
ACE Delegation Script), 147, *147*,
146–148
staying focused on, 24
Internal e-mails/messages, 158–159, 201
Internal improvement goals, 63, *63*,
66–67

J

Judgment
Release judgment to compassion
(step 4, CCORE), 29–33, *30*
using good judgment vs. "judging," 14

K

Koko (gorilla), 15

L

Leaders, A+, 94–96, *96*, 213–216, *214*
Leadership. *See* Entrepreneurs and
CEOs; Self-Leadership
Leadership Conversations Cheat Sheet,
243–245
Leadership Toolbox, 235–242
Leading Edge Teams, xxvii
Leveling up
acceptable behaviors and, 50, 126
for building emotional endurance,
125–126
to Vision (V) state, 50–53, *52*, *53*, 93
Listening, active, 178–179
Lower spiral
defined, *10*, 11
stealth lower-spiral behaviors, 17–21
See also Self-protection

M

Map Out Your Structure (Role Clarity,
Agreement 3), 230, *230*
Meetings
Meeting Agenda That Never Fails,
209–213, *210*
reluctance about, 206–207
types of, 207–209 (*See also* ACE
Teamwork)
Metrics
measurability of goals, 58–59
metric tracking vs. People Part,
xi–xiii
Micromanagement vs. secure relationship, 106

N

Norms, violation of, 155–156

O

Observe thoughts and feelings (step 3, CCORE), 28–29, *29*
Organizational culture. *See* Culture That Drives Excellence
Over-responsibility, 17–19

P

Pausing to self-regulate, 23–24
People Part, xi–xxxvi
  business as team sport and, xxi–xxii
  Business Part and People Part, *224*
  developing human performance and, xxii–xxviii
  goals of, xxviii–xxx
  importance of, xi–xiv, xvi–xxi, xxvi–xxviii
  people as problem and solution, xiv–xv
  Seven Agreements, overview, xxxi–xxxv
  teamwork and agreements, xxiv–xxvi
  working together as heart of, 216
  See also Agreements
Perfectionism
  secure relationships vs., 109–110
  in vision, 55–57
Performance of individuals. *See* individual performance gaps
Perspective of individuals. *See* Individuals, perspective of
Peter Principle, 95
Power of the Pause (Self-Leadership, Agreement 1), 228, *228*
Practice Appreciation and Apology (High-Trust Relationships, Agreement 4), 231, *231*
Practice Effective Delegation (Conscious Agreements, Agreement 5), 232, *232*
Practice Successful Renegotiation (Recognize Change and Renegotiate, Agreement 6), 233, *233*
Prioritizing
  of goals, 63, *63*, 65–66
  monitoring priorities, 210–211
Problem-solving. *See* Recognize Change and Renegotiate
Professional development, role clarity for, 94–97
Psychological safety
  creating safe environment to discuss change, 168–170
  for high-trust relationships, 111–118, *118*
Purpose and benefits ("Why" step in ACE Delegation Script), 147, *147*, 148

R

Rationalization, 13
Reaction as self-protective response, 6–9
Recipient-led delegation, 154
Recognize Change and Renegotiate (Agreement 6), 167–193
  GAPA formula for, 173–179, *174* (*See also* GAPA formula)
  individual performance gaps and, 180–189
  Practice Successful Renegotiation (exercise), 233, *233*
  recognizing a gap in agreement, 168–173, *169*
  reflection about, 193
  for succeeding in ever-changing reality, 167
  success story, 190–192
  takeaways, 192
Relationship building. *See* High-Trust Relationships
Release judgment to compassion (step 4, CCORE), 29–33, *30*
Renegotiation. *See* Recognize Change and Renegotiate
Resources, 247–248
Responsibility, deflection of, 19–21
Role Clarity (Agreement 3), 77–101
  defining business structure for, 80–82, *81*, *82*
  as everyone's responsibility, 92–93
  individual perspectives of roles and, 89–90

Map Out Your Structure (exercise), 230, *230*
overview, 78–80
professional development journey and, 94–97, *96*
reflection about, 101
"slowing down to speed up," 89–90
stages of business growth and development, *83*, 83–93, *85*, *86*, *88*
as structure to enable teamwork, 77–78
success story, 98–99
takeaways, 100

S

Secure relationships, 105–111. *See also* High-Trust Relationships
Secure self, Engage (step 5, CCORE), 34, *34*
Self-blame, 16–17
Self-Leadership (Agreement 1), 1–41
as basis of company culture, 197
CCORE Empowerment Process for, *25–30*, 25–34, *34*, 36–37 (*See also* CCORE Empowerment Process)
for critical thinking, performance, and effective interaction, 1–3
defined, xxiii–xiv
discomfort and, 36–37
drivers of human behavior and, 4–9
example, 34–36
How's This Working for Me? Test, 32–33
Leadership Conversations Cheat Sheet, 243–245
Leadership Toolbox, 235–242
overview, 221–223, *223*
pausing to self-regulate, 23–24
Power of the Pause (exercise), 228, *228*
putting it all together, 34–36
reflection about, 41
renegotiation and, 169–170 (*See also* Recognize Change and Renegotiate)
self-protection vs., 1–3, *10*, 10–22
self-regulating for, *23*, 23–24
success story of, 38–39
takeaways, 40

Self-protection
avoiding behavior, 12–13, 129–130
blaming and defending for, 14–15
building high-trust relationships and recognizing tendencies of, 126–130
denying and rationalizing for, 13
example of, 1–3
high-trust relationships and recognizing tendencies of, 126–130, *127*
judging for, 14
lower spiral of, *10*, 11, 17–21
reaction as, 6–8
recognizing, overview, 10–12
self-blaming and, 16–17
Seven Agreements
Agreement, defined, xxvi
overview, xxxi–xxxv
"Showing up." *See* Self-Leadership
"Slowing down to speed up," 89–90
SMART (Specific, Measurable, Achievable, Relevant, Time-Bound) goals, 67–68
Special-purpose meetings, 207–209
Standard operating procedure (SOP), 163–164
Starbucks, 7–8
State of the American Workplace Report (Gallup Organization, 2017), 215
Stealth behaviors, 17–21
Strategic goals, 63, *63*, 64–65
Strategic Planning on the Back of a Napkin (Goals, Agreement 2), 229, *229*
Stress
active listening and problem-solving, 179
self-protection as reaction to, 126–130

T

Talking tentatively, 197–200
Teamwork
attracting A+ leaders/A Players, 94–96, *96*, 213–216, *214*
autonomy of team members, xxiv
business as team sport, xxi–xxii, 221–223, *223*

conscious agreements as mechanism of, 135–136

goals and team input, 59–60

problem-solving with (*See* Recognize Change and Renegotiate)

role clarity as structure to enable teamwork, 77–78

team huddles, 207–209

See also ACE Teamwork; High-Trust Relationships

Top-down management

authority vs., 180–189

People Part vs., xvii, xix

Trust. *See* High-Trust Relationships

path to desired future with, *63*, 62–67

perfectionism problem and, 55–57

Sketch Out the Back of the Napkin (exercise), 229

SMART goals for, 67–68

Vision (V) state, 45–53

leveling up to, 50–54, *52, 53*, 93

from point A to V, 45, *45*

successful navigation from A to, *48*, 48–50, *49*

thinking from V state, 46–48

vision, defined, 45

V

Villain/Victim Test, 31

Visionary Master Plan (VMP), 54–71

creating effective goals with, 44

defining V state for, 55 (*See also* Vision (V) state)

fundamental keys to, 57–60, 70

importance of, 60–62

as living document, 68–71

W

What, Why, How, What If, Follow Up, Finish steps (ACE Delegation Script), *147*, 146–154

Wins, sharing, 210, 213

Wizard Test, 30–31

ACKNOWLEDGMENTS

Life is a team sport, just like business, and all my achievements were made possible by the support, guidance, mentorship, and contributions of many important people in my life.

First my mom and dad, Herb and Mona Hyman, who included me in dinner table discussions about the Coffee Bean, sparking my business interest that grew into passion. Then entrusting me to grow the family business (during my 20s) before I could fully understand the risks I was taking—I'm grateful it worked out. ;-)

To Nathan Pratt, my former husband of 13 years and Executive VP at Coffee Bean, who worked alongside me and supported me even through the tough parts. And to all the amazing managers and leaders who learned with me along the way.

My forum members from Entrepreneur's Organization and Young President's Organization, along with my Sock 'em Dogs forum, whose support and encouragement kept me going when I was convinced that I was both failing in business and losing my mind.

Special thanks to the following people—without their support and guidance I wouldn't have focused on the People Part of my business and achieved the success I have. Jeff Walker, who added me to his Platinum Plus Mastermind (despite the fact that I didn't have a launch business) and went above and beyond in endorsing and advocating for me as I created new programs and services. Sebastien Night, who stayed up with me until 3 A.M., designing my first workshop, then my first pitch, and then continually helped me keep my courage to try new stuff. Victoria Labalme, not only for teaching me how to be "me" when presenting on stage and on camera, but also for being my rock and boosting my confidence when I needed it most.

My many clients who believed in me, kept reengaging me, and achieved truly transformational success in your businesses and incredible leadership teams. I so appreciate your trust in my work—especially a few who went over the top: Reid Tracy, Margarete Nielsen, Craig Murray, Michael McIntyre, Adee Cazayoux, Erico Rocha, Susan Peirce Thompson, and Jeff Walker.

Thanks to the Platinum Plus members who participated in every new leadership and team program I created and provided unwavering support.

My business partner and mentor Mark Samuel, who encouraged me to grow my business beyond an individual consulting practice and to embrace my humanity-based leadership and teamwork methods.

USM, for teaching me that compassion is the antidote to emotional pain, that suffering isn't required to have a good life, and that I'm "good enough" exactly "as is."

My Leading Edge Teams' Team—with extra gratitude to Barbara Schindler, our COO and Executive Coach and Entrepreneurial Business Consultant, whom I borrowed from my business partner seven years ago and never gave back. This business and book would not be possible without her tenacity, drive, and nonstop belief in the People Part and how we help our clients. This book would still be an idea that I might do "sometime" if it wasn't for you.

To Heather McGonigal, our Director of Programs and Executive Coach, whose dedication to the integrity of our programs and to our clients' results (despite major challenges) has been beyond all expectations and boosted my confidence in the good nature of humanity. Thank you not only for being by my side, every step of the way, to create this book, but for taking the lead in this journey with your writing and teaching expertise, along with your compassionate heart that kept pulling me back in.

To Jim McGonigal, our Creative Content Manager, whose artwork simplified and brought to life the humor of the People Part, and whose cartoons and characters made our work so much more approachable. The graphics are such a critical part of our teachings, and your hand drawings are masterful.

To Jackie Crystal, our Executive Administrator, thank you for keeping my life on track through not only managing my crazy calendar, but demonstrating such professional leadership in anticipating my needs and providing solutions on this book writing journey.

To James Pratt, our Writing and Social Media Intern, who not only brought a young perspective and lots of energy to the writing and editing of the book, but also entirely restructured the book to represent my vision.

To Judy Dippel, for adding your support wherever needed and helping me to realize all the stories I had to share.

To Reid Tracy, Hay House CEO, for not only hiring me to develop the Hay House leaders and team but also giving me this opportunity to impact so many more leaders' lives through this book. To Margarete Nielsen, Hay House COO, for being coachable and developing into a truly extraordinary leader who represents what's possible with this work. To Patty Gift, VP and Publisher, for constantly promoting my work and boosting my confidence so I could actually write this book. To Anne Barthel, editor extraordinaire, for all the ways you so generously worked with me through this process by providing the support, expertise, and caring partnership that I needed to get this book out into the world. Thanks to the whole Hay House book team and the publicity and marketing team. Additional thanks to the many Hay House leaders and managers who have embraced and demonstrated the People Part.

To my siblings—we share a unique experience being Herb and Mona's kids—I'm grateful for our bond and wonderful family connection.

To my children, Grace, James, Justin, and Joey, you inspire and surprise me every day with your courage to take your own unique paths, while at the same time staying connected as siblings. Your quick wits are unmatched for insulting yourselves and joking with each other, and you've taught me a whole new love language that makes my life better.

To David MacMahan, my husband—thank you for being the best life partner ever. I can't adequately express how important you've been to my own growth and development, which was critical for this book. Speaking of, thanks for always being a good sport and allowing me to use you (and us) as a subject for my examples.

You showed me that long-term partnerships could keep growing and improving, despite life's many unavoidable challenges—something I was highly skeptical of before meeting you. Your investment in our marriage and family went above and beyond what normal people would do. The support and stability you provided created an environment where our family could thrive and I could have time to pursue the business of my dreams. Thank you. I am excited for our new phase together as empty nesters, cheering you on courtside and exploring the world together. I would not want to do any of this without you.

ABOUT THE AUTHOR

Annie Hyman Pratt is the founder of Leading Edge Teams, located in sunny Southern California. Annie and her leading edge team do business consulting and executive coaching, in groups and one-on-one, online and in person. They have an unparalleled track record of helping businesses achieve massive, sustainable, team-driven growth.

Annie started her business education around the dinner table, hearing her mother and father talk about their entrepreneurial business, the Coffee Bean & Tea Leaf. Annie worked behind the bean counter in her teen years and then went to college at nearby UCLA, where she graduated with a degree in Economics/Business and became a certified public accountant. Her solid grasp of numbers and business landed her immediate employment doing business valuation consulting with one of the prestigious Big 8 accounting firms in Los Angeles—a very auspicious start.

At age 22, Annie took the reins and became the CEO of her family business. A trailblazer for women in business, she 10X'd the business to 70-plus stores around the globe, and then led the company through a highly successful sale.

After the sale of Coffee Bean, Annie moved into interim C-suite executive work and top-tier business consulting. She became an expert in guiding companies through rapid growth and complex turnarounds while working within diverse industries. Annie's experience with so many different types of entrepreneurial businesses is especially rare, giving her a unique understanding of what it takes to succeed and how the People Part plays a greater role than ever.

Annie's specialty in the People Part was further cultivated through her study at the University of Santa Monica, where she learned what it really takes for human beings to transcend their "quick to judge" nature and instead work together to reach their full potential.

Annie believes your people are the most valuable asset in your business!

While building her expertise and reputation, she also partnered with David (her husband) to build a thriving blended family. Annie is a proud mother of James, Grace, Justin, and Joey, and a dog mom to Pepper.

Hay House Titles of Related Interest

THE SHIFT, the movie,
starring Dr. Wayne W. Dyer
(available as an online streaming video)
www.hayhouse.com/the-shift-movie

***

HIGH PERFORMANCE HABITS:
How Extraordinary People Become That Way,
by Brendon Burchard

LAUNCH: How to Sell Almost Anything
Online, Build a Business You Love,
and Live the Life of Your Dreams
(Updated and Expanded Edition),
by Jeff Walker

RISK FORWARD: Embrace the Unknown
and Unlock Your Hidden Genius,
by Victoria Labalme

All of the above are available at your local bookstore,
or may be ordered by visiting:

Hay House USA: **www.hayhouse.com**®
Hay House Australia: **www.hayhouse.com.au**
Hay House UK: **www.hayhouse.co.uk**
Hay House India: **www.hayhouse.co.in**

We hope you enjoyed this Hay House book. If you'd like to receive our online catalog featuring additional information on Hay House books and products, or if you'd like to find out more about the Hay Foundation, please contact:

Hay House, Inc., P.O. Box 5100, Carlsbad, CA 92018-5100
(760) 431-7695 or (800) 654-5126
(760) 431-6948 (fax) or (800) 650-5115 (fax)
www.hayhouse.com® • www.hayfoundation.org

———

Published in Australia by: Hay House Australia Pty. Ltd.,
18/36 Ralph St., Alexandria NSW 2015
Phone: 612-9669-4299 • *Fax:* 612-9669-4144
www.hayhouse.com.au

Published in the United Kingdom by: Hay House UK, Ltd.,
The Sixth Floor, Watson House, 54 Baker Street, London W1U 7BU
Phone: +44 (0)20 3927 7290 • *Fax:* +44 (0)20 3927 7291
www.hayhouse.co.uk

Published in India by: Hay House Publishers India,
Muskaan Complex, Plot No. 3, B-2, Vasant Kunj, New Delhi 110 070
Phone: 91-11-4176-1620 • *Fax:* 91-11-4176-1630
www.hayhouse.co.in

———

<u>**Access New Knowledge.**</u>
<u>**Anytime. Anywhere.**</u>

Learn and evolve at your own pace
with the world's leading experts.

www.hayhouseU.com

Listen. Learn. Transform.

Listen to the audio version of this book for FREE!

Gain access to powerful tools and life-changing insights from world-renowned experts—guiding and inspiring you as you work toward your goals. With the *Hay House Unlimited* Audio app, you can learn and grow in a way that fits your lifestyle . . . and your daily schedule.

With your membership, you can:

- Learn how to take your writing to the next level, start and build your business, and create abundance in all areas of your life.

- Explore thousands of audiobooks, meditations, immersive learning programs, podcasts, and more.

- Access exclusive audios you won't find anywhere else.

- Experience completely unlimited listening. No credits. No limits. No kidding.

Try for FREE!